Hypersexuality
and Headscarves

New Anthropologies of Europe
Matti Bunzl and Michael Herzfeld, editors

Founding Editors
Daphne Berdahl
Matti Bunzl
Michael Herzfeld

Hypersexuality
and Headscarves

Race, Sex, and Citizenship
in the New Germany

DAMANI J. PARTRIDGE

Indiana University Press
Bloomington and Indianapolis

This book is a publication of

Indiana University Press
601 North Morton Street
Bloomington, Indiana 47404-3797 USA

iupress.indiana.edu

Telephone orders   800-842-6796
Fax orders   812-855-7931

Manufactured in the United States of America

Library of Congress Cataloging-in-Publication Data

Partridge, Damani J., [date]
  Hypersexuality and headscarves : race, sex, and citizenship in the new Germany / Damani J. Partridge.
       p. cm. — (New anthropologies of Europe)
  Includes bibliographical references and index.
  ISBN 978-0-253-35708-3 (cloth : alk. paper) — ISBN 978-0-253-22369-2 (pbk. : alk. paper) — ISBN 978-0-253-00531-1 (electronic book)   1. Political anthropology—Germany. 2. Race discrimination—Germany.   3. Sex discrimination—Germany.   4. Citizenship—Germany.   5. Minorities—Germany.   6. Foreign workers—Germany.   7. Post-communism—Germany.   8. Germany—History—Unification, 1990.   9. Germany—Politics and government—1990–   10. Germany—Race relations.   I. Title.
  GN585.G4P28 2012
  305.800943—dc23
                                                                          2011032354

1 2 3 4 5   17 16 15 14 13 12

This book is dedicated to the four generations of women who have sustained and supported me: Jasmine Josephine Bose Partridge, Sunita Bose Partridge, Dr. Josephine Aona Valiera Allen, Carrie Gwendella Allen, and Dr. Deborah Partridge Cannon Wolfe.

Contents

Acknowledgments

Writing this book has taken much longer and has been much more arduous than I expected. I would like to begin and end by thanking my daughter, my partner, my mother, my grandmothers, my father, my siblings, my nieces, my aunt, my uncle, my cousins, and my friends for creating an environment that helped me to know that writing this book wasn't the only story. I would like to also thank all of those who participated in the research that led to this book. While some of the people overlap, I owe its completion to both of these groups.

Specifically, I thank Eka Neumann, without whom this book would not have been possible. She introduced me to many of my major contacts and discussed my ideas with me in detail from the perspective of an activist and an intellectual. I also thank Anthony Kwame Kongolo, who was an engineering student and student advisor at the Technical University in Berlin at the time; he introduced me not only to Eka, but also to a side of Berlin life that has become central to my understanding of citizenship and processes of exclusionary incorporation in Berlin and post-unification Germany. I thank Barbara and Erhard Friedemann and their children, my host family in East Berlin with whom I lived for several months when I arrived in 1995, for taking me in as a "foreign" son and introducing me to a critical history of the German Democratic Republic and German "re"unification as they lived it and reflected on it. I also thank my first host families, the Moritzes (including Andreas Wünderlich), the Tamgüneys, and the Beckhusens in Brake and Frieschenmoor, who cared for me and made me feel at home when I arrived in West Germany as a sixteen-year-old Rotary Youth Exchange student in 1989. Thank you to the members of the Initiative of Black Germans (now known as the Initiative for Blacks in Germany) for granting interviews and allowing me to participate in some of their events, including the planning of Black History Month. Thank you to the asylum seekers in Brandenburg and Mecklenburg-Vorpommern and to others in Berlin for telling me your stories, for allowing me to film, and for feeding me. I hope you think that this book does your lives justice.

Thank you to the schoolchildren, their teachers, and principals for being open and sharing their desires and fears. Thank you to the women and men, friends and acquaintances who have frequented dance clubs or who traveled to or from Africa, or dreamed of traveling there. Thank you to the members of the Anti-Racism Initiative in Berlin and to the members of the Active Equality Working Group (Aktive Gleichstellungs AG). Thank you to Fereshta Ludin for agreeing to an interview after having already become disenchanted with much of print and television media. Thank you to Sevim Çelebi, who not only allowed me to live in her home, but who has become a friend. Thank you to Anjuli Gupta and Biblap Basu for allowing me to live in their home and for reading my work and engaging in discussion and debate. Thank you to Awino Kuerth for undertaking a summer intensive study with me and discussing critical texts on "race" and belonging in contemporary Germany, even while she was working on her own dissertation. Thank you to Myong Lee for becoming a friend and inviting me over almost daily for dinner after I left my host family and was trying to establish myself in Berlin. Thank you to Wolgang Kaschuba, who welcomed me as his guest and read and commented on portions of my work on so many occasions at the Institute for European Ethnology and Humboldt University in Berlin.

Thank you to Andrés Nader, who introduced me to other sides of Berlin and let me stay with his family, and who has become a critical friend and interlocutor. Thank you to Branwen Okpako and Jean Paul Bourelly for letting me stay in their flat and for being such close friends. They have both always had incredible insights on so many topics. John Goetz also has become a great friend and important interlocutor; he let me live for free in his apartment and use his office, and he allowed me to dip my toes back into the professional world of media production. Furthermore, he introduced me to Isabella Kempf, who is one of the best researchers I have ever met. I did not know that information could be found so quickly.

Franziska Nauk read portions of my work, corrected my German, and became a friend. Viktoria Bergschmidt regularly asked great questions, uttered great insights, and was willing to look over my German at the last minute on critical occasions. Janet Lassan and Johannes Elwardt made Berlin a loving place by letting me stay in their flat, experience their children, and share many fabulous meals.

Kristin Kopp has been a critic, a great friend, and an interlocutor in Berkeley, Berlin, Tübingen, and Vienna. I am grateful that she invited me to become part of the BTWH—Berkeley, Tübingen, Wien (Vienna), Harvard—network, which has been so inspiring over the years. Thank you to Michi Knecht for sharing her office in Berlin and for telling me about conferences, books, and interlocutors with whom I was unfamiliar.

Thank you to Kristine Krause for important insights on migration and Africa, and for help with my written German. Thank you to Moritz Ege for inspiring work and great conversations. Thank you to Neco Celik for coming to show his films in Michigan and Rhode Island, for giving that tour of Kreuzberg for a friend's seminar, and for helping me to think about Berlin in new ways. Thank you to Özcan Mutlu for granting interviews on multiple occasions. Thank you also to Tamara Hentschel, who gave me access to the archives of Reistrommel. I am grateful to everyone else who participated in my research and who made my life livable and enjoyable in Berlin, including Hans Kreutzjans and Elke Bickert, who have recently become friends; they let me stay longer in their flat and introduced me to great skiing.

While I originally met her at the House of World Cultures in Berlin, at Cornell University Leslie Adelson invited me to participate in her DAAD-sponsored faculty seminar on German studies and the post-national imaginary. While I was back in Ithaca, New York (the place where I grew up), she also read and commented on the text that was the framing of this book.

Between Ann Arbor and Berlin, Susanne Unger was a great research assistant, who read an early version of the entire manuscript and transcribed tapes and videos with precision. She has been an important interlocutor.

I am grateful for the institutional support that helped to finance trips to Germany beginning when I was sixteen. In particular, I thank Rotary International; the Fulbright Foundation; the Graduate Opportunity Program, the Anthropology Department, the Center for German and European Studies, the Foreign Language and Area Studies Program, the Townsend Center for the Humanities, and the Institute for International and Area Studies, all at the University of California, Berkeley; the Lowie/Olson Funds; the National Science Foundation; the Alexander Humboldt Foundation, which has funded several trips; and the Simpson Memorial Fund.

At the University of Michigan, I thank the Department of Anthropology and the Center for Afro-American and African Studies and their staffs for their generous institutional and financial support. I also thank Dean Homer Rose Jr. for awarding me faculty enhancement awards from the Rackham Graduate School.

I thank all of the people in the United States who read my work and inspired me. Thank you to Aihwa Ong for mentorship, for teaching and advising, for writing countless letters, and for reading drafts of my work at record speeds and offering detailed critical feedback. Thank you to Judith Butler for inspiring me and helping me to find the courage to think and write outside of the prescribed borders of discipline and ideology through her teaching, writing, and mentorship. Thank you to Allan Pred (we all miss you) for frequent meetings, for comments and encouragement, and for that high five when I got the position at Michigan. Thank you to Paul Rabinow and Alexei Yurchak for critical feedback. I also thank Nancy Scheper-Hughes and the graduate students of her dissertation writing group. I thank those who participated in a year-long series of discussions at the Townsend Center for the Humanities. In addition, I thank Margaret Lavinia Anderson and members of her German history seminar. I also thank Miriam Ticktin for reading my work, being a good friend, letting me read her work, and inviting me to conferences. I thank Duana Fullwiley for engaging me in critical discussions over the years and helping me to find funding. Thank you to Irene Wang for her encouragement and inspiration. Thank you to Nitasha Sharma for her encouragement and feedback.

I thank Andrew Shryock, whose mentorship has been unparalleled. Not only did he read the entire manuscript in its various iterations from the moment I got to the University of Michigan until now, but he was always available to give the best possible advice. I thank James Jackson for asking me to apply for a position at the University of Michigan, for his mentorship, and his leadership. I thank Kelly Askew, who has also been a fabulous mentor and is also responsible for my coming to Michigan, for reading and commenting on this work, and for helping to make Ann Arbor a fantastic place to live. I thank Kader Konuk, Rita Chin, Robin Queen, and the other members of the Turkish German Studies Group for being part of an invaluable network and for commenting on aspects of the emerging book. I also thank members of my anthropology writers group at the University of Michigan, including Miriam Ticktin, Eduardo Kohn, Rebecca Hardin, Julia Paley, Gayle Rubin, Elizabeth Roberts, and Nadine Naber. Tom Fricke became a mentor at a critical time in my career and even came to see me in Berlin, where he was invited to present some of his groundbreaking work.

In addition to Tom Fricke and James Jackson, the other directors and chairs of my two departments, including Angela Dillard, Kevin Gaines, Conrad Kottak, Katherine Verdery, and Judith Irvine, have also been incredible mentors who have given feedback on my manuscript and crucial advice. I thank the members of Katherine Verdery's East European writing group, including Alaina Lemon, who gave critical feedback on one chapter of this book.

At the University of Michigan, the Center for Afro-American and African Studies organized a manuscript workshop which included John Borneman, Paul Johnson, and Sabine Broeck. I thank them for their feedback. I am also truly grateful for the comments and support of the other attendees, including Stuart Kirsch and Rita Chin, who encouraged me to retain my focus on a collective of noncitizens who could not be reduced to one ethnic or racial group. In addition, I appreciate the presence and comments of Judith Irvine, Kathleen Canning, Kevin Gaines (who took copious notes that he sent me after the event), and Rebecca Hardin. I met John Borneman in Berlin on several occasions after the workshop to discuss his comments, but I am, of course, responsible for the decisions that have resulted in this book.

At Indiana University Press, I thank my editor, Rebecca Tolen, who has been kind and helpful as I made the final push to get this book done. I also thank Matti Bunzl and Michael Herzfeld for accepting this book as part of their series. I thank Andrew Shryock and Dominic Boyer for encouraging me to send it to them in the first place. I also thank Dominic Boyer, Esra Özyürek, and Sander Gilman for their critical comments on this work. Additionally, I would like to thank Jane Cavolina (external to the press) and Merryl A. Sloane for their fabulous copyediting.

Finally, I would like to convey my thanks to Sunita Bose Partridge for putting up with me, for loving me, and for being encouraging and supportive in so many ways. I cannot imagine life without you. Thank you, Jasmine Bose Partridge, for being that inspirational spark in my life and for your brilliant violin and piano playing and your beautiful voice. Thank you, C. Gwendella Allen, for helping me to learn my multiplication tables and pointing me in the right direction. I miss you. Thank you, Deborah Cannon Partridge Wolfe, for expecting nothing less than the terminal degree and for all of your support. I miss you too. Thank you, Father, for always being within reach. Thank you, Mother, not only for bringing me into this world, not only for demonstrating unconditional love, but also for being a mentor and a role model. Finally, thank you to everyone else whose names I have not mentioned, including my schoolteachers, my professors, my violin teachers, my dance teachers, my crew coaches, my friends, my colleagues, and my family. (In this book, except where first and last names are used together, I have invented pseudonyms.)

Earlier versions of chapters 2 and 3 have been previously published as follows: 2009. "Travel as an Analytic of Exclusion: Becoming Non-Citizens after the Fall of the Berlin Wall," *Identities: Global Studies in Culture and Power* 16(3): 342–366; and 2008. "We Were Dancing in the Club, Not on the Berlin Wall: 'Black' Bodies, Street Bureaucrats, and Exclusionary Incorporation in the New Europe," *Cultural Anthropology* 23(4): 660–687.

Hypersexuality
and Headscarves

Prologue

As the '68 generation reaches retirement age, it becomes ever more apparent that Europe needs immigration to support its aging population, but unemployment rates are nearly 50 percent for so-called immigrant youth, many of whom were born in Europe. In this context, Germany and Berlin are not exceptional, but exemplary sites for an investigation of the future of Europe and the future of global noncitizens, particularly when one thinks of this future in relation to the aftermath of socialism and the post-9/11, intensified turn against Islam. In 1989, street protesters in East Germany made public claims that the state be held accountable to their desire, asserting *Wir sind das Volk* (We are the people). This call for democratic accountability, however, turned into nationalist fervor, expressed in the subsequent chant *Wir sind ein Volk* (We are one people); the emphasis shifted from democratization to the two Germanys' "re"unification[1] as the path toward social and economic prosperity. From the first moment of flag-waving, it was already clear who was to be included in that "we," even if there continued to be hierarchical differentiations between West and East Germans and between Western and Eastern Europeans. Even so, just prior to the Wall's fall, a pluralistic future seemed possible, at least from the perspective of anti-racist activists in West Berlin. Multiculturalism, even if a problematic concept, was not yet a tainted term.

Was It a Peaceful Revolution?

Many scholars have described 1989 in terms of a "peaceful revolution."[2] The affirmation of this claim, however, depends on whose lives are taken into account. This assertion is too centered on the experiences of *das Volk* (the ethno-national community) and not enough on the noncitizen, including those who have German passports but whose complexion leads analysts and the normative public alike to see them as foreign, or not to see them at all.

Real Citizenship Reform in 2000?

Just over ten years after the Wall fell, on January 1, 2000, the German parliament instituted a new legal order under which the children of those who had lived in Germany for at least eight years with a legally recognized permanent resident status could legally become German citizens without having to naturalize. Most would still have to choose one country to which to belong by age twenty-three, for example, if their parents held Turkish citizenship. Up until that point the only way that children of Turkish descent or Turkish parentage could become citizens was to submit to the discretionary power of local German bureaucrats, who would decide whether they fulfilled the requirements for formal German belonging. After 2000, under Social Democratic and Green Party leadership, a more universal citizenship seemed possible.

But there were impossibilities inherent in these new proclamations, and, at best, they have led to exclusionary incorporation for noncitizens. In local communities, for example, Germany has developed a parallel form of not-quite-democratic accountability called *Ausländer Beirate* (foreigner advisory councils) to represent the interests of foreign residents to elected officials in local government. I sat on such a council in 1999–2000, during one year of my research, in the so-called immigrant neighborhood of Kreuzberg[3] in Berlin as a representative of the local Anti-Racism Initiative. I was not persuaded of the efficacy of these institutions other than as an official version of exclusionary incorporation: the presence of noncitizens is formally recognized, but there is no chance of equal participation. These councils are purely advisory.

Remembering the Wall's Fall: Anti-Racism, Anti-Anti-Semitism, and Noncitizenship

The fall of the Berlin Wall must be considered in relation to the massive outpouring of violence against noncitizens and those thought to be non-Germans. Returning to Berlin in the unusually cold winter of 2010, I wanted to follow up on the contemporary relevance of the fall of the Wall to the politics of noncitizenship. It was in this context that I met with anti-racism and anti-anti-Semitism activist Anetta Kahane. Just at the end of the German Democratic Republic (East Germany), she became the *Ausländerbeauftragte* (foreigner representative) for East Berlin, and in 1991 she founded the *Regionale Arbeits-stelle für Ausländerfragen, Jugendarbeit und Schule* (Regional Center for Foreigner Questions, Youth Work, and Schools) and in 1998 the *Amadeu Antonio Stift-ung* (Amadeu Antonio Foundation). Amadeu Antonio Kiowa was an Angolan former contract worker (one of the "temporary immigrants" who were invited to work in the eastern bloc economy of labor shortages as part of the global network of Communist brotherhood/sisterhood; see Verdery 1996) in East Germany. He was killed in the aftermath of the fall of the Berlin Wall. As the foundation puts it:

> Amadeu Antonio Kiowa was a contract worker from Angola who lived in Eberswalde in the state of Brandenburg. In the night of November 25th, 1990, a group of about 50 neo-Nazi youths carrying baseball bats went through the city on a "hunt" for blacks. They found and assaulted three black men at a bar: two Mozambicans were severely injured but escaped, while the 28-year-old Amadeu Antonio Kiowa fell into a coma from which he did not recover. He died two weeks later.
>
> Amadeu Antonio Kiowa was one of the first fatalities of racist vio-lence following Germany's reunification. Five of the young culprits were convicted by the court in Frankfurt/Oder and received sentences ranging from probation to at most four years in prison. It was never established who dealt the fatal blow. Amadeu Antonio Jr. never got to know his father: he came into the world a few weeks after Amadeu Antonio Kiowa's death. Today he lives with his mother and his three siblings in the state of Brandenburg [Germany]. (Amadeu Antonio Foundation 2010)

In the post-Wall context, street violence is linked to the absence of adequate bureaucratic accountability to these maimed and murdered subjects. Here, we begin to see the implausibility of the claims of peaceful revolution at the cen-ter of post-Wall "freedom." From the perspective of noncitizens, 1989 was the beginning of a new violence.

I went to talk to Kahane about the links between her work, the fall of the Wall, and post-Wall violence. We met in her office, which is located in the extremely hip revamped center of Berlin, which is also a historically Jew-ish quarter that continues to sustain some Jewish German institutions, pri-marily via the post-Wall emergence and increased presence of Russian Jewish immigrants. Kahane is the daughter of German Jewish parents who were also committed socialists. Although she had been in the running to become the post-Wall *Ausländerbeauftragte* for Berlin after the CDU (Christian Democratic Union, the center-right party) stalwart went into retirement in 2003, her one-time, brief role as an *Inoffizielle Mitarbeiterin* (unofficial informant) for the STASI (the East German secret police) made her ascendance to this position politically impossible (see Kahane 2004).

It was the beginning of the week and she had just come back to Berlin from Dresden, where a coalition of protesters had successfully blocked the procession of a major neo-Nazi demonstration. In spite of this success, she was somewhat irritated that the *Evangelische Kirche* (the German Protestant Church) had taken so much credit for it without also acknowledging their partial responsibility for the deportation of Jewish Germans during the Holocaust. Her uncle, she said, had been deported from Dresden.

In our conversation,[4] it became apparent that she was also troubled by an event she had attended the night before, a symposium on structural racism in Germany, sponsored by a coalition of groups in honor of Black History Month. She was annoyed, in part, that people at the event blamed capitalism for the persistence of racism. One Afro-German woman, she said, argued that things had been better in East Germany. During our conversation, Kahane countered:

> *The fall of the Wall just laid it [racism] out in the open. That means, it just made it public. It was already there. It's not as if the change* [die Wende] *came and then, all of a sudden, the heavens fell. . . . It was really* Volksgemeinschaft *[the East German official term for "national community"]. And that's how people talked . . . about the Poles, about the Blacks, about the Vietnamese, and so on. About the Jews. That was simply the reality. That was daily life.*

Kahane argued that the turn to violence against noncitizens or those who were perceived as such did not happen "because capitalism came." At this suggestion, she laughed mockingly. "It's because that's how the people were." She continued:

> *The mood, from my perspective, was exactly the same in the '80s. It didn't surprise me at all. . . . The people, lots of people, said, "Huh? What's going on here? Where are all of these Nazis coming from?" I said: "Where were you living?" . . . Since the middle of the '80s, there were so many Nazis in the GDR [East Germany]. And the mood, the xenophobia, the racism, the anti-Semitism. It could be felt everywhere. There was a reason that I couldn't stand it any longer.*

After meeting Kahane, I thought it important to also get another perspective. I decided to go to the office of an old friend, activist Biblap Basu, who works for an anti-racism advice center called Reach Out, in Kreuzberg, a prominent immigrant/student/bohemian neighborhood. I ran into him on the street as I arrived at the center. He seemed surprised and happy to see me. I was only in Berlin for a few days, so I was happy that he was there and, as it turned out, he had a great deal to say about the post-socialist moment and the emergence of massive racialized violence. His comments had a lot to do with (implicitly, if not on the surface) citizenship and the production of noncitizens after the fall of the Berlin Wall. Even though he is also fluent in English, we conducted our conversation in German. He allowed me to record:

> *My analysis is that . . . this vehemence, this concentration of racist attacks and . . . racist violence in that time period . . . came about because the West German state delivered the message, "People from the GDR, Germany is yours," already just before the fall of the Wall. "Germany is yours and you are the rightful," so to say, "owners of Germany. And don't let anyone take it away from you. And there are lots of people who are sitting in boats and who want to come here, and who want to make your lives difficult. Or they already live in Germany, but they don't have any right to Germany. This land doesn't belong to them. Be careful. Be on alert." That, approximately, was the message.*

The message that Biblap Basu recounted was, of course, not literally said. But the message is revealed in legal discourses and legislative debates, in institutional settings and newspaper accounts. As many have noted, East German citizens were legally always citizens of the West German state even before the fall of the Wall (see Borneman 1992). I will interrogate both Kahane's and Basu's claims about the emergence of violence, but I also will reveal the broader processes that led and continue to lead to the production of noncitizens.

Basu concluded:

> *The GDR was not an anti-racist state, but the GDR was also not especially racist. [It was not] more racist than the FRG [Federal Republic of Germany, or West Germany]. . . . What was present in the GDR that was not present in the FRG was a state sanction against an openly racist attack . . . and the people were not allowed to act openly in a racist manner. That was . . . the GDR. In contrast, in the FRG . . . such sanctions did not exist.*

My aim is not to advocate a return to the socialist past, but to think critically about this past in the context of the future of noncitizenship, and to examine 1989 as a key moment in which the claims of freedom also enabled violence.

An Ethnographic Entrance

Nearly nine years prior to these conversations, in 2001, I was in Berlin to work on a film for the American cable network MSNBC about the National Party of Germany (NPD)—a far right party. Hired as an associate producer, my idea was to focus, in particular, on the noncitizens living in so-called *National befreite Zonen* (nationally liberated zones, or what I had come to call neo-Nazi zones), regional spaces that were supposedly foreigner-free, having been "liberated" by young neo-Nazis, many of whom were in some way affiliated with the NPD.[5] My contribution would be to add the perspective of the impact, spread, and influence of a neo-Nazi party, based on the experiences of those perceived to be non-nationals living in the zones in which the NPD was receiving the most support measured by the party's success in elections and in the recruitment of young people. While one should refrain from contributing to the stigmatization of the East as "less developed," "backward," and "more racist," one should nevertheless note that all of the *Zonen* were in the former German Democratic Republic (East Germany).

As we worked on the film one day, on the grainy image of a TV tuned to CNN in an asylum hostel where I was directing my portion, I saw airplanes crashing into the World Trade Center in New York City. The cameraman, Guillermo (from Peru), and I were sitting down for a lunch hosted by a resident of the hostel. I immediately called one of the film's producers in Berlin and told him what had happened. He had not yet heard and asked who I thought could have orchestrated this. "Osama bin Laden?" I mused.

That evening, Guillermo and I stayed overnight at a hotel. I didn't leave the hotel that evening, and we spent a lot of time at the bar watching German television, which showed looped images of people jumping from the World Trade Center buildings. I remember a German man at the bar saying something about George W. Bush and worrying that this could be the beginning of World War III. During the subsequent days and weeks, the state-financed German television station showed Palestinian women in headscarves celebrating (as it turned out, they didn't know what had just happened), as well as images of women in headscarves walking through their neighborhood in Berlin-Kreuzberg.

The fear of sleeper cells was central to the ensuing discourse. At some point, one of the MSNBC producers asked if I thought any of my contacts in Greifswald might know any of the attackers. I thought this was an absolutely ridiculous question, but as it turned out, al-Makadi (a student-imam in the university town) had been the imam of one of the September 11 "death pilots" in Greifswald, and the producers used my interview with him in *The Making of the Death Pilots*, a film that at the time it was released was the most-watched documentary on MSNBC.[6]

In further reflecting on that period, I am struck by the fact that the enormity of September 11 obscures the everyday terror of people of color living in these zones. In *The Making of the Death Pilots*, there is no reflection on their experiences of terror in the context of the destruction of the World Trade Center and the massive loss, hurt, fear, and violence, not even in Germany. Could there be a link between the experiences of this terror and the willingness to become a "death pilot"?

Given what was turning out to be the important German dimensions of the attack on the World Trade Center (all of the suspected pilots had studied and convened in Hamburg before going to Florida to learn how to fly), our focus as filmmakers quickly switched from neo-Nazis to the social production of the death pilots and the planning of the Twin Towers attack. We had footage of some of the neo-Nazis, with whom we had become familiar in Germany, protesting in support of the attack. But in the context of September 11, that protest seemed marginal, and that film was quickly dropped; we moved on to examine much more pressing matters—from the perspective of Americans and the Euro-American world.

Before I left Germany that year, however, I completed my own short documentary film called *neo-nazi zone*. Even while these globalized events were taking place, I believed that one should not forget the local implications for the noncitizens living in these spaces. Years later, when President George W. Bush first visited Chancellor Angela Merkel in Germany, he came to the same region where I had been filming. (Chancellor Merkel had grown up in this area.) When Bush came, some of the local and national media criticized the sudden infusion of capital to repave roads and to provide security measures to make it safe for an American president at war. Similar criticisms reemerged when the G8 summit was held in the same province at an exclusive hotel while the general public was kept at an extreme distance. I returned to the area to observe the protests and the police response. While some of the protesters made mention of the persistent racial violence in these zones, there was little or no mention of it in the mainstream press. Interestingly, because of the exceptional presence of so many police officers and so much media, with the exception of the threat of fire hoses being unleashed, this was the one post-1989 moment in which I felt safe in this region.

Neo-nazi zone: A Filmic Encounter with the Persistence of Post-Wall Violence

After a four-hour drive, we arrive at the asylum home, where 300 asylum seekers stay. When I see the police officer with the bulletproof vest gripping his rifle (smiling, with two kids on either side of him), I wonder whether he is there to protect them or to keep them from leaving.

Inside the temporary barracks (defined by its narrow hallways and plain, sterile, white walls), we find whole families living in one room, and we meet an Iraqi man who has been living in the same room for five years. His shutters are closed and he sits there alone.

> *Me [voice-over]:* Mit den Nazis, wann war das? *[With the Nazis, when did it happen?]*[7]
>
> *Him:* Drei Mal . . . *[Three times . . .]*
>
> *Me [voice-over]:* *He tells me he's been beaten up three times by skinheads.*
>
> *Him:* Achtzehn Menschen. *[Eighteen people.]*
>
> *Me [voice-over]:* *He has trouble speaking German. He hasn't had access to German courses for the whole time he's been living there.*
>
> *Him:* Polizei Rostock weiß. *[The police in Rostock—the main city in the region—know.]*
>
> *Me [voice-over]:* *Television seems to be the only way that he can have access to any outside world. Television is his world outside the asylum home. [The camera zooms in on his television, which shows a mosque, and we hear devotional singing.]*
>
> *Him:* Aber ein oben, das machen— *[But one upstairs did this—] [He wraps both hands around his neck and looks up through metal-framed glasses toward the ceiling, his tongue sticking out slightly over his bottom teeth as if he has already breathed his last breath.]* Tot machen *[Made (himself) dead].*
>
> *Me [voice-over]:* *He tells me that the person upstairs has killed himself and the person next door has also killed himself. And he's also sick. He doesn't want to stay here. He wants to leave.*
>
> *Him:* [I'm] Forty-six-years [old].
>
> *Me:* Excuse me?
>
> *Him:* Forty-six years.
>
> *Me [voice-over]:* *He starts crying, and I'm not sure how to respond. All I can do is ask him how old he is. He says that he's forty-six (although he looks at least a decade older, his hair—including his beard—is almost completely gray).*

I ask him what he does during the day. He tells me, he just wants to go visit his brother and cousins in West Germany.

Him: *I'm very tired. [A tear falls from the corner of his eye after a large drop has formed.] I also want to die.*

Me [voice-over]: *He tells me that he also wants to kill himself.*

Him: Kleines Zimmer. *[Small room.]*

Me [voice-over]: *He's been sitting in the same room for five years.*

Him: Sitzen. Ein Jahr. Zwei Jahre. Drei Jahre. Fünf Jahre. *[Sitting. One year. Two years. Three years. Five years.]*

Scene ends with a kid pointing toward the police officer's guns

Kid: Du hast Pistolen. Du hast zwei Waffen. *[You have pistols. You have two weapons.] [Actually, one gun appears to be a semi-automatic rifle.]*

Police Officer: Mmmmm hmmmmmm.

Me [voice-over]: *As it turns out, the asylum compound is on [actually near] the Baltic Sea, next to a major vacation destination for German tourists.*

Cut to a view from a car on a rural road approaching a new town

Me [voice-over]: *Now we're driving to Anklam on the Polish border. The lawyer has told me that this is one of the most dangerous cities in Mecklenburg-Vorpommern [a federal state].*

Me [voice-over]: *I go to the police station first to find out what the state of things is. [I walk across the street and go inside a building marked* Polizei. *We see a police officer with four stars affixed to each shoulder of his uniform.]*

Police Officer: Es gibt so eine Dynamik und dann entwickelt sich diese Gruppendynamik, dass man dann aus der Situation heraus so aggressiv reagiert.

Me [voice-over]: *The police officer begins by explaining to me that there's a situation in which young people, German people, when they're in a group, and they've drunk alcohol, they start to become aggressive.*

We reenter the conversation slightly later

Police Officer: Ich sag mal, Anklam ist eine ganz kleine Stadt, hat nur sechzehn oder siebzehntausend Einwohner, uhmm und jeder. . . .

Me [voice-over]: *He tells me that Anklam is a small city with only 16–17,000 citizens and that people who have a different color of skin, they stand out.*

Police Officer: Ja, es gibt keine. *[Yes, there aren't any.]*

Me [voice-over]: *He claims that the situation in Anklam is different from big cities like Hamburg or Berlin.*

Police Officer: Es gibt keine Anonymität . . .

Me [voice-over]: *There's no anonymity . . .*

Police Officer: . . . wie in Berlin oder in Hamburg. Und wo es über Jahr und Jahrzehnte, es gehört einfach dazu, dass es auch dort . . . [. . . *such as in Berlin or Hamburg. And where over years and decades, it's simply part of normal life, that . . .]*

Me [voice-over]: He says people in those cities are used to foreigners.

Police Officer: Das war nach der Wende etwas völlig Neues für das flache Land. *[He motions with his hands back and forth, to show the flatness of the region.]*

Me [voice-over]: But after the fall of the Wall, this is completely new for Mecklenburg-Vorpommern, what he calls the flat lands.

Police Officer: Sicherlich, dann auch, eine völlig Neue Situation so wohl für die Menschen als auch für die Asylbewerber.

Me [voice-over]: He says that this is a completely new situation for the people and for the asylum seekers. [One should note that he differentiates between "people" and "asylum seekers" in his understanding of the implications of the fall of the Berlin Wall.]

Me: Was heißt "National befreite Zone"? *[What is a "nationally liberated zone"?]*

Police Officer: National befreite Zone das ist ein Begriff der. . . . *[Nationally liberated zone is an expression.]*

Me [voice-over]: I ask him what a National befreite Zone *is and he assures me that in Anklam it doesn't exist.*

Police Officer: Hier in Anklam gibt's keine National befreite Zone. Also, ich wüsste nicht, dass es hier eine gibt. *[There aren't any nationally liberated zones here in Anklam. At least I am not aware that there are any here.] [He smiles slightly.]*

Me [voice-over]: But then he goes on to tell me that Nazis define a National befreite Zone *as a place where asylum seekers are never supposed to go.*

Police Officer: Ein bestimmter Teil der Stadt, wo niemand etwas zu suchen hätte. *[A particular part of the city in which no one, in their right mind, would venture to visit.]*

Me [voice-over]: He tells me that if I know anything about a National befreite Zone *in Anklam, I should tell him.*

Police Officer: Ein Asylbewerber darf dort nicht hin. Wenn Sie dazu was wissen, müssen Sie mir das sagen. Also, ich kenne das nicht. *[An asylum seeker is not allowed to go there. If you know something about this, then you must tell me.]*

Cut to next scene

[*We hear the sound of the rental car's turn signal and then see three young, heavyset men with shaved heads (skinheads?) walk in front of the car. All of them, one after the other, stare at the Afro-Peruvian cameraman and me through our windshield.*]

Me [*voice-over*]: Just as we were leaving the police station, we ran into the Nazis. In order to make this film work, I knew I had to interview them.

Cut to next scene

[*Image of me driving the car, smiling nervously*]

Me [*to Guillermo, the cameraman, who is offscreen, because he's filming*]: Ich habe Angst.

Subtitle: I'm scared.

Me: Wieso hast du kein Angst vor den Nazis. [*I look toward the cameraman*]

Subtitle: Why aren't you scared of Nazis?

Guillermo: Achhhh. Ich steig aus und dann sage ich zu denen, "Hallo."

Subtitle: Come on. I'm going to get out of the car and say hi.

Guillermo: Ich weiß das nicht, Mann . . . [*I don't know, one . . .*]

Me [*voice-over*]: I don't know what to do.

[*Eventually, we stop the car in front of the stand where the NPD (the far right party) is handing out information. One of the young men immediately holds one of the pamphlets up to hide his face, as our camera is pointed toward the group.*]

Guillermo: Was ist das? [*What's that?*]

[*The leader shouts to us as we roll down Guillermo's window. In front of the table where they are pamphleting hangs a banner:* Freiheit ist immer die Freiheit der anders Denenden! *(Freedom is always the freedom of the one who thinks differently!)*][8]

Leader: Schönen guten Tag. Haben Sie eine Filmerlaubnis? [*Very good day to you. Do you have a film permit?*]

Me [*not in the picture, shouting from the car*]: Können wir ein kurzes Interview machen? [*Can we do a brief interview?*]

Subtitle: Guillermo: *No.*

Leader: Ihr Nummernschild ist registriert und sie werden eine Anzeige erhalten. [*We've written down your license plate number and we're gonna notify the police.*]

Me [*voice-over*]: We drive around the block several times. I'm not sure about the legal situation or whether the Nazis are just bluffing, so I call the producer.

[*As we drive around the block, the camera is still focused on the Nazis pamphleting. The leader appears to be talking on the phone. As Guillermo zooms in, he finishes his conversation. Another young party devotee gives us a sarcastic smile and a "thumbs up." From one angle, we can see an old BMW with an NPD flag draped over part of the roof and coming down over the driver's and back passenger's windows. There is another banner on the hood of the car and an NPD picnic umbrella (the kind that most political parties in Germany use to announce their presence in public spaces) behind the car, next to the table full of flyers.]*

Me: *John, it's Damani. We're in Anklam and [the leader] Spiegelmacher's here. [I know who he is because another part of the team, including Guillermo, has been filming him at NPD demonstrations.]* NPD Leute *[people] with lots of Nazis, like, pamphleting.*

[Guillermo snickers in the background. The camera is focused on me talking on my cell phone.]

Me: *Yeah, we did, but what's the rule? Like, they said they're going to call the police. Is that okay? It's legal, right? Guillermo wasn't sure if it was legal. Yeah, it's on the corner of the street in downtown Anklam. You are? Okay. No, no, no. It's outside, on the corner. They're pamphleting.*

[Spiegelmacher is handing pamphlets to people passing by. One woman walks by with a baby stroller. While she doesn't take the pamphlet, an older woman (her mother?) who seems to be walking with her takes one and folds it in half as if to make it small enough to fit into her jacket pocket or purse.]

Me: *Should I worry about getting beaten up? Yeah, it's getting dark. All right, all right, all right. Thanks. Goodbye.*

[After hanging up, I sigh loudly once again, and Guillermo chuckles]

Cut to next scene

[Spiegelmacher appears in the center of the frame with my microphone in front of his mouth]

Me *[voice-over]: When I get there, my hand is shaking. I'm cold. During the interview, I know that my hand is shaking, and I want it to stop. I don't want them to think or to know that I am scared.*

Me: Haben Sie im bezug auf Gewalt eine Veränderung nach der Wende bemerkt? In Bezug auf Gewalt gegen Ausländer? *[As it concerns violence, have you noticed a change since the fall of the Wall? In terms of violence against foreigners?]*

Spiegelmacher: Also, diese Veränderung kann man ja nicht bemerkt haben, da die DDR . . . *[Actually, one couldn't have noticed this change, since the GDR . . .]*

Me *[voice-over]: Maik Spiegelmacher is one of the leaders of the neo-Nazi party of Mecklenburg-Vorpommern. I asked him if he's noticed a change since the fall of the Wall in terms of violence against foreigners. He says that this isn't possible because, actually, East Germany was a nationalist state and they didn't have a problem with foreigners. He speaks eloquently and goes on to say that multiculturalism has not functioned anywhere in the world, that people should live next to each other, but not mix.*

Spiegelmacher: Wenn jeder Mensch, in seinem Heimatland, in seinem Volk behütet aufwachsen und leben kann, dann hat er garantiert von sich aus nie den Drang in irgendein anderes Volk hineinzugehen. Auf keinem Fall. *[When every person can grow up protected in his homeland, in his Volk (nation, folk), then I would guarantee that he won't be compelled to go into another nation. No way.]*

[The film cuts between Spiegelmacher speaking, young people taking pamphlets from the stand, the image of the NPD umbrella, and then an image of a "White Power" sticker on the back of the old BMW. It has a clenched fist, the same sign that one might have seen at a solidarity demonstration or that Nelson Mandela gave after he came out of prison in South Africa, except this time the clenched fist is white.]

Me [voice-over]: It feels strange shaking the hand of someone I know tried to kill someone else with a baseball bat. And he tried to identify with me. He told me that he didn't want Germany to have something like American slavery. That doesn't make any sense.

[I think Spiegelmacher's point is that the only reason for the presence of the Other in Germany or in the U.S. is for purposes of exploitation. He is arguing for a National Socialist vision of contemporary life in which the state provides for and protects the national Volk. This vision, however, cannot be thought of apart from his previous attempt to kill a Moroccan immigrant with a baseball bat, for which he was convicted and has served jail time. Street violence remains part of the logic of purity and protection, particularly after the Wall, when the East German state has fallen apart and many former East Germans have had to move to West Germany to find jobs and to create viable economic lives.]

Cut to Greifswald

[Image of me outside the Studentenwohnheim *(student dormitory), walking toward the prayer scene inside an East German one-story, unrenovated* Plattenbau *(concrete prefabricated) building in a sea of renovated high-rises]*

Me [voice-over]: The next day we go to Greifswald, a university town in a northern part of Mecklenburg-Vorpommern, to get a different perspective, the perspective of students.

Cut to inside the prayer scene

[Al-Makadi sings (the call to worship?), closing his eyes, with his head turning toward the light and back toward the wall, his fingers (all five on each hand)

touching either side of his face. Then, we see him in a line with other men, arms crossed, standing, with their heads slightly bowed, whispering prayers. There is also one child standing among the young men.]

Me [voice-over]: The warmth of the prayer scene makes me feel at ease. Inside, I can feel at home.

Cut to interview with al-Makadi

Me [voice-over]: Al-Makadi has lived in Greifswald for the past ten years. A general medicine and then dentistry student, he is also the de facto imam for the Muslim students who live here. Al-Makadi says that before he came to Greifswald, he had lots of contact with students from Yemen who studied here and who said that Greifswald was amazing, incredible, but he says that was before the fall of the Wall. For me, it is beginning to become clear that the fall of the Wall had a great deal to do with the establishment of the neo-Nazi zones.

[As I am talking on the voice-over, the film cuts between the image of the interview and a news report on ZDF (Germany's number-two, state-funded television station). On the screen, we see the television news headlines and the news anchor reading a report. The headline reads: Wieder gewalt gegen Ausländer *(Once again, violence against foreigners). Under these words is a map with dots and the names "Greifswald" and "Ueckermünde" in yellow. In white capital letters and a slightly larger font is the name "Mecklenburg-Vorpommern." Before my voice comes in, the viewer can hear the announcer say:* Nach Auschreitungen gegen Ausländer . . . *(After riots against foreigners . . .)]*

Cut to al-Makadi's dorm room

[As I recall, we asked him to put a prayer mat on his bookcase. We also featured his books with Arabic script at the center of our frame, establishing him visually as a religious figure. At this point, our film had begun to be about September 11 and the making of the death pilots. The pilot of the plane that crashed in Pennsylvania had been a student in Greifswald and knew al-Makadi. We had interviewed the former student's German landlady in Hamburg, who described him as a lovely young man who had even attended the funeral of the landlady's husband. He had a cousin who still lived in Greifswald. He had grown up middle class in Cairo and attended a Catholic school. I wondered to what extent the experience of living in Greifswald, among hostile neo-Nazis, had contributed to his radicalization.]

al-Makadi: Da kam die Leute und wollten uns angreifen. *[The people came and wanted to attack us.]*

Me [voice-over]: He describes the attack in October 1992. He speaks perfect German and is very charismatic. Neo-Nazis came to attack their dorm. The former students with [the help of] German students had to defend themselves. The police came, but didn't do that much.

The film has cut to a scene of the evening of the attack with police in riot gear casually patting down the apparent attackers. The viewer also sees the burning remnants of Molotov cocktails on the sidewalk as police walk by. Cut back to al-Makadi

Me [voice-over]: They typically arrest people, al-Makadi said, but let them go after two or three days.

al-Makadi: Und dann plötzlich findet man, dass man ohne Hand oder ohne Bein oder. *[He makes a clicking sound to indicate that someone has gone insane.]*

Me [voice-over, translating al-Makadi's words]: And then, all of a sudden, they were without a leg or an arm or they've gone crazy.

Cut back to scene of the attack with police arresting some of the young male attackers

[Two adults are talking casually to the police in front of the half-full paddy wagon.]

Me [voice-over]: He says that students ask why they don't organize to do something against the Nazis. The police and the state aren't doing anything.

al-Makadi: Ich dachte die Polizei, was weiß ich, werden auch was machen, aber wir merken, dass wirklich die Leute nichts machen, also, die Polizei zu mindestens. Die nehmen die Leute fest aber, die machen nichts mit denen. Am Ende, [nach] zwei, drei Tagen, werden die [wieder] frei gelassen. Und [dann] machen die Leute weiter. *[I thought that the police, or someone, would also do something, but we realized that the people weren't going to do anything, at least the police weren't going to do anything. They arrest the people, but they don't do anything with them. In the end, after two or three days, they let them go. And then they continue doing what they were doing.]*

Cut to al-Makadi sitting at his desk with a replica of a human skull, doing something with its fake teeth. His university textbooks are open.

[The camera pans to a view, through the open window, of the renovated high-rise Plattenbau apartment buildings in al-Makadi's neighborhood.]

al-Makadi [voice-over]: Also, ich kenne Greifswald viel mehr als meine Heimat San'a, wo ich jetzt da wohne.

With the very last words, the viewer sees al-Makadi speaking onscreen

Me [voice-over]: When I ask him if he's scared, he says no, that he knows Greifswald better than his hometown of San'a. He's lived here for ten years. But he's worried about the new students who come to Greifswald.

al-Makadi: Die Leute haben Angst. *[These people are scared.]*

Cut to a close-up of a young Sudanese student with sunglasses and a baseball cap (worn to disguise his identity)

Me [voice-over]: We then go to the center of Greifswald, an area that a number of people have told me is safe. On the street, I see a group of young foreign students and ask them if they are willing to do an interview. It turns out that one of them has been attacked. At 7 PM [one day] in April, he had gone alone to the bathroom of the shopping center behind him. Here, the skinheads attacked him. One of them hit him on the back of the head, and the others kept kicking him while he was lying unconscious on the ground. Later, when he came to meet his friend, he was bleeding, and no one helped him.

Sudanese Student: Hat niemand mir geholfen. *[No one helped me.]*

Cut to one of his friends standing next to him, without hat or glasses

[He is standing in front of the store with at least three friends. Both asylum seekers and foreign students in the area tell me it is necessary to move in a group when walking around in these zones.]

Me [voice-over]: After hearing the story, I ask the students if they are going to stay in Greifswald. They tell me that after their preparatory year [language training in preparation for their studies], they're going to leave. They're going to go to another city where they'll be treated like human beings. To Stuttgart or Berlin, where there aren't any racists.

The Friend: Man kann dort wirklich wie ein normaler Mensch [leben]. Die Leute dort sind normal, [die] machen nichts. Es gibt kein Rassisten. Keine. Nichts. Die sind ganz normal. *[One can actually live like a normal human being. The people over there are normal; they don't do anything [violent]. They aren't racists. Nothing. They are totally normal.]*

Cut to an evening scene, leaving one of the towns, and a slow-motion shot of our driving by a group who look, to me, like skinheads. As I recall, they yelled something at us and I sped up to get away from the threat of danger (thus the need for slow motion).

[The final credits include our return to Berlin and Bob Marley singing about chasing "those crazy baldheads out of our town." That was a different context, but it also made sense for the end of this film.]

These film scenes, rendered as text, raise a number of additional questions about mobility, space, post-socialism, multiculturalism, violence, and citizenship. These are precisely the questions I will explore in this book.

Introduction: Becoming Noncitizens

In 1989, the fall of the Berlin Wall seemed to symbolize the ushering in of a new era that would forthrightly introduce universalized bodies to "freedom." The fact that so many people were "freely" dancing on the Wall apparently proved that human desire had willed this end. But this new freedom and the expectations that accompanied it also produced "noncitizens," not only stateless people or war survivors who attempted to enter Europe's borders, but also those who experienced the celebration and the fall firsthand, for whom this end meant an immediate loss of any certain claim to belonging.

At the center of a global political and economic shift, the fall of the Wall and the push toward East and West Germany's unification emphasized "Germany for the Germans," East Germans "not being treated like niggers any more," more stringent regulation of the borders for those non-Europeans and non-Germans who were not already permanent residents, and the fulfillment of the right to consume. These occurrences together produced the conditions under which new incorporations of noncitizens (understood to include all those not seen as German) would be exceptional and conditional, and often rely on informal regulations and individual discretion. The regulation of citizenship and the production of noncitizens would be attached to both formal and everyday invocations of national sovereignty.

The "noncitizen" is the central figure in this book.[1]

The state does not care for her or his body like it cares for the citizen's, as can be seen in policies and the everyday realities of noncitizens' health, education, policing, housing, and employment. In Germany, for example, there is a nearly 50 percent unemployment rate among young Turkish/Turkish Germans. One-third of the people in prison are Turkish or are the children of Turkish immigrants.[2]

Since the Wall fell and asylum in the new Germany has become increasingly difficult, in order to become formally incorporated into the national polity, noncitizen Black men have had to live up to hypersexual fantasies to gain the attention and recognition of White German women who might agree to marry them, thus getting them access to papers to stay in the country.[3] Furthermore, the mainstream German media and mainstream German social scientists have been speaking of and writing about a parallel society that refuses to "integrate," arguing that some people are living in Germany without belonging or conforming to German norms. They are, the argument follows, holding on to their "old," "traditional," "foreign," "different," "macho," "Muslim" ways and not becoming European. The argument against the possibility of dual citizenship (before a law forbidding it went into effect on January 1, 2000) was particularly directed against Turkish nationals, and posited that they would have divided loyalties and it wouldn't be clear that, when push came to shove, their commitment to Germany could be trusted.[4] While this law also apparently opened up the possibility of naturalization, the conditions of its passing highlight the need for a closer examination of contemporary citizenship.[5]

As the notion of a parallel society has persisted, there has been little discussion of the normative society's role in producing it. There has also been little mention of Germany's commitment to those who purportedly live within that parallel society. Furthermore, in the formal legal arena, in exceptional cases, some can still officially become dual citizens; European Union citizens can vote in communal elections. In this respect, "Turks" are neither exceptional nor European. In practice, the national media and the average White German call the people who live in the parallel society *Ausländer* (foreigners)—i.e., those who are participating in a life that is *nicht normal* (not normal). Following the logic of Michel Foucault, one might say that they have refused the processes of normalization, that is, "of becoming normal." Looking more closely, one might ask about the specific ways in which the process of becoming citizens (a process that demands normalization) has been refused to them.

I will show that the production of a so-called parallel society is not a simple refusal to integrate. It is also a politics that cannot be adequately understood by an analysis of resistance. The status of noncitizens is not based simply on personal refusals to become normal Germans, but more complexly on the impossibility of this becoming. The process of "foreign" incorporation is not one of normalization, but one of differentiation. The regimes of governance that regulate the incorporation of noncitizens are operating under a politics of exclusionary incorporation. This process of becoming noncitizens, made more acute by the fall of the Wall, is relevant to a range of subjects, including those who would (in a more equitable world) like to become normal Germans, and at least on the surface would willingly give up the possibilities to "queer" (see Butler 1993) national subjectivity from within, in order to be subjects who will be understood as part of the family.[6] While biopower, the governmental power to foster and manage life, may be in effect for the normative population (see Foucault 1990), by taking care of the national population through a politics that attempts to maximize the potential of national bodies via good health care, good education, and a reliable defense, biopower definitely creates different results in those instances in which subjects are becoming noncitizens. Headscarves, hypersexuality, murder, and even suicide are the symptoms of a politics that officially recognizes incorporation, but unofficially makes it a challenging, if not dangerous, act. I am not arguing that formal state institutions systematically or intentionally murder noncitizens, but situations of willful neglect may ensue from this politics and, further, it has systematic corporeal consequences.

In this context, one should note that to be foreign does not necessarily mean one is officially without German or European citizenship. It might suffice just to have "Black" hair or "Black" skin. For example, at a parent-teacher evening at my daughter's bilingual school in Berlin, one of the other parents, who had a complexion resembling that of an African American, awkwardly introduced herself: "He [my husband] is American, and I am German, even if it doesn't look that way." "Not looking German," of course, alludes to the fact that not belonging is related not only to questions of culture, as the notion of parallel societies implies, but also to the way the physical body gets read by the mainstream society.

Technologies of Exclusion

In analyzing the processes of becoming a noncitizen, following but also significantly modifying Foucault's insights—since an analysis of normalization is not adequate—I have developed the term *technologies of exclusion*. These are the social technologies of governance, representation, and population construction that have the effect of (sometimes unwittingly) managing and producing noncitizen bodies. Following the insights of Benedict Anderson (1991) and Arjun Appadurai (1996), I include in these technologies media regimes which are involved in the construction of national audiences for the evening news, sit-coms, national soap operas, and even the German *Popstars* (a show like *American Idol,* but emphasizing the creation of a pop group as opposed to

an individual celebrity). In this context, management of the national population and its noncitizens is conducted explicitly through formal laws and social
policy, but also in the arena of popular culture.

The actual sites of the negotiation and deployment of laws, policy, popular
culture, and even physical violence are central to my analysis. There are many
unexpected places for and types of noncitizen production. The sites I consider
include neighborhoods, schools, asylum camps, and dance clubs as evidence
that the forms of management involve not only guarding the border, but also
exoticizing and consuming the Other.

The significance of technologies of exclusion in these arenas is the extent to
which they show us that the path of those within the nation-state is not necessarily toward citizenship, but potentially toward becoming noncitizens. Neither
path is straightforward, but there is a trajectory toward noncitizenship observ-
able in Berlin and other German cities, towns, and villages that I see as part of
a larger global pattern. I first entered Germany in 1989 and stayed for a year at
the moment in which the nation and the world were simultaneously claiming
the universalization of citizenship and the apparent freedom it entailed. Yet the
fall of the Wall was a particularly important moment for the intensification of
the process toward becoming noncitizens. We, as students, researchers, activists, and artists, need new terms to understand this process.

In the past, German technologies of exclusion have included technologies of
war in southwestern Africa and technologies of genocide in Europe, including
gas chambers and formal laws of racial exclusion. But after genocide, how do
technologies of exclusion persist? How do they shift? What are the continuities
and what are the differences? Understood more broadly, to what extent does liberal democracy contain the demand for its own exception? English philosopher
John Locke (1988 [1690]), for example, sees the justification for government
codified in the protection from outside forces, the indigenous forces violently
displaced in the case of America, in the protection not only of the colonizing
European community, but also of private property.

In writing about exclusion and the extent to which "the state of exception
is becoming the rule," borrowing from Walter Benjamin, Giorgio Agamben
(1998) points toward the persistence of the technology of the concentration
camp in the form of the asylum camp. It persists not only in the way that it
concentrates people in a confined space, but also in the way that it continues
to work as an exceptional space in relation to national laws and foreign trea-
ties. Although seemingly old technologies of exclusion persist, their purposes
and means are shifting. While marking difference, asylum camps and even

deportation prisons also allow entrance into Europe and into the European nation-states. Under what conditions, and at what costs, are those bodies to be incorporated?

The politics of exclusion has already been successfully articulated in a number of other places. I concentrate here on the emerging realities of exclusionary incorporation.

Exclusionary Incorporation

The concept of exclusionary incorporation is an extension and critique of Yasemin Soysal's idea of incorporation via "universal personhood" into Western European welfare states. In her famous sociological work, *Limits of Citizenship: Migrants and Postnational Membership in Europe* (1994), she compares the incorporation policies of Western European states and finds that in spite of significant differences in the way they incorporate non-nationals into their national polities, there are strong tendencies to incorporate in every case.

Using the language of "host countries" and "guest workers," while admitting the permanence of the so-called temporary workers, Soysal acknowledges the contingency of the nature of belonging for the so-called guests. An emphasis on the official accounts of institutions and social service agencies, however, does not reveal the particularity of exclusion. In her analysis, Soysal writes about institutions and laws as evidence of guest workers' incorporation, while conceding that "the existence of a complex of legal rights and privileges may not dissolve discrimination and empirical inequalities" (1994: 134). She continues: "There is always an 'implementation deficit,' a discrepancy between formal rights and their praxis" (ibid.). It is precisely the empirical inequalities that make the technologies of exclusion visible as they hide behind broader apparent inclusion. While many in Germany have access to schools, for example, in spite of the absence of formal citizenship, an analysis of exclusionary incorporation demands a closer look at the conditions and constraints of incorporation. Soysal emphasizes generosity at the expense of closely analyzing the absence of equitable rights and the production of noncitizens.

The daily experiences of permanent residents and other "foreigners" in Germany suggest the limits of citizenship, not as a general analytical category—as Soysal argues—but as a mode of incorporation. Citizenship in Germany (and elsewhere) operates as an exclusionary construct in both its formal legal and broader social dimensions. Soysal sees this exclusion primarily at the level of political rights. She considers labor rights and social services to be relatively inclusive in Western Europe, and contends that permanent residents have nearly the same rights as citizens. Even though she suggests that there is political exclusion, she is still more optimistic than daily experience suggests, emphasizing noncitizens' participation in labor unions and local foreign advisory committees (1994: 129).[7] A closer analysis of social practice, however, reveals a different reality.

Soysal claims that because ideas of human rights were expanded after the (old) nation-building project was completed in many nation-states, those projects can be distinguished from contemporary nation-building projects inasmuch as national citizenship is no longer as central to ideas about rights. The nation-building project in Germany and Europe is ongoing, particularly because of Germany's East-West unification and post–Cold War processes of Europeanization (see Borneman and Fowler 1997: 119). As this project continues, the guilt that helped establish a universalization of rights in the first place, in acknowledgment of Nazi atrocities, is fading as the postwar generation takes over.

Germany Is Not an Exception

Germany's articulations of modern citizenship in the postwar and post-Wall eras are typical. As cultural geographer Allan Pred (2000) has argued, "even in Sweden" cultural racisms are becoming the norm.[8] In other words, using Pred's adaptation of Marx, "the specter haunting" Germany is also the specter haunting Europe. Germany is not taking a "special path," or *Sonderweg*, but a European path toward the future that is related to a reconfiguration of the politics of "freedom" after the Wall "in which African children, men, and women are dying in sinking boats on the Mediterranean, just trying to get in" (see Partridge 2008).

Points of Intervention

In the production of noncitizens, the day-to-day implications of technologies of exclusion and exclusionary incorporation go beyond the binary opposition suggested in the friend-enemy distinction that for Carl Schmitt (1996 [1932]) is fundamental to the founding and articulation of politics. This is a new methodological approach for understanding the ways in which noncitizen bodies get produced.[9] It is not that most Europeans want to kill noncitizens, but caring for them is not central to the logic of the European nation-state or the supranational body, even though these states insist on universal notions of citizenship and rights.

In *States of Injury*, political theorist Wendy Brown argues: "Historically, rights emerged in modernity both as a vehicle of emancipation from political disenfranchisement or institutionalized servitude and as a means of privileging an emerging bourgeois class" (1995: 99). She goes on to note, "Not only did bourgeois rights discourse mask by depoliticizing the social power of institutions such as private property or the [bourgeois] family, it organized mass populations for exploitation and regulation, thus functioning as a modality of what Foucault termed 'bio-power'" (ibid.). There is, in other words, a contradiction in the universal claims of bourgeois democracy, which simultaneously protects and disenfranchises subjects both external to it and produced in negotiation within it. Furthermore, "freedom" coexists with coercion, such as the coercive processes involved in making a subject "normal." This is exemplified by the example of the intersex newborn, whom doctors in the U.S. have traditionally made female, arguing that "it is easier to make a pole into a hole" than the reverse (see Chase 1998) and that the child will suffer socially if the parents do not make the decision to have this surgical procedure done to their child.[10] But what of the physical and psychological consequences of normalization, and what happens when it is impossible to make the subject normal or even for the subject to pass? An analytic of noncitizenship opens up a space for thinking about how the foreign subject is incorporated into social and political life without being totally excluded. Noncitizenship also suggests a different trajectory for incorporation than the social justice and freedom that citizenship regimes claim to produce. In "Hegel and Haiti," Susan Buck-Morss points out:

> By the eighteenth century, slavery had become the root metaphor of Western political philosophy, connoting everything that was evil about power relations. Freedom, its conceptual antithesis, was considered by Enlightenment thinkers as the highest and universal political value. Yet this political metaphor began to take root at precisely the time that the economic practice of slavery—the systematic, highly sophisticated capitalist enslavement of *non*-Europeans as a labor force in the colonies—was increasing quantitatively and intensifying qualitatively to the point that by the mid-eighteenth century it came to underwrite the entire economic system of the West, paradoxically facilitating the global spread of the very Enlightenment ideals that were in such fundamental contradiction to it. (2000: 821; emphasis in original)

This is a more pointed demonstration of Wendy Brown's notion of the contradictions of bourgeois democracy. In Buck-Morss's example, slavery is a form of exclusionary incorporation inasmuch as European prosperity and democracy require it, and its goal is not death. Through this example, we also learn that the type of freedom that Europeans call "universal" is in fact White and European. We see this, Buck-Morss argues, precisely in the need for the Haitian revolution that follows the French one, which more inclusively links citizenship to Blackness, the exception to universal freedom as it was otherwise articulated in the European and American revolutionary contexts.

To understand the differentiating process of producing noncitizens as opposed to normal subjects, Germany works as a national case with transnational, even global, significance. Writing about the supranational implications of the memory of Auschwitz, anthropologist Matti Bunzl suggests, "The very project of the European Union, in fact, is regarded by many of its greatest champions as nothing if not the antithesis to Nazism and the Holocaust" (2005: 501). In response, anthropologist Dominic Boyer links this assertion back to the German case: "During our conversation, [then chancellor Helmut] Kohl spoke at length of the distinctive burden of German history owing to Nazism and the Holocaust and then explained that his energetic push for greater European cooperation and union was 'the only possible solution to German history'" (2005: 523). In Germany and by extension Europe, the Nazi past and the European response to it seem to preclude the reoccurrence of mass murder or death camps, and the right to claim asylum in Europe emerges out of attempts at atonement for the perpetration of this mass murder. The fall of the Wall suggests a localization of this universalization of rights. And finally, the new German citizenship law enacted in 2000, a moment at which the German government recognized naturalization[11] as a more universal political possibility, seemed to ensure a movement away from blood as the proof of belonging.

Germany is an interesting case because in spite of all these apparent shifts toward a universalization of rights, exclusion continues to persist at the core, as if there can be no universalization without necessarily compromising "the Other," thus producing noncitizens. Exclusion in this case is a way of keeping people out, even while keeping them in, a way of making them into noncitizens. Universalism as an ideology, as Brown suggests, hides its own injustice. In this sense, the turn in Europe to address genocidal forms of exclusion does not mean that new forms of exclusion will not be produced. In fact, claims that seem to demonstrate the ability to learn from past atrocities actually produce a semi-legitimacy for supranational forms of exclusionary violence. After the fall of the Wall, individual European nation-states and Europe collectively again declared the realization of universal freedom. Many observers, however, witnessed an upsurge of nationalism against noncitizen workers, students, refugees, and racialized subjects, who experienced the most intense impossibility of belonging precisely during the period that included the Wall's fall, the end of the Cold War, and the two Germanys' unification, times when the possibility of universalized unity seemed greatest.

Using philosopher Giorgio Agamben's insights, one could argue that this is precisely a moment at which one can see the distinction between being (simply) human and being a citizen. Writing about the French *Declaration of the Rights of Man and of the Citizen,* Agamben concludes:

> In the phrase *La déclaration des droits de l'homme et du citoyen,* it is not clear whether the two terms *homme* and *citoyen* name two autonomous beings or instead form a unitary system in which the first is always already included in the second. And if the latter is the case, the kind of relation that exists between *homme* and *citoyen* still remains unclear. From this perspective, Burke's *boutade* according to which he preferred his "rights of an Englishman" to the inalienable rights of man acquires an unsuspected profundity. (1998: 127)

In the German and French cases, the slave's, the guest worker's, and the refugee's bodies make it possible to see the split between *homme* and *citoyen.* Susan Buck-Morss's example of the necessity for a revolution in Haiti, even after the French revolution, also makes this clear.[12]

The production of national citizens happens alongside the production of noncitizens. Refugee camps, as scholars like Agamben reveal and as my book will make clear, operate as sites in which universal rights are regulated in national and local settings. Because refugees are not citizens of the nation-state in which they currently reside, their bodies are regulated differently. Insofar as national and supranational sovereignty dominate as political forms, rights (both in imagination and in practice) will continue to be regulated and produced in terms of national and supranational (in this case, European) interests.

Through bodies in expected and unexpected locations, the workings of state and suprastate power in national and international law become clearer. In schools, in dance clubs, in the preparation for factory work, and in the communities of former West German guest and East German foreign contract workers, the persistent relevance of citizenship and the workings of the technologies of exclusion and the processes of exclusionary incorporation that produce noncitizen bodies are apparent.

Gaining rights has become a bifurcated process whereby incorporation into the national polity relies on recognition and exclusion. East Germans gain recognition through their "Germanness," while "foreigners" get sent home. Asylum is an emblematic case that at first appears to challenge the exclusiveness of unification. But it reveals the human rights discourse as a form of exclusionary incorporation, whereby groups are incorporated into the national polity only to the extent that they can be tolerated (see Brown 2006) or their claims for the need for protection and care are officially and nationally recognized (see Ticktin 2006). In Germany and elsewhere, technologies of exclusion persist in spite of various forms of incorporation (Soysal 1994) into the national polity.

Soysal writes about the limits of citizenship. I am interested in citizenship's limit. One should note that rights require recognition, and that recognition is part of the process that produces noncitizens, those who Talal Asad (1993) argues are "learning to become different." This different becoming is not only a slowly evolving social process, but at times a requirement for incorporation. Soysal thinks that questions of membership have become less relevant, but they continue to remain central (see Hall, Held, and McGrew 1992).

Sites of Engagement

In chapters 1 and 4, I consider technologies of exclusion in terms of the bodies of labor migrants and their descendants in the aftermath of the Wall, and the movement toward realizing that they could become permanent residents even if they remained noncitizens. Noncitizen bodies in both East and West Germany can be described as "leftover." In West German schools with high "immigrant" populations, teachers call their students *Restkinder* (leftover kids), referring both to the lack of their utility in the contemporary nation, and to their future in the job market. Like leftover food, the rhetoric implies, no one really wants them. They are crudely viewed as the excess of a bygone era. In the former East Germany, both official and informal responses to the former socialist brothers and sisters (from countries such as Vietnam, Mozambique, and Angola) make a description of their social status as leftover also apropos. The post-Wall vision of the European future does not have them in it, even if they remain in Europe. By looking at what happens to these leftover bodies before, during, and after the eras in which they were heavily employed in and needed for factory work, the leftover subject position reveals much about citizenship in contradistinction to the universalizing claims European nation-states such as Germany make about this socio-legal form of belonging. Here, technologies of exclusion include medical devices (such as condoms) and other tools that reference the (past) utility of labor migrants' bodies and a fear of (future) reproduction. Amid this consistent fear of reproduction, after the possibility of factory work has ended, the life experiences in schools in West Berlin of the former foreign workers' descendants suggest the production not of future workers but of the unemployed.

In East Germany, restrictions that included deportation for having children in the socialist republic, little free time, and the active discouragement of social or sexual relationships with German men or women revealed the ways that foreign socialist laboring bodies were turned into machines, much as they were in the pre-unification guest worker era in West Berlin and West Germany. In East Germany, the policy specifically dictated that migrants would be sent home if they refused to work. Condoms were handed out upon arrival, a technology of exclusionary incorporation that kept foreign workers working without other responsibilities to families in the German Democratic Republic.

The condom reveals the official recognition of the possibility of pleasure (i.e., having sex outside of reproduction), but in this context, pleasure does not become an adequate political articulation of liberation or freedom, at least not for those incorporated through exclusionary means. While Foucault suggests "bodies and pleasures" (1990) as a new liberatory articulation in the context of the normative regulations that constrain sexual expression or other "deviant" bodily articulations—a regime in which norms regulate the possibilities of potentially normative bodies—technologies of exclusion necessitate a different politics and a different orientation toward the possibility of pleasure.

Tolerance, as opposed to citizenship, is one critical realm in which technologies of exclusionary incorporation operate (see Brown 2006). Tolerance as an ideology suggests the explicit and public refusal that citizenship is truly universal. As political theorist Wendy Brown notes, one tolerates that to which one is actually averse: "since tolerance requires that the tolerated refrain from demands or incursions on public or political life that issue from their 'difference,' the subject of tolerance is tolerated only so long as it does not make a political claim" (ibid.: 46). I take this argument a step further: discourses and practices of tolerance reveal sites of power and some of the conditions under which noncitizens will be managed. Tolerance, Brown argues, suggests the limits of the possibilities offered by a rights discourse. Broad calls by government agencies to "tolerate difference" suggest not only a differential access to possibilities of belonging, but also the limits of tolerance itself and the limits of citizenship as a universal form of belonging. The nation tolerates different cuisines, foreign music, and some religious expression, but wearing a headscarf is increasingly viewed as an intolerable act. Sexual availability, on the other hand, is a national expectation, particularly as it concerns the exotic Other.

Chapter 2 discusses the possibility of travel, which is closely allied with consumption—the defining feature of post-Wall freedom. Travel is linked to technologies that produce excluded bodies in spite of their persistent presence. Black bodies in Germany, for example, always symbolize travel, even if Black subjects want to make claims as Germans, that is, as both cultural and legal citizens within the nation-state. As with the headscarf, as I will discuss in chapter 5, the modes in which travel and its accompanying bodies of knowledge produce noncitizen subjects are not a process that moves in one direction with victims at the other end. It is a process of "self-fashioning and being fashioned" (Ong 1996), given the available resources. In chapter 3, I demonstrate how this process takes place by looking at sexualized encounters in Berlin club scenes between White German women and Black men, including occupying soldiers. As will become clear, on the other side of consumption are the technologies that produce consumable bodies. In this process, photographic and cinematic technologies and post-Wall legal constraints take center stage as they reconfigure men's and women's bodies, producing forms of knowledge about them and images of them that can easily be consumed.

For Muslim women, wearing a headscarf is a response that disrupts the possibility of being used. It is an articulation of both piety (see Mahmood 2005) and resistance. Linking the demands for hypersexuality and the intensification of the choice to wear headscarves, chapter 5 asks: If Muslim bodies are already differentially regulated, that is, if there is no real possibility for Muslim subjects to become White German citizens (and German citizenship is in some way always linked to Whiteness), then what could the desire to remove the headscarf be about other than freely consuming Muslim bodies? How are modes of consumption related to the desire to remove the headscarf? How are technologies of exclusion related to wearing it in the first place?

In the conclusion, I return to the following questions: Can citizenship be adequately contested as the ground upon which new belonging can take place, or must an altogether new politics be conceived? How can an analytic of noncitizenship work as the ground for such a new politics?

ONE

Ethno-patriarchal Returns: The Fall of the Wall, Closed Factories, and Leftover Bodies

Although socialist ideology and its adherents would vehemently make claims to the contrary, under "actually existing socialism" (see Verdery 1996)—in spite of an international rhetoric that claimed understandings of universal rights and belonging—socialism in the national context revealed social differentiation as official policy. The production of noncitizen bodies in these cases was achieved through technologies including abortion and contraception, forced removal, and ghettoization. Socialism included national economies that differentiated labor power, as in the examples of temporary work and temporary workers in the postwar period in West Germany. What happened to East Germany's foreign contract workers after the two Germanys' unification is consistent with their status in other socialist, social democratic, and capitalist states. Indeed, as others have suggested, *state capitalism* may be the more helpful terminology for understanding the East German case and its noncitizen workers.

The differentiation between types of belonging can be seen in the care provided for the East and West German citizens compared to the production of noncitizen bodies. It can also be seen in the rush toward unification, which reemphasized national belonging and linked Germanness with social, political, and economic rights—undergirding on an official level what neo-Nazis were articulating with baseball bats on the reunified streets.

Backgrounds of "Temporary" Workers and Their East and West Contexts

Both *Gastarbeiter* (guest worker) and *Vertragsarbeiter* (contract worker) are terms that suggest foreignness in each of the two Germanys; these terms also suggest futures constructed in terms of limited stays. The invitation to both of these kinds of workers during the Cold War in West and East Germany, respectively, was also a response to the economic necessity for more laborers, beginning with the invitation to Italian workers in the late 1950s to come to West Germany, and in the 1960s with the state-to-state contracts that allowed *Vertragsarbeiter* (first from Poland, later from Vietnam, Mozambique, and Angola, among other socialist brothers/sisters) to come to East Germany.

What happens when the so-called temporary worker overstays his/her contract or his/her "guest" status? The relevant issues here are: What happens to the configuration of his/her rights, what happens to his/her body, and what are the possibilities for his/her political participation? In the initial East and West German formulations, he/she was never a citizen, and there was no plan for permanent immigration or naturalization. Furthermore, in almost all cases, the kind of labor for which the guest or contract worker was brought in was physical. In other words, not only the economy, but also their age would limit the utility of these workers. Here, I want to distinguish the politics of economic utility from those of rights, security, or care.

With the financial crisis of the 1970s, the guest worker jobs began to disappear from West Germany, but there was no political possibility (perhaps because of the background of the Holocaust) of forcing people to leave who wanted to stay, and eventually the federal government implemented a family unification policy, which allowed immigrants who had participated in the guest worker program to bring family members to West Germany, with some notable restrictions (see Chin 2007).[1]

In East Germany, the fall of the Wall led to the disappearance of East German state-owned factory jobs; many were initially bought cheaply by West German entrepreneurs, but then ultimately closed—with the West Germans arguing that East German factories were too inefficient when compared to West German production. Legally (at least initially), however, the contracts of the foreign socialist workers had not run out. While the new unified German government was encouraging them to leave, they had a legal right to stay.

In the cases of both West German *Gastarbeiter* and East German *Vertragsarbeiter*, what will become apparent below is what happens to "visiting" bodies after they are no longer needed for the economy; what happens to the workers' social and political mobility will also become apparent. With the implementation of family reunification policies in both East and West Germany, the further question emerges: What happens to their progeny?

East Berlin, 1995

Large sections on the outskirts of East Berlin were easily distinguishable from the outskirts of West Berlin even long after most of the Berlin Wall was in museums, on postcards, in living rooms, and in desk drawers. High-rise housing complexes and low-rise buildings from the 1970s shared the same prefabricated socialist East German architecture. The first time I saw it, I was reminded of the projects I used to see from the highway on the way out of New York City. But before the Wall fell, these portions of the East German capital were sites of privilege. They had telephone lines and gas (as opposed to coal) heating, they were relatively new, and there was easy access to shopping, youth centers, and schools.

Now they stand as a reminder of a past era of socialist modernity. These high-rise buildings not only allowed for convenient worker housing, but also made it possible for East German officials to concentrate foreign contract workers into segregated complexes. When the Wall fell, West German Christian Democratic politicians said that these buildings were an eyesore and should be removed. At the very least, they wanted to remove the monuments to socialist leaders and activists and to change the street names. Many East Germans saw this as an erasure of their history. The scents of socialism were gone: the familiar smells of cleaning chemicals that are no longer produced, the outside smells of factories that are now closed, and the smells of East German cars that are now in rare supply (see Berdahl 1999). But in addition to the changes in the physical landscapes, which still for the most part remain on the edges of the eastern German cities, there are living bodies left over with no clear sense of future purpose. These are the bodies of former factory workers who came from Mozambique, Angola, China, North Korea, Cuba, and Vietnam.[2]

In the post-socialist context, even former Eastern European citizens' bodies got reimagined and reconceived. Eastern European women, who used to be seen as equally contributing members of the nation, at least ideologically, were remade in new national images. Now there is a traffic in women's bodies from Russia to Germany. The German-Czech border is lined with young recruits to prostitution. In the unified Germany, East German women's bodies are thought of more explicitly in terms of family duties and childbirth, particularly in the projections of West German political rhetoric from the Christian Democratic Party. Unlike the White German women, the former foreign contract workers' bodies are no longer useful to the nation, since the factories are now closed, so these subjects of exclusion are forced to become entrepreneurs. The press represents Vietnamese former workers largely as part of what they call a "cigarette mafia"—people at urban express train stations (e.g., the S-Bahn in Berlin) covertly selling cigarettes without collecting the mandatory state sales tax (see Bui 2004).

Politicians use these representations as justification for the removal of those who did not "go back" after the initial moment of euphoria when the two Germanys unified. In 1992, youths attacked asylum homes and former contract worker housing complexes in East and West Germany. In a number of cases, local German residents applauded as Molotov cocktails shattered glass windows. Young people stood below and repeatedly shouted, "Foreigners get out!" The *Frankfurter Allgemeine Zeitung* (*FAZ*) wrote, "At the end of 1989, there were 170,000 foreigners of whom 90,000 were factory workers living in the German Democratic Republic" (Frankfurter Allgemeine Zeitung 1993), and "foreign students, trainees, and workers had come from the other countries in the 1970s." At the time the Wall fell, the paper estimated that there were 60,000 Vietnamese, 15,000 Mozambican, and about 1,300 Angolan contract workers (ibid.: 6). The paper also estimated that there were 8,500 Cubans, although the Cuban government did not allow these workers to stay.

> For the foreign contract workers, the Maizière government [GDR] decided on June 13, 1990, to give these workers an equal status to the German workers. After the business and currency union and the unification with the Federal Republic of Germany [West Germany], the contract workers were offered state aid. If they agreed to return [to their country of origin], they would receive 3,000 German marks [approximately US$1,700] and a return airline ticket. (ibid.)

According to the *FAZ*, most took the 3,000 German marks and the prepaid flight. Others, however, claimed asylum in the new Germany. "At present [May 17, 1993] there are still about 12,000 former contract workers in Germany almost all of whom are Vietnamese. They want to stay here" (ibid.). Anthropologist Pipo Bui has described the return of Vietnamese migrants in terms of mass deportations via airplanes.[3]

In 1995, over a year and a half after this *FAZ* account and several months after I returned to Germany to begin a project on the daily life and politicization of Afro-Germans, another widely read West German publication reported, "Actually, the federal republic wanted to send 20,000 rejected asylum seekers, 10,000 illegal migrants and 10,000 former contract workers from the German Democratic Republic back to their homeland. . . . 'We are of course making sure that refugees won't be exposed to any repression in their homeland,' the

Free Democratic politician reassures" (Focus 1995: 26–27). As former contract workers also pointed out, those who did not immediately agree to take the 3,000 German marks on the condition that they leave Germany could not count on getting that money later. *Focus* magazine, however, following the public policy lead, concluded positively about the politics of return: "The employment prospects for the return don't look that bad. Siemens and BMW are showing lots of interest in Vietnam. Edward Reuter [Daimler-Benz] will deliver trailer trucks and buses to Asia. [Werner] Hoyer [state minister of the German Foreign Office] says: 'The entrepreneurs need well-trained labor with a knowledge of the German language right away'" (ibid.). The politicians' perspective reflected global trends in regionalizing cheaper factory work (see Beck 2000). Since the cost of living is lower in Vietnam, German factories could pay Vietnamese workers much less there, and the German social welfare system would not have to pay for workers who had contracts for jobs that no longer existed in now closed East German factories or in Eastern Europe more broadly. The national thought process was, "Now they can be contract workers back in Vietnam, *where they belong*." But many did not go back, and they fought for the right to stay in Germany, in spite of their confrontations with German labor and immigration policies and violence on the street. Ironically, due to the lack of language training during the socialist period, those workers who did return had little knowledge of the German language.

Leftover Bodies: East Berlin *Neubauviertel*[4] after the Wall

1995

As I walk home at night to my dorm in Berlin-Lichtenberg, I carry with me the weight of my color and see no escape. This is supposed to be one of the most dangerous sections of Berlin, notorious for skinhead attacks. When I tell an African German woman that I haven't had any problems yet, she tells me that I could live here for a whole year without running into trouble, or I could get thrown off the train on my way home. Another woman tells me the story of an African man whom skinheads tried to throw off a packed train in the middle of the day, *"und niemand hat was dagegen getan."* And no one did anything to stop it. That was just two years earlier.

After reading my graduate school application, a prominent anthropologist at New York University writes back saying that she is worried about my safety and refers me to a recent *New Yorker* article by a former leader of East German neo-Nazis. The train station in Berlin-Lichtenberg was the headquarters for his group and their activities.

When I return home from the university, or visit with friends, or go out in the morning, I regularly see young men with closely cropped hair and wonder about their political allegiances, trying not to look too closely and also trying not to look scared. At night, I sometimes wait for the bus, instead of taking the earlier subway, calculating that this mode of transportation will somehow be safer in the dark, because more people are concentrated in the same compartment and I have direct access to the driver should a group of young skinheads get on.

One friend from Cameroon, who is a student advisor at the Technical University and who has lived in Berlin through the period of Germany's reunification, tells me stories every day about people who have been attacked. From his perspective, and from the perspective of many other people of color I meet in Berlin, post-socialist East Germany and East Berlin are the locus for attacks. Having lived with a family from East Germany for three months, I am aware of the stigmatization of East Germans and East Germany. I continually ask them if I am safe and I negotiate my fear of skinheads with my identification with East Germans as another marginalized group, seen by West Germans, Western Europeans, and Americans as backward.

1999–2000

I begin doing research with former Vietnamese contract workers and their children on the edge of Berlin-Lichtenberg and Marzahn, another notoriously dangerous district. This time, as a form of protection, I take taxis, which I can only afford as a result of a generous fellowship. It wouldn't have been possible during my Fulbright year (1995–1996). It hadn't even occurred to me then. I got used to living in fear. Now, five years later, when I get to the western edge of Lichtenberg on the streetcar (which, unlike the U-Bahn, allows me to see who is waiting at the next stop), I get off and go to a nearby stand where taxis are always waiting. One day, however, I don't want to pay for a taxi. I think, "Why should I?" and decide to continue on the streetcar. And then, along the way, a number of youths get on. They don't look exactly like skinheads, but they also don't show any outward signs of friendliness toward me, and I am scared. I am the only person of color, the only person with black hair. After surviving this trip, I decide that this fear is not worth it. That is the last time I save money by not taking a taxi.

The Center

After the fall of the Wall, the possibility of movement in public space is dramatically transformed. Who can move and how they move are at issue. Official and unofficial discourses and acts (two terms that meld into each other) help to constitute a national space that already existed, even in the socialist era, but now the rules of movement have been altered just as the consequences of noncitizenship have been transformed for people of color and for people with black hair.

The Vietnamese cultural center was once also a political center, founded to end police brutality and skinhead attacks and then later used as a vehicle to fight for the rights[5] of former contract workers who wanted to stay in Germany after working in East German factories. The children of the former contract workers refuse to admit to me that they are afraid of being beaten up. Many of the former contract workers agree with their children, but the youth coordinator talks a lot about the fear. Although she is at first skeptical about my presence, once I start teaching English she slowly reveals the various details of the danger, and the fear. She says that most of the teenagers and young adults learn to drive as soon as possible so that they can avoid having to take public transportation, where they might face skinheads directly. One night, when she is driving me home to Berlin-Kreuzberg, she tells me that two young women who frequent the center live close to the Lichtenberg train station, one of the most dangerous areas. Ingo Hasselbach, the famous East German former neo-Nazi, said it was the center of neo-Nazi activity before the Wall fell (Hasselbach 1996). My White American roommate ends up getting attacked there.

A former GDR university student came to the center to apply for a job teaching German. He was originally from North Vietnam, and came back to East Germany as a group leader for Vietnamese contract workers in a leather factory. He recalled the period of change from East Germany to unified Germany:

> At the time it was especially bad with the skinheads, . . . the Republicans [a far right party], the skinheads. . . . They hunted the Vietnamese. . . . As a result, lots of colleagues went back to Vietnam.
>
> Were you scared?
>
> One has fear. . . . At nights [you can't go] on the streets. . . . When one goes somewhere, then it's better to go together with two or three people. . . . Then I bought a car. A car is much safer. On the S-Bahn and U-Bahn [the regional train and subway], there are lots of skinheads. . . . I was also attacked by three skinheads . . . here in Hohenschönhausen [East Berlin] . . . 1990.
>
> It was eight o'clock at night. . . . There weren't lots of people on the train, but the people are also scared. . . . They look away. They don't come to help. . . . [The skinheads] are boys . . . brutally strong. . . . And the people are scared.

What did you do?

I could have returned their blows, but I was alone. . . . I was scared of the consequences . . . [since] my residency [status] was not secure. . . . The police didn't know which legal system they were supposed to implement . . . even the police . . . they weren't sure about their work. It was that bad at the time. I didn't go to the police. That wouldn't help. I just held myself so that there wouldn't be any worse consequences. At the time, I was also naive. . . . I was scared that if I hurt someone, I would lose my residency status. . . . I just let [the skinheads] do it. . . . That's how bad it was. . . . 1990 was a bad time period. . . . My head was all bloody.

Describing a similar event that occurred in 1996, a former contract worker for the East Berlin public transportation line, who was in the Vietnamese army before coming to East Germany, recalled:

I have fought in the past. . . . Did you see? On television. . . . I have already fought. . . . 1996 in the afternoon. . . . One day in the East . . . in Friedrichs-felde Ost [East Berlin] . . . I badly hurt one [skinhead]. . . . They were telling my friend to "Get lost. Get lost." . . . lots of insults . . . and I hit one [with my foot] right away. . . . I did it right away.

There were five there, but five with fear. . . . They got in the S-Bahn and went away. . . . Here, when you drive with a car, there's no problem. On the S-Bahn or U-Bahn or bus . . . sometimes you'll hear . . . "Foreigners get out . . . foreigners . . . foreigners get out . . . foreigners," always, "Foreigners get out" or "Fidschi" [a racist term used against people of Asian descent].

In my apartment . . . my neighborhood is nice . . . no problems . . . but walking on the street . . . on the S-Bahn.

In Lichtenberg, I fought with five young Germans. . . . One was injured and then they were scared.

Contextualizing the Violence: The Way the Wall Fell

An African German[6] woman, Annette from Leipzig (East Germany), who is formally a citizen and who actively participated in the demonstrations that led to the end of the East German state, recalled her experience of unification, the changes symbolized in the social imagination, and how this imagination shifted:

In the fall of 1988, I told someone who was in the Party,[7] a high officer in the FDJ [Free German Youth, the official socialist youth movement], "In one year, everything is going to be different. And I am sure that I am right." And I was right. . . .

And then everything happened; the Monday demonstrations[8] were in full swing. People gathered at the Nikolai Church. And then there were more, and more, and more people. At 4 PM, all of the businesses closed. . . . The streetcars stopped running, because there were people everywhere.

Once, I wanted to go there with my friend. We went, but we couldn't get to the church, because soldiers were standing in front of us—in front and behind with machine guns. That was the first time that I was really scared, because I didn't know what was going to happen. We were probably a group of thirty people. I think that most of the people wanted to go to the church. We did too. But we couldn't. We were trapped. We couldn't move to the left or the right. They were standing in front of us and behind us. Their expressions looked very menacing, but they were all around our age.

How old were you?

We were nineteen. I was nineteen. And . . . we stood there for at least an hour. And then they let us go on, without telling us why we had been stopped in the first place. They simply let us continue. We couldn't make it as far as the church though, because the area had all been blocked off. That was at the beginning of the summer.

In the beginning, people would ask secretly: "Are you going on Monday?" Later, it was clear. Everyone went . . . people of all ages were there. Then the pictures came on television, even in America, I can imagine. But then . . . at a particular moment, the right-wing people started to come.

When?

A few months later . . . in autumn, lots of them started to join the movement, marching with us. And for me, that symbolized the end of the real intent.

Why?

Because most of us had gone to the demonstrations so that we could . . . quote unquote, Be Free, so that we could travel, so that we could consume, so that we could buy everything that we wanted. Most of the people didn't want to overthrow or leave the GDR. We just wanted to travel to places we wanted to see and then come back home.

The thought was never to give up on the GDR . . . to sell our country at some flea market on markdown. But things happened differently. The country was sold anyway. And the people . . . myself included . . . we allowed it to happen. We didn't do enough to stop it. Then right-wing radicals were there. Then I also stopped going, because I was scared of them and their phrases: "Germany for Germans" and the like.

Once a woman called out to me. We were marching around the train station, and then I heard the woman calling. She was walking toward us and said: "You are marching in the wrong direction." I didn't understand.

What did she say?

"You are marching in the wrong direction. You are marching with the wrong people." When I turned around, I understood why. [She laughs] Behind me were the Nazis.

The whole ring around the train station was in motion. The scene was full of people. It was so full that you wouldn't have been able to stand. I was there with my sister. . . . They were just a few meters behind me, the idiots. I then left quickly with my sister. And then came the reaction: "Germany for Germans!"[9]

Yeah, yeah, and you know the rest.

A centrally located church in Leipzig was the place where the movement that would lead to the end of the East German state began (see Maier 1997). In Annette's recounting, it is clear that the movement toward unification and the call for new rights were symbolized by a moment of exclusion. As she noted, it was the desire to consume that drove people en masse to West Berlin. "You couldn't even get on a train," she said. "People were trying to squeeze underneath." She went to West Berlin long after the initial offering of 100 German marks,[10] which the West German government gave to East Germans to introduce them to West German consumption. They had already been fed West German television images, commercials, and the *Voice of America* through the radio waves and television signals that reached over the Wall—except in the area around Dresden, which could not receive the signals because it lies in a river valley, and which East Germans outside of the region called "Tal der Ahnungslosen" (Valley of the Clueless).

Recounting her experience of going to a West Berlin bank to pick up her 100 marks, she remembers, "I was embarrassed. A family from Thüringen [an East German state] was in the bank saying, 'It's our right [to collect the money].' They didn't have to give us the money. I just bought some *Currywurst* [sausage with red sauce and curry powder] and fries and went back to Leipzig."

It was the notion of limited goods, including the desire to have a one-to-one exchange rate and to live on par with West Germans, that limited accessibility to the nation and to the dominant conception of rights (as articulated by the family from Thüringen). Exclusive notions of belonging became apparent just as the possibilities of consumption were confirmed. Even with official citizenship status, certain bodies were nevertheless marked as East German, noncitizen, or Black—and repositioned.

With unification, programs in schools in West Berlin and in low-income immigrant neighborhoods, which had helped facilitate the articulation of pluralistic modes of belonging in the West German nation, were suddenly cut.[11] In the streets of Kreuzberg (a West Berlin district on the border with East Germany), as a university student of Turkish descent recounted, there were massive street battles between Nazis and Turks. Former East German contract workers' rents were increased, just as they lost their jobs; this was much like the situation for East Germans, but the contract workers had no guarantees and no immediate right to German citizenship and its social and material protections.

The words of demonstrators in Leipzig before the Wall fell quickly changed from "We are the people" (*Wir sind das Volk*) to "We are one people" (*Wir sind ein Volk*). The linguistic shift indicates not only a push for the two Germanys' unification as a resolidification of a fractured nation, but also a change from a conception of citizenship based on universalized rights (i.e., equality, liberty, and justice) to rights based on blood or, more specifically, on belonging to the German nation. An assertion of "the people" (*das Volk*) indicated those in whose interest the socialist state claimed to be operating, while an assertion of "one people" (*ein Volk*) suggested the commonality of all Germans, regardless of state regime.[12]

The fact that these phrases were uttered in East Germany in 1989 signals a change in a revolutionary moment from a position that advocated a reformulation of actually existing socialism in terms of a new conceptualization of citizenship and rights in the socialist state, to a position that undermined the socialist state altogether and instead looked for unity with West Germany through an ethno-national concept of the reunifying state. One should note that the West German state (the Federal Republic of Germany) maintained the latter conception of citizenship throughout the postwar era, calling all East German citizens its citizens and at times even buying them from the East German government (see Darnton 1991; Borneman 1992).[13] Furthermore, the reclamation of rights based on an ethno-national status was simultaneously a reclamation of rights based on a male status—i.e., the gendered right to once again be head of the household and father of the nation, again reconfiguring the status and articulation of East German women's bodies. As one sees around the world, nationalism is racialized and gendered, both in its official rhetoric and in its daily articulation in courtrooms, in bedrooms, in parliamentary proceedings, and on the street.

East German men who made assertions about their need to reclaim their status as heads of households and fathers of the nation relied on undoing state forms of paternalism as heard in state-sponsored ideology and policy: "socialist brotherhood," "equal pay for equal work," "free day care," etc. The real effects of socialist policy included vastly increased numbers of women in the workplace and in higher education as well as the importation of foreign labor and university students from countries like Poland, Vietnam, Mozambique, Angola, Cuba, North Korea, and China. While supported by socialist ideology, this policy also functioned in terms of transnational socialist industrial practice. In other words, attempts at alleviating the double burden—working both inside and outside the home—were attempts to free up time and to free up workers just as the importation of foreign labor made it possible for Eastern European, and specifically East German, states to produce at much higher levels than would otherwise have been possible. Katherine Verdery, drawing on the example of Romania, discusses the position of women in the Eastern European socialist states: "The zadruga-state's [state as extended family] interests in their labor-power led it to take upon itself some of women's 'traditional' nurturing and care-giving roles" (1994: 231). These so-called traditional roles included day care, food preparation, and cleaning, all of which the state mediated through guaranteed early child care places, a vast cafeteria system, and easy access to modernized cleaning equipment. Inasmuch as socialist governance emphasized various forms of equality, Verdery continues, "The zadruga-state's usurpation of familial-patriarchal authority is now giving way to policies and attitudes aimed at recovering that lost authority for men in nuclear families" (ibid.: 251).

The more foreign labor the state imported, the more resentment East German citizens had against these foreigners, particularly when foreign and, increasingly, East German women's bodies were "left over" after the fall of the Wall. In this sense, the end of socialism led not only to the desire to recover patriarchal masculinity, but also to attempts to rebuild East Germany as an ethno-national state that would be joined with West Germany. Recovering a national identity was directly tied to reclaiming masculinity, both of which were then linked to rights and freedom.

In a post-unification letter to East German author Christa Wolf, West German philosopher Jürgen Habermas quite perceptively described the formation of nation-states and implicitly the change in demonstrators' chants from "We are the people" to "We are one people":

This political mobilization required an idea with consensus-building power that could appeal more strongly to hearts and minds than could the ideas of a people's sovereignty and human rights by themselves. This need is filled by the idea of a nation; it is this idea that first makes the inhabitants of a state's territory aware of a new, politically mediated form of belonging together. It is national self-awareness—which crystallizes around a common origin, language, and history, the sense of belonging to a people—that first makes subjects into citizens, that makes them feel that they belong to the same political community and feel responsible *for each other.* (Habermas 1997: 172)

In other words, German-German unification and rights were necessarily exclusionary, as the reformulation of state institutions was directly linked to a limited ethno-nationalist social imaginary.

The "voting by foot" that took place as trainloads of East Germans left the East as soon as the GDR opened its borders not only symbolized national identification, but also access to the Mercedes, BMWs, and McDonald's hamburgers that GDR residents had heard about.[14] Nationalism worked like a promise that the East Germans, too, could have access to these commodities and to West German wealth. Perhaps most important, freedom meant the freedom to consume however much and whatever one wanted (see Verdery 1996; Berdahl 1999), assuming one had the necessary resources. In his campaign for unification and in subsequent election campaigns, Chancellor Helmut Kohl and his party counted on this feeling. Only in the election that brought Social Democrat Gerhard Schröder to office in 1998 did many East Germans acknowledge that, with an unemployment rate approaching 20 percent, national feeling alone could not guarantee wealth.[15] The election results indicated this feeling of betrayal. High vote totals for extreme right-wing parties, however, have shown that the disappointment can sometimes lead to a more rigid nationalism based on the idea that "the foreigners are taking our jobs."

Nationalism, however, predates the end of socialism in formerly socialist countries. An upsurge of neo-Nazi and skinhead groups in central Eastern Europe throughout the 1980s has been widely noted (see Hockenos 1993; Hasselbach 1996; Kühnel 1998; Kürti 1998), and anti-Communist sentiment was often articulated as anti-Soviet and anti-Russian sentiment. In central Eastern Europe, Communism was an ideology that was imposed from outside. Nationalism is a reassertion of "the natural" in terms of both its racial and its gendered articulations. The formation of separate nation-states was part of a path that could have led to the undoing of nation-states altogether. But this never happened. Inasmuch as there was an earlier repression of nationalist sentiment, it returned vociferously after the fall of the Wall. Inasmuch as socialist states marked ethno-national difference, a belief in difference was socially maintained, which can be seen in the socialist production of noncitizen bodies.

While East Germany did invite students and workers from other socialist states, they were put in separate housing and monitored closely. When it was found that a worker from Vietnam, for example, had become pregnant, she was immediately sent back to Vietnam (see Hentschel 1997). A former factory translator who first came to East Germany as a student recalls the experience of having his wife visit while he was working in East Germany: "Before the Wall fell, she came to visit here once. When she became pregnant, the factory made me send her home." Forced removal worked as the operative technology of exclusion in these cases. In fact, having relatives visit at all was unusual. Translators and group leaders, however, had special privileges, and sometimes even their own rooms.

The vast majority of foreign workers were put in separate housing with at least four to a room. East German regulations stipulated "one mattress with a box spring, one blanket, one pillow, two light towels, two dark towels, one tea cup, one saucer, one flat plate, one deep plate, etc." (Spennemann 1997: 11).[16] Workers who were trying to sleep were often awakened by other workers who had to get up to go to their shift. Visitors between 10 PM and 5 AM had to receive special permission from East German authorities, and each housing complex had an East German watchperson who had the power to send workers back to their country of origin.

A woman originally from Hanoi whom I got to know over the course of several months described her experience as a worker in an agricultural machine factory in East Germany. She came from Vietnam when she was eighteen:

> I came to Bischofswerda . . . near Dresden. A small town . . . lots of mountains and valleys. . . . It was nice for me. No problem. . . . The people are nice. No problem.
>
> [I lived in a] housing complex . . . with only Vietnamese. . . . [There were] six buildings . . . 370 men . . . 30 women. . . . There was not much space for women.
>
> How was the work?
>
> Hard . . . drilling. . . . It was hard for me. Everyday, I had to cut almost forty pieces . . . with three machines, always more. . . . Every piece was from three to four kilos. I started on the first of November 1987. We had to work through three shifts. . . . This week [the morning], . . . next week [the night shift]. . . . We changed. I was scared of the early shift . . . I can't get up early. . . . I had to get up at approximately 4:30 AM. It took me forty-five minutes

to prepare and eat breakfast. . . . We had to take a bus . . . fifteen to twenty
minutes [on] a bus. . . . We ate lunch or dinner together . . . at the cafeteria
in the factory. . . . Four women live together in a two-room apartment . . .
different shifts . . . [so we were never home on the same schedule].
    Did you have to always be quiet?
    Yes . . . when one came back. For example, my friend had the early shift . . .
I had the night shift.

In spite of these difficulties, many East Germans had the perception that
"the foreigners" had the best housing conditions and were buying up all of the
consumer goods—thus, they thought, the difficulty of finding desired goods in
East German stores. A U.S. journalist, Paul Hockenos, quotes a young man
talking about his perception of East German skinheads at a youth club in Dresden (part of the former GDR) in 1989: "On some things like the niggers and
fidschis, the skins say it like it is. . . . They come here from the third world and
get everything that they want, just because they're communists. But now that's
come to an end" (1993: 2–3). The speaker simultaneously rejects both socialism
and foreigners.

In practice, though, the vast majority of noncitizens in socialist East Germany were there because of their utility, not because of their ideology. East and
West Germany divided the possibilities of migration into geopolitical spheres,
but this did not stop either the socialist or the capitalist country from participating in world markets or trying to produce at the least possible cost to their
populations and industries. In each case, laboring noncitizen bodies were part
of the national equation.

Unification

In spite of the pre-unification utility of noncitizens' bodies, West German
industrialists viewed East German factories as entirely inefficient. With
unification, the new (often) West German owners closed East German factories, and the noncitizen bodies were left over. In West Germany, noncitizens
were replaced by East German workers, by West German and European Union
factories, and by machines (see Candan 2000). If foreign contract workers took
the money offered by the state to "go home," they lost any right to permanent
residency. Many accepted the offer, but some later fought for and obtained the
right to stay. For the larger group, their initial exclusionary incorporation—
i.e., separate housing and stricter regulation of their bodily and social practices

in socialist East Germany—became criteria for their later removal. They had never truly belonged.

The fact that East German authorities distributed birth control pills to Vietnamese women upon arrival (see Hentschel 1997) implicitly acknowledged their approval of extramarital sex while restricting the possibility of Vietnamese babies. Pleasure is not the central site of regulation, but bodies are. Technologies like birth control, which can produce desired bodies and restrict others, are useful to the nation, given the costs of the unproductive years of childhood and parenthood. But even within the socialist context, noncitizens performed jobs the East Germans least desired; furthermore, their work guaranteed them few rights other than access to the East German mark[17] and the ability to send one moped home a year.[18] The able-bodied workers' presence, however, signified the need for a larger population to maintain the necessary level of production. The housing complexes where former contract workers and foreign students lived became the first sites of attack during the period of unification, linking official ideologies of national belonging to street articulations. Molotov cocktails and baseball bats became the operative technologies of a new national production that was everywhere imagined to be natural.

Initially jobless in East Germany and a member of the Party, Tamara Hentschel applied for and was offered a job as a watchperson in foreign contract worker housing in East Berlin. She became active over the policy of sending Vietnamese women back to Vietnam when they became pregnant. She was eventually able to organize housing for these women in East Germany and get permission for them to stay. She continued to be active as unification approached and police and neo-Nazi violence against contract workers became a regular occurrence.

> Are you scared when you get involved?
>
> *I have been affected by the violence . . . in the time when things were happening with Rostock. The same thing was planned in Berlin and we had to protect the housing complex day and night. . . . We had to walk through, past these people . . . I mean, I was pretty well known, but not that famous that one knew my face. . . . Unnoticed, [as] a woman, [I] could go through. The left-wing people came from Kreuzberg [in West Berlin]. . . . They blew up the [neo-Nazi] house . . . and then you just heard how they yelled . . . "Shit!"*
>
> *If they hadn't blown up the [neo-Nazi] house, then the [contract worker] complex would have burned. . . . That was the only time when I was really [scared].*

Otherwise, I would go alone during police raids into the [contract worker] housing complex. . . . The police had a picture of me. . . . Every time that there was a raid, the Vietnamese all had my telephone number. . . . The police, of course, didn't know that. Then it was also the case that neighbors in other buildings [would also call]. I would write everything down, everything they said. Then I would call Amnesty International and SOS Racism. The problem was that when [the West German left-wing activists] came from Kreuzberg, everything was already over. I was always alone there. That was the problem.

[Some] colleague[s] from ARI [Anti-Racism Initiative] . . . they did a street watch. Then I told them what kinds of things I was experiencing . . . that I didn't know what to do any more, because I'm always alone. Then they said, we'll sit down together and make a record of everything I remembered. After we wrote down everything, we went to the press. And then it finally stopped.

How are things now in terms of violence?

The police are restrained. . . . After this initial publicity, then the Vietnamese said, first of all, I'll go to Reistrommel and they'll write this down. Then it stopped. But the violence from right-wing people is increasing again . . . in this part of the city . . . yes . . . in the East . . . but also in Brandenburg and Schwerin [parts of the former GDR]. . . . The societal climate needs to be changed.

We are trying to stay in contact with each other [the anti-racism groups]. . . . That's not the problem. There's a latent racism. . . . There is a state-sponsored racism.

State-sponsored racism?

The election speeches alone, the racist remarks. . . . The intensification of legal restrictions is also racist . . . the law of asylum requirements . . . that they are accused of coming here to receive social welfare.

[While some] doctors are ready to work without money . . . we have had emergency cases in the hospital where the police were called, even by doctors. This is actually a violation of their professional ethics . . . but there will always be people [who do such things].

One sees even the professional medical separation between citizens' and non-citizens' bodies.

The Gender of Unification and Renationalization

Assessing the fall of the Berlin Wall and the two Germanys' unification through the lens of gender and through White German women's bodies further reveals the ways in which these events worked as an exclusionary enterprise, claiming universal freedom and in fact producing newly gendered subjects. While the East German state related to its female citizens and their bodies in terms of the heterosexist norms of motherhood and marriage, it also enforced an ideology of gender equality. This was not equality based on demands triggered by massive social movements, but planned equality determined by state bureaucrats, and practices introduced and maintained through state-funded social institutions. In addition to guaranteed day care and formal laws that guaranteed equal pay for equal work and equality within the family, there was also the right to abortion without restriction and the right to divorce.

Even though in practice women were concentrated in certain professional sectors and failed to reach high levels of management and responsibility at the same rate as men, in a number of technical fields they represented 50 percent of the labor force. This has never been the case in West Germany. In East Germany, education was almost completely equalized in terms of the percentages of men and women represented at each level. With the fall of the Wall, however, women, along with foreigners, lost their jobs at a much higher rate.

Nationalist men in the broader post-socialist context wanted to return women to the home, and some women agreed with the sentiment. Journalist Slavenka Brakalic quotes from an interview with Czechoslovak writer Eva Kanturkova: "It seems that a woman's dream here is to stop working in the labor force. The fact that most women have jobs is not a signal of equality. It is a form of slavery being forced to work because one wage can't support a family. To be equal we must be free to choose whether we want to go out to work or work at home" (1990: 40, col. 1). In a piece titled "Women after Communism: A Bitter Freedom," E. Matyania remarks, "Today, liberation does not mean escaping from domesticity. It means acknowledging the family's role as a refuge, a place providing shelter from a paternalistic state that always knew 'what was best for the people.' And so today, for many Czech and Slovak women, liberation means precisely a return to the family" (1994: 6). It is not clear to what extent this position is true for East German women. A post-socialist form of paternalism that included West German women complicated their situation, as some charged that East German women neglected their families during the period before unification, that mothers refused to stay at home. Conflict between East and West has positioned East German women differently and has resulted in different bodily articulations. While abortion rights were being restricted in countries like Poland after the fall of the Wall, East Germans fought hard to maintain this right, which had been very restricted in West Germany. The resulting compromise was more stringently regulated than the previous East German law but more permissive than what the West German government had formerly allowed.

Alongside practices that point to the re-gendered and re-racialized body as central sites of social and legal contestation in emergent nationalistic movements that predate the fall of the Wall, one finds increasingly rigid distinctions between the public and the private highlighted within these unification battles and their emergent nationalisms. With the fall of socialism, as sites of political articulation moved from private discussions in the home among family and friends to the public streets, the home reemerged as the "natural" place for women. In this sense, post-socialist activism highlights and creates a masculinization of politics at the same time that it excludes the foreigner from citizenship and from politics, and rejects conceptions of a global Communist brotherhood/sisterhood and the equality of women. These nationalistic articulations must be understood as direct responses to the socialist state and its ideology. Just as the emergent nationalistic discourses and practices (and their requisite technologies) rely on distinguishing men from women, culture, as a critical component of nation, takes on new significance.

Unification gained international legitimacy through claims of universal freedom. Rights do appear to be truly universal. But access to these rights relies on an exclusionary enterprise and the production of new subjects who neatly fit within the boundaries of the new nation. The repression of masculine dominance and forthright national identification under the East German regime led to a situation in which freedom was understood as the possibility to reclaim these forms of belonging. Subjects with rights became those who could successfully claim belonging under the new conditions. These conditions forced those who stayed, the leftover students and contract workers, into informal economies or into working for themselves. In addition, they did not have the same access to social welfare as did the East Germans, many of whom also lost their jobs as a result of the factory closings and structural readjustments.

A former group leader for Vietnamese contract workers and a graduate of an East German law school, originally from North Vietnam, notes:

> It's too bad that I can't practice my career. . . . I came to Berlin at that time . . . I worked for a factory. I saw the fall of the Wall on television, by accident. We wanted to go to West Berlin, but it was already nighttime, too late to go to West Berlin.
>
> At the end of 1989, my factory closed. . . . They had to close the factory, then we [the employees] were gone.

I always tried to find short-term work, . . . jobs for a year or so. I am unemployed [frequently]. Then I worked at the unemployment office, for a notary, . . . at the city hall, . . . for a nonprofit. . . . Then that came to an end. In the meantime, I've always been unemployed for a little while.

I'm in the process of starting my own business. It's damned difficult in Germany. According to West German law . . . we, as East German lawyers . . . we have problems.

I've had a German passport for a long time . . . even before the fall of the Wall. I don't have a paper problem. But the content . . . I'm still a foreigner, just like before.

If my career is restricted, then I can't do anything. I work with other lawyers and clients. They are dumber than me, but I get 30 German marks, and they get 3,000. I give them instructions about how they have to do things.

The Vietnamese and the others have to do the dirty work, because they have to survive. When it comes to work, foreigners don't have a chance.

A former GDR factory translator, also originally from North Vietnam, who studied engineering in an East German university, recalls his experience after the fall of the Wall:

I've done almost everything. At first I worked as a window cleaner in Baden Württemberg [West Germany] . . . and then in an architectural firm. In Berlin, I worked on an assembly line. And now I'm working here [at Reistrommel]. I can't find any work any more, and they don't want to hire foreigners.

I've almost decided to [go back to Vietnam]. . . . I've been away for a long time. I don't have any work, or a place to live. Nothing. In Vietnam one doesn't receive unemployment, no welfare, nothing. That's why I've decided to stay here.

Now I've become German . . . two months ago. I can't do anything else. It's too late to go back to Vietnam. My wife and my children are here. My sister and brother are all in Vietnam.

Before the change of regimes, [my wife] was here to visit me once. When she became pregnant, the factory required me to send her back home, because she was pregnant. After the change of regimes, I was able to bring her back here . . . in 1995.

I ask how he survived this time without his family.

[I]t was very hard. I couldn't go back and I wasn't allowed to bring her here, because of my residency status. . . . 1993 was the Family Reunification Act.

There was still a problem with residency. One has to have work, an apartment, and money to support the family. So I tried to meet all of the criteria. . . .

Capitalism was very new to us. We didn't know what capitalism was. At school we just learned about the bad parts. In capitalism, there are also good sides, for example, materially things are much better. We used to have so many needs. But intellectually, one is immediately confronted with xenophobia and social insecurity. One has to fight to survive.

Why Do People Stay and What Happens to Their Bodies?

There is a similarity in the ways the preconditions for the present situation were produced in the former GDR and in West Germany before the fall of the Wall. Immigrants are blamed for their lack of integration when, in fact, German interests produced the forms of exclusion for which the leftover workers are now criticized. Contract workers received only one month of language instruction, mostly to learn the words that they would use in the factory. They were needed for their productive labor power, for their bodies. Scholars, activists, and contract workers have often quoted the phrase *Arbeiter wurden geholl und Menschen sind gekommen* (Workers were summoned and people came). They came with translators and group leaders who could oversee and manage them, and translate their bodies into machines. As one former contract worker noted, these laborers only received very specific training for their particular tasks in their respective factories.

However, all the former contract workers, group leaders, and translators with whom I spoke saw better prospects in staying in Germany than moving back to Vietnam, where they said there were no job prospects at all. Furthermore, they said that they stayed so their children could succeed. Some brought their children from Vietnam many years after unification, and some have children who were born in Germany. Many of the children are already doing well in school. The individuals and families continue to live in East Berlin because of their familiarity with the East, because East Germans have gotten used to seeing them, and because there are other former contract workers who live there. The neighborhoods in which former contract workers tend to live are also much cheaper than those in West Berlin or West Germany.

TWO

Travel as an Analytic of Exclusion: The Politics of Mobility after the Wall

In the relatively homogeneous and closed society of the GDR, Blacks were presumed to be exotic, foreign, and different—patterns of attribution similar to those found in other countries. To be associated with such attributes in the GDR meant also to be regarded as part of "another" society, definitely not as part of the GDR proper, but as a foreigner whose stay is limited.
—*Piesche 2003*

Mobility within Europe is now considered as much of a basic right as citizenship, and civic affiliation is no longer purely a national matter.
—*Göktürk et al., 2007*

I've been arguing that ethnography (in the normative practices of twentieth-century anthropology) has privileged relations of dwelling over relations of travel.
—*Clifford 1997*

If consumption was the principal mode of envisioning post-Wall freedom, the ability to travel was the principal signifier of this possibility to consume. Part of the significance of the Wall and the Cold War discourse against it had to do precisely with the fact that it impeded travel, and thus impeded freedom. How do the symbolics of travel, though, work in relation to noncitizens? How did the fall of the Wall and its association with travel-as-freedom affect them? How did it configure their bodies?

The magazine cover featured on the billboard (figure 2.1) frames vacations and travel through the figure of a Black woman's body (in zebra print, one should note) and the symbolics of a clearly non-German beach. Posted next to

Figure 2.1. *Endlich Ferien!* (Finally Vacation!), billboard, Berlin, summer 1998.

a regional train station in the center of a treeless boulevard in (East) Berlin, the words and the image are all about getting away. But could this woman be German? Could this advertisement be an expression of her own vacation? Or does the image of her body necessarily represent travel outside Germany? How might the representation of her body as a symbol of mobility, fantasy, and travel produce her as a noncitizen? In the context of post-Wall Berlin, we should read travel not only as a seasonal possibility, but also as an opportunity central to what it means to be a citizen. Travel hints at the relatively recent possibility (now material as well as imaginary) for White East Germans to visit non-socialist, non-European destinations with new legal, economic, and racial flair—in particular, to realize freedom as an exotic fantasy. But what does this fantasy do to Black bodies? As an analytic, travel, even more than identity, reveals a great deal about what it means physically to become a noncitizen.

Traveling through the "Black" Body: Setting the Scene

Referencing the hypersexuality that Black bodies represent in European spaces (see Partridge 2008; Linke 1999; Gilman 1985; Fanon 1967), Blackness (in Northern Europe, in particular) must always represent some exotic there and not here, since the implication is that Black bodies have traveled from somewhere else in order to come here. The journey I have taken will make it possible to see citizenship via Blackness, when Blackness signals travel.[1]

My Arrival

I first came to live in East Berlin straight out of Amherst College in 1995, when I was twenty-one. I had already visited East Berlin as a teenager, during the time when the Wall was falling, when entrepreneurs were lined up along the crumbling wall and renting out hammers or were themselves chipping bits of newly spray-painted pieces to sell to tourists—including me. But this was the first time I would really get to know the city. I had lived for a year as a Rotary exchange student in a small town in West Germany when I was sixteen, but now I was entering a world in which the realities of unification and the end of the Cold War had had more time to settle in. A year before I left Amherst, my German professor gave me a copy of *Farbe bekennen* (Opitz, Oguntoye, and Schultz 1992), also known as *Showing Our Colors: Afro-German Women Speak Out*. The book is about the lives of Afro-Germans in German history and in contemporary life. It immediately drew me in. As I wrote in my Fulbright application:

> [T]he Afro-German's daily life exists as a challenge to a history and understanding of the "normal" German that comes through childhood songs, books, teachers, friends, parents, and the news media. Unlike African Americans, Afro-Germans are immediately seen as foreigners because of the color of their skin, and in every encounter, their sense of home, country, and belonging are taken away from them, until and if they can explain who they are and why they are there. To most, Afro-Germans don't belong, even though Afro-German history dates back for centuries—since or possibly before German colonialism in Africa. "I am African, but I'm German, too. African in appearance, German in thinking, behavior, and the way I move: in those respects I'm European" (Opitz, Oguntoye, and Schultz 1992: xxi), one woman explains.

I went to Berlin in 1995 to research the "daily lives and politicization of 'Afro-Germans' in East and West Germany after the Berlin Wall," and in the back of my mind, I also thought of my own identification with my Turkish German host family on my earlier stay in 1989–1990. Their daily experiences of discrimination seemed close to my own in the United States, although Blackness in Germany was configured quite differently than it had been in the States, given the particular U.S. histories of lynching, slavery, and fear (see Fehrenbach 2005). In Germany, I was exotic, not feared. Furthermore, in Germany there is no common history of Black migration (see Campt 2004b). In this respect, the stakes of my investigation moved from racialist identity politics toward an investigation of citizenship, defined by sociologist Bryan Turner as a "set of social practices which define the nature of social membership" (1993: 4). One should note that "social membership" encompasses but is not equal to the more narrowly defined legal regime.

Thus, Afro-Germans can be legal members without seeming to belong. As the head of the Berlin chapter of the *Initiative Schwarze Deutsche* (Initiative of Black Germans) told me six years after the Wall fell: "At the unification party, I saw a young, blond, blue-eyed youth. He symbolized for me the new Germany." Another African German friend, originally from East and later West Berlin, remembers that when she went to the city center after the Wall fell, East German fathers with their families told her, "We are now here. You can go home." Clearly, her body was read as having traveled to Germany from elsewhere, and thus she disrupted the emerging image of German unity. And yet this emerging unity and "freedom" would be based, to an important degree, on freedom as travel. One was free to the degree to which one could move across borders without major restrictions. On the former border with East Berlin, on the American side of the former Soviet sector, the still frequently visited Checkpoint Charlie Museum is largely made up of narratives of East Germans trying to travel outside of the German Democratic Republic by getting over the heavily guarded Wall and into West Berlin. The museum is devoted to technologies of escape.

Travel as an Analytic

In the post-Wall era, examining travel is an important way to examine citizenship and the process of becoming noncitizens. Particularly within the context of the Cold War and the fall of the Berlin Wall—when travel represented liberty (see Borneman 1998; Asher 2005; Göktürk et al. 2007) and the Iron Curtain was a central symbol of Soviet-bloc repression and Western European and American freedom—seeing citizenship through travel helps us think beyond the problematic discourse of immigration, which naturalizes noncitizenship and successfully diverts any hard-hitting analysis of exclusion. John Borneman's (1998) work has been particularly concerned with travel-as-liberty as it relates to East Germans; I am concerned with East and West German desire (to travel, in particular) as it relates to noncitizen subjectivity. It is not just the ability to travel that is important, but the conditions, regulations, and imaginations under which that travel takes place.

In European popular discourse, the framing of post-Wall racial violence in terms of xenophobia as opposed to racism or exclusion reveals one way in which a popular social logic associates bodies with travel. It even psychologizes and individualizes certain forms of violence (see Fehrenbach 2005), failing to see them as necessarily part of the power of national sovereignty, which is substantiated through street fights as well as parliamentary debates and new laws.

The tendencies of European immigration politics (in which allowing immigration has been seen as the progressive stance in a country that, according to former Chancellor Helmut Kohl, didn't have a history of immigration) are tied to more forthright neo-Nazi violence. In the post-Wall/unification moment, the German federal government took the stance that "foreign" contract workers and "foreign" students in East Germany should return to their "natural" homes. The relationship between travel and displacement (terms that Caren Kaplan [1996] takes up in her work) reveals a great deal about the relationship between travel and citizenship. It is not that normalized national subjects don't travel, but that their travel is configured differently.

How one travels or how one is perceived to have traveled became critical issues in the post-Wall moment in which "no fewer than 1.4 million people emigrated from the former East Germany to West Germany between 1989 and 1993, whereas only 350,000 moved to the East" (Göktürk et al. 2007: 13). Furthermore, while many could emigrate to the West since East German citizens were always considered to be citizens of West Germany (see Borneman 1991), many non-German noncitizens, particularly in East Germany, had to claim asylum just to get the right to stay. As Andrew Asher has pointed out:

> While East Germans might be mapped as second-class Germans, they are still first-class "Europeans" enjoying full rights to freedom of movement within the EU. With their movement within the EU qualified for a "transition period" of up to seven years, Poles are currently positioned as second-class "Europeans," but are moving toward first-class status. With no rights to movement in the EU, Ukrainians are positioned as third-class "Europeans" or excluded altogether. (2005: 136–137)[2]

Even this apparently straightforward legal image is complicated by the presence of Black Germans who are legal residents and German by birth, but who still undergo the threat of racial violence that originally accompanied the fall of the Berlin Wall. Even though they are German, their mobility and freedom are constrained by their Blackness, which is almost always read as foreign.

Travel as an analytic of exclusion allows us to see the ways in which the post-Wall moment and associated technologies of exclusion, including legal regimes, and popular fantasies of travel make some subjects more mobile and severely limit the mobility of others, delegitimating their attempts to travel. Seeing citizenship through travel makes it possible to see travel as liberty, but also in terms of constraint.

Europe Is for White Europeans

In 2001, I was filming my contribution to an MSNBC documentary on the National Party of Germany (NPD), a neo-Nazi party that continues to have some strength in eastern Germany. I had decided to focus my piece on refugees in asylum hostels and foreign students who live in what German journalists had come to call *National befreite Zonen* (literally "nationally liberated zones"), or what I call neo-Nazi zones, places where it "is difficult for people of color to move" (as John, a resident of an asylum camp, put it) without risking getting beaten up or killed. I had demanded a rental car and refused to go to these places alone. Nor did I stay overnight except once, on the evening of September 11, 2001; I didn't leave the hotel, which served as my fortress, until I saw the sunlight. These were the conditions of my travel.

Just after arriving in Greifswald, a seemingly quaint university town, I saw some young students of color. I approached and asked them about the lives of people of color in these zones. They immediately understood what I meant, and introduced me to a friend from the Sudan who had recently been attacked by right-wing youths in the town. They had hit him on the back of the head with a blunt object and knocked him unconscious in the middle of the day in a shopping center in the center of the town. "And nobody helped me." He repeated, "And nobody helped me." It became clear that, at least for people who could be seen (or imagined) as foreigners, moving in a group was a necessary condition for moving through these towns at all.

On a tour of this region, Isaac Obuba, a middle-aged Ghanaian man who was a social advocate for refugees, acted as our guide. He had come to East Germany to study shipbuilding, and ultimately got married, had children, and stayed. I asked him and others, with the exception of children, to speak in English, even though this was sometimes more difficult for them, because the original film was for American television. Much of our subsequent conversation, however, took place in German. He told me: "NPD and DVÜ [another radical right party] . . . they're all against foreigners here. . . . In the night or sometimes in the day, they attack foreigners here." When I asked why he stayed under such conditions, he replied: "If we all choose to run away, it means they've won. . . . I also pay tax[es] here, and from these tax[es], they live." But in a meeting in an asylum hostel in Anklam, a small town with a notable neo-Nazi presence, he told me: "It's very dangerous here nights to move here as a foreigner. I can tell you a fact: [for] ten years, I haven't been to the cinema. I don't go at night with my family anywhere. Not in Anklam, not in Greifswald, and not around here. [At] night, I don't move on the street."

In the same asylum hostel, a brown-skinned and dark-haired woman from the former Yugoslavia and her children told me that her husband had been attacked. Her eldest son said that his school is full of neo-Nazis. The two brothers (one is ten, the other is thirteen) told me that it is not possible to feel safe in this town. The younger one told me that big kids in the school call him "shit foreigner," "nigger, African, and asshole." Their mother talked about an attack on the asylum hostel, young Nazis throwing Molotov cocktails, trying to burn them. She said that they killed a former resident of the hostel (see Partridge 2001). Her husband came home, they called the police, and the Nazis disappeared.

On another day, Obuba took me to a camp at Saal. I noticed graffiti on the wall of an old silo in large letters just before the entrance: "Skinhead Power." At the hostel, the press spokesperson for this region, northeastern Vorpommern, met us, partially because I had press credentials, and I asked about the prevalence of this sentiment. Even though he denied that there was an organized presence of neo-Nazis in this town, he described an incident in which a whole group of "Romanian people" in the camp were attacked by youths from the area.[3] "One group of German people came to this *Heim* [home], and they [fought] again, and one [person] from . . . Romania lost his life." He explained the upsurge of violence:

> *I have lived in North Vorpommern for twenty-five years, and I was born in Rostock [in East Germany]. Until 1990, we [didn't] have problems with skinheads. It was [repressed by the] government, [by the] regime. Maybe we had problems in the underground, but not to visit on the people here. The problems with skinheads happened with the switch from GDR to Germany, you know what I mean?*

In East Germany, there was "pressure," he said. In the post-unification moment, asylum camps were introduced to East Germany as a federal (West German) attempt to spread the "economic burden" of the hostels, which are supported by combinations of local and national funds. The camps clearly act as technologies of exclusion.

I talked to some other people in the camp. One man spoke to me through an informal translator, who was also a resident. Translating from Arabic into English, the translator explained:[4]

> *He has been in* Deutschland *for five years. . . . The mother and father were already dead for two years. . . . He just wants help. . . . He wants to get out from his dilemma here. He says, "I am suffering. Where should I go?" He cannot go back to Iraq. He wants his freedom. He says that he is suffering here. "You [he refers to me], or the judge, or* Deutschland, *or anyone who can help."*

The man had earlier gone to Sweden to escape the violence, but returned. The translator interpreted the middle-aged Iraqi man's story:

> *[A right-wing youth in the town] tell[s] Salem that, "You have to leave* Deutschland. *. . . What are you doing here? You have to leave* Deutschland." *So Salem decided to run away from* Deutschland, *because they decided they may hit him [or] kill him. There were also fifteen people sitting behind the trees. They hit him . . . and he ran away. . . . Those people followed him. . . . The guard phoned the police. The police [took] the* Ausweiß *[IDs] from those people. The doctor made a report and sent this report to the police.*

Salem then spoke for himself, in German: "*Ich bin Angst vor zurück* [sic], *und Iraq und so* [I am fear of going back to Iraq, and so]." I asked the translator to ask Salem what his life in Germany is like. "He says that his life here is just like hell." Because he went to Sweden without the permission of the German government, Salem lost his right to *kleines Asyl* (little asylum—a partial form of recognition), but he cannot be shipped back to Iraq, so he has to remain in the asylum camp in a seemingly permanent limbo.[5] Only those whose cases have been fully recognized can leave. The camp is a double trap. Right-wing youth know where it is, and its residents cannot leave legally, unless they "go home."

In the same hostel, I met a young man from Togo. Our discussion moved to the question of travel. "If it's so bad here, then why do people stay?" I asked him. "Why don't they move to a different part of Germany, even if they cannot, as a result of the German and European laws about the mobility of refugees, move to a different part of Europe?" Obuba interpreted the man's response: "Supposing they want to go and visit somebody in Hamburg. . . . It means that they have to go to [another town] for permission. . . . The last time he went to Hamburg, he was caught. They gave him a penalty to pay, about 600 marks [approximately US$300]." The man showed me the court document from the *Amtsgericht* (regional court) in Hamburg. "If he doesn't pay this amount, they can imprison him for sixty days, two months." "Why can't he leave the area?" I asked. He replied: "These are the laws they have here." The hostel resident noted that their situation is much like the situation of East German citizens before the fall of the Wall. They also could not easily travel to the nearby city of Hamburg, which was then on the other side of the Wall. Obuba: "These restrictions, now they've imposed these restrictions on them."

It becomes clear that state authority is complicit with neo-Nazi violence. Not only does the state no longer suppress neo-Nazi violence, it forces people of color to live in neo-Nazi zones. It makes sense to compare the immobility of these refugees to the previous limited mobility of East Germans, who also needed special permission to travel from Saal to Hamburg before the Wall fell. The difficulty of westward travel, however, did not expose the less mobile subjects to imminent violence, as is now the case.

I asked the young Togolese man about his leisure time: "Do [you] go to the *Diskothek?* Do [you] go out to party?" Obuba translated: "In the night, they don't go to the *Disko*. They hide in the room here. That is why this one person [who lives in the same room as the Togolese man] is going mad. He hides in the room here. He doesn't go anywhere."

The Transference of Restricted Travel

Whether one came as a student or as an aide to the GDR economy depended on the ideological status of the country of origin. If the country of origin had—after having gained independence in the course of the cold war—decided to lean towards a Western market-based economy, chances of being admitted to study in the GDR (mostly in medicine or engineering) were very good. This was because the education of the future intelligentsia had to be paid for in foreign currency (meaning U.S. dollars). Countries that saw themselves as part of the socialist bloc did not have to pay for education; often they would not have been able to do so in any case. The GDR bore all related costs for workers from socialist countries, which could be used for propaganda purposes as an expression of solidarity. Citizens of other socialist countries who were admitted to the GDR had to accept, however, that these agreements meant working in the production sector rather than pursuing university studies. A two-class system developed in which the country of origin often clearly indicated whether a particular foreigner was studying or working. People from Ghana, Nigeria, Zambia, and Iraq mostly came to study. In contrast, people from Angola, Mozambique, Egypt, Ethiopia, Kenya, Vietnam, and Cuba went into socialist production and started—according to the economic needs of the GDR—an apprenticeship in labor. Members of this latter group were usually employed in areas where workers were in short supply. This was especially the case in the textile and chemical sectors and in fine mechanics such as the assembling of radios and razors. The foreign workers represented a simple economic calculation for the GDR; even at the beginning of the 1980s there were still approximately 180,000 foreign workers who provided necessary services to the GDR. The import of low-wage workers was, therefore, not solely a feature of West German politics, although the numbers of guest workers were significantly higher there. (Piesche 2003: 40–41)

In the post-Wall aftermath, opportunities for travel were reversed: the West German government wanted all foreign GDR workers to leave Germany. Highlighting this process, the nonfiction film *Farewell GDR* (Azevedo 1991) opens with a scene of a Black Mozambican man on a motorcycle on a road near the ocean. A White East German woman sits behind him, holding him tightly. The film is about leaving East Germany. During the Cold War, Mozambique officially represented another socialist land in cooperation with the eastern bloc, yet this moment of symbolic solidarity has passed and the politics of freedom-as-travel have shifted. Significantly, before the Wall fell, as one Mozambican man in this film notes, "In Mozambique the people didn't understand what socialism was. Only the government itself knew what socialism was." In other words, socialist ideology as practiced in Mozambique was neither particularly liberating nor repressive. Mozambique had no "iron curtain." Its citizens could travel, and a number of them went to the GDR to make money, attend the university, or purchase new technologies. As the film makes clear, on arrival, they also found German women and nudist beaches (images that also link their travel to their desire).

The film cuts frequently between Mozambique and Berlin; the viewer isn't always sure which place she is seeing. White East German women can now physically travel to places they could (for the most part) only fantasize about before the Wall fell. The technology of film produces a time-space compression (Harvey 1990)[6] that happens through the vehicle of the Black body in the sense that the travel destination is now Mozambique for African men and German women. With the fall of the Wall, the significance and the meanings of travel have shifted. In the film, a road here fades into a road there, and into rooms and other intimate spaces. The viewer wonders whether she is here or there. At the same time, the masses of East German cars driving through concrete landscapes contrast sharply with women walking with bundles on their heads. Despite this aesthetic of confused location, the socialist era's material disparity becomes clear in discussions of Mozambicans' need to escape hardship (in Mozambique) versus a desire to "experience their culture" via travel beyond Germany (to Mozambique) after the fall of the Wall. Recalling the time before the Wall fell, one Mozambican man says, "I was a daydreamer. I always wanted to leave Mozambique, even for a short while. I was tired of the hardship. That's why I went to the GDR." Another man recalls, "I wanted to have a German child with a German girl, then my child would be properly dressed, clean, and well fed." Now, the hope of this moment has faded for Mozambicans, while White East Germans can realize it fully.

Africa as the West: Blackness and Travel before the Wall Fell

In spite of the normative claims that even East Germany was part of a wealthy European continent to which Africans wanted to travel, in fact, as demonstrated in the quotation from Peggy Piesche above, there existed a two-tiered system of African presence in East Germany. Among the more privileged, such as African students, their presence in East Germany could more easily be associated with the West. Foreign students could cross into West Germany and had access to dollars and Western commodities. In the cases of students in particular, their bodies, seen as exotic, could serve as a visible opportunity for travel. This functioned even within and partially because of narratives of a global socialist brotherhood/sisterhood. These narratives, however, were complicated by the presence of East Germans of African descent, who were perceived to be foreign even though they had been born in the socialist nation. As Annie Horn, then twenty-three, a dance and performance student who has one African diasporic and one German parent, explained, when a break-dance film came out in East Germany in 1986, "I started to get lots of love letters." Break dancing was seen as a desirable cultural form from New York. Her body (or, more precisely, her complexion) became the physical marker through which some people imagined that they could travel in fantasy, if not reality, to the U.S. East Coast. A former law student, originally from Angola, who had studied in the GDR, recalled:

*We, as students, . . . had stipends in German marks and dollars. We had
lots of money—we couldn't even spend it all. You could have a woman for
the whole night, even for the whole weekend. The student dormitories in the
GDR were the biggest brothels I've ever seen. They slept with you just to see
videos. At the time when I came, the big thing was* Rambo. *I had Michael
Jackson videos. One can't imagine it. . . . The foreign student dormitories
were the biggest brothels, because there wasn't anything else to do, except for
going to the movies.*[7]

Significant here is the Angolan student's access to *Rambo* and Michael Jackson as foreign (Western) commodities, which represent a differentiated ability to travel. In spite of his equating the student dormitories to brothels, it is not clear that the women who entered into relationships with the students saw themselves as prostitutes, but more likely as women in search of adventure. While he interprets access to White German bodies as a form of prostitution, he fails to see the ways in which he too is providing a service.

It is apparent that East Germans could travel through the Black body and that the Black body was and is produced—in movie images, on magazine covers, and even through American television (to which many East Germans had illicit access)—as a site of travel. Travel in this context is not simply a metaphor. Its possibility, its restrictions, its fantastic imaginings, and its material practices relate directly to configurations and reconfigurations of citizenship.

East German Imaginaries of Travel

In conversations and interviews conducted from 1995 to 1996, a number of people from East Berlin and East Germany spoke of Africa as the West, partially because some of the African students had access to Western money and were able to travel to West Germany. The East German government restricted marriage to Africans for fear of escape or journey outside of its well-defined borders, but within its borders, one could travel through the Black body. It stood as a means of departure, even if only imaginary or temporary. It also stood for the Other, for what was not German. Intimate contact with this body was like crossing the Wall and going to a new land.

Ulla, a woman who lived all her childhood and the pre-fall part of her adult life in the GDR, tells a story about a Guinean man she met in a Rostock[8] club before unification. She recalls: "We met while dancing. In the clubhouse, I went to the African men because my sister told me to, because they were good dancers. . . . Two years later, my daughter was born." White boys in that club beat up the African men, since they didn't want these men taking "their" women. Ulla says that she didn't dance with them simply because they were Black, but because "they came from a different world." She adds that they could just as well have been French. Whether Ghanaian or French, the Black body as a visible and material entity signified the possibility of travel.

In post-Wall East and West Berlin, there are a number of clubs whose dancers are primarily Black men and White German women. I met Katharina, then nineteen and from Potsdam, in the Strike Club, which featured "Black music," and again later in a university café. As we talked, she took out her daily planner and removed pictures. They were all of young Black men. As she thumbed through them and showed me the faces, she explained that she *hat eigene geliebt* (has loved some), *andere gemocht* (liked others), and *hat einer für fünf Jahre geliebt* (loved one for five years). They were, she told me, from Germany, Moscow, parts of Africa, and the United States. Katharina had spent a great deal of time in Moscow. Before the Wall fell, legally she could only travel east, but through the Black body, she could travel "west" wherever she was.

Restricting Movement and Reconfiguring Liberty: The Fall of the Wall through the Eyes of Black Subjects

The former Angolan student who studied law in the GDR describes the events surrounding the fall of the Wall and unification:

> *At some point, that which everyone had already sensed would happen happened. At some point, the system [couldn't] be maintained. Then the demonstrations started, in which many foreign students also demonstrated. And we were also welcomed. But we were also scared, because things were getting out of control. And then, when it came to the fall of the Wall, the fear took hold of us. The fear of not knowing what would happen to oneself. The studies that you had already started, if you would also be able to finish . . . if the education would be recognized . . . fear that you would have to go home. Fear—because the GDR didn't exist any more—if the treaties were still valid. There was a special fear that students had. Fear that they would lose this privileged status. We had had dollars. The normal GDR citizens hadn't.*
>
> *We lost this privileged status. All of a sudden, you couldn't get a girl by offering her chewing gum. This fear was affirmed. Then the East Germans started to attack the foreigners.*

Me, personally, the time period between '89 and '93, I call this time a civil war for foreigners. It was a civil war against the foreigners. This designation is justified, because people were killed. It was December 1990. There, the Germans, the soccer team, won in Italy. Until '93, it was a war, from the perspective of foreigners.

The worst off, the people who suffered the most in this period, were the foreign workers. Because they didn't have any protection—most of them were in their dormitories on the outskirts of the city—and most of these were totally wild zones. There, the skins could do as they pleased. They were organized with the worst people. Usually, the student dorms were in the middle of the city. . . . The problem started on the weekend, when most of the German students went home. And they went [home] every weekend. In Weimar, . . . we couldn't even go to get our groceries. It wasn't just the skins, . . . it was the whole population. All of this rage that they had back then—forty years without having freedom. They took a lot of their rage out on us—even old grandfathers and grandmothers. And when you weren't beaten, the looks you received in this time. They were sickening. You couldn't turn to anyone. You called the police. The police didn't come.

One should also note that this was all new for the police. The police hadn't experienced this before. They didn't know how they should deal with it. I would say that the GDR citizens, they were the ones who abandoned us. They left us alone with our problems. Before the Wall fell, we were welcomed. We brought our culture with us. We brought our life with us. But after the Wall fell . . . I resent them for that even now.

In this whole period of change, there were lots of people, lots of people who benefited . . . as they reconnected. But lots of foreign youth were the major losers. Lots of people had to leave this country from one day to the next. The state gave lots of these GDR foreign workers 3,000 German marks in order to get them to leave the country. In lots of countries, the pro-socialist governments fell apart. You went back to your country and the government said, "No, your education doesn't count," or "You can't do anything here."

Lots of students didn't go home. You lost six to seven years of your life. Many went to other countries. Many became alcoholics. Many academics [and] foreign students . . . many one finds as dishwashers, especially in Indian and Italian restaurants. And that hurts. For me, those are the double losers. We are the double losers, and it pains me, it pains me a lot.

Similarly, a man from Mozambique who originally came to East Germany as a secondary school student and then later as a worker, recalls:

I worked here [in East Berlin] at the cable factory Oberspree. Lots of Mozambicans worked there at the time, my fellow compatriots. And the contract was for four years. In the middle of the contract, die Wende came. [We] went out seldom on the weekends . . . there was so much extremism. . . . We were [attacked] daily . . . [by] 100, 200 Germans. . . . There were fights every day. We were lucky that none of us were severely injured. Every day there was violence. We called the police, but the police didn't come. Or they came, laughed, and said, "Whatever," and drove on. We didn't have any protection.

We contacted our embassy, but they didn't do anything either. Then we went to our companies' advisory boards. They said, "You must all go home . . . we can't do anything else to help." The people came with sticks and hammers . . . with everything that one can pummel someone with. We didn't have windows [in our apartments] any more. The watchpeople didn't come any more. We had to defend ourselves. We rotated . . . around the clock. No one went away from the home without being armed . . . to go shopping or anything else.

Yeah, and since most of us had been in the army [as child soldiers], we were reluctant to go home [to Mozambique]. What we experienced here was nothing in comparison to what we had experienced at home. Even when one of us got hurt, no help came. But when we hurt someone, then came the police. Only, we didn't go to them, they came to us—the hooligans.

We were lucky that we could speak good German. In that respect, the police couldn't do anything to us. The others, as a result of their fear, packed their bags [and] fled toward home. At that point, we then had to do everything ourselves . . . go to the authorities, look for work. . . . We didn't have anyone we could ask. Nothing like a citizens administration office, a city hall, or an ombudsman for foreigners. It didn't exist. There was no place for us to go.

Many were without work, without any means to support their existence. As a result, we had to help ourselves—whoever had even a little bit of money. Given this history, it is a miracle that I'm here and can talk to you.

And since most [East] Germans had a lot of money, but could only exchange a certain amount at a one-to-one exchange rate, they came to us. And we had the money exchanged for them with the stipulation that we receive food or some money. Many Germans came to us. That was our salvation. We didn't get the 3,000 German marks [that workers who left got]. That was our punishment.

In both cases one sees a collusion of state and everyday forms of social regulation in order to make a previously mobile population almost completely immobile (with the exception of those who went "back home"), partially as a result of acts of structured terror.

From another perspective, Ingo Hasselbach's *New Yorker* article reveals:

> It was after the Wall came down, in the fall of 1989, that I began to take neo-Nazism seriously. I crossed into the West and spent a few months drifting back and forth between a friend's house in Berlin and a refugee camp for East Germans in Hamburg. The West German neo-Nazis came to the camp looking for new recruits and, like any political group or religious organization, offered literature. The first material I received was about what they called "the Auschwitz lie." . . .
>
> This was a revelation beyond words. No gas chambers! No mass murder of the Jews! It had all been Communist lies, like so much else. . . . And in this moment of relief and joy we recruits passed from being simply rebels against the G.D.R. to being true neo-Nazis. Even as citizens of the G.D.R., we'd grown up with German guilt. We'd been told that millions of innocent people had been gassed by our grandparents, and even though we were always told that *our* Germany had not been to blame—that it had itself been a victim, like the Jews—we still felt guilty. (1996: 42)

West Germany became the site for new possibilities, even for White East German neo-Nazis, while former socialist brothers and sisters had to hide in their rooms or fight for themselves if they chose to stay in East Germany.

Refusing to Represent Travel: Black German Politicization

In the early 1980s, May Opitz (later, May Ayim) and Katarina Oguntoye, two Afro-German women, along with Audre Lorde, developed the term *Afro-deutsch* to establish a politicized identity within the West German context and a connection to other people of color globally. Their politicization grew out of a feeling of increased repression, invisibility in the West German feminist movement, and the subsequent need for solidarity and public recognition. In 1986, Opitz, Oguntoye, and Dagmar Schultz published the first edition of the book *Farbe bekennen* (*Showing Our Colors*) in an attempt "to go public" (1992: 9) as Germans who are Black. The book sparked the growth of several organizations, including ADEFRA (a Black German women's group) and the Initiative Schwarze Deutsche (ISD, Initiative of Black Germans; more recently renamed the Initiative for Blacks in Germany), through which Afro-Germans, Asian Germans, and other people of color in Germany have published a quarterly magazine and organized events and protests (see Fehrenbach 2005). The establishment of these organizations and the planning of annual events such as Black History Month make clear the strong ties to African American politicization and the U.S. civil rights movement. In Germany, however, this politicization has taken place predominately in the West and it began before unification.

Carl Camurça, who was the head of the Berlin chapter of Initiative Schwarze Deutsche when I interviewed him, described his emerging politicization from his teenage years to the present: "First came my gay coming out, and then my Black coming out." He says that the ultimate goal of the Initiative of Black Germans is to achieve national recognition as Germans who are Black. At the same time, he emphasizes, "I am a Black German and not a German Black." He adds, "Goethe is also a part of my culture." He rejects a diasporic notion of Blackness and claims Germanness as his. His form of Blackness refuses to travel. For him, Goethe represents a unifying symbol of German pride. A hyphenated identity of Afro-German or Black-German, though, blurs the distinction between self and Other. It destabilizes an imagined purity that was established through legally defined bloodlines, at least until January 1, 2000.

One wonders, however, in which ways Camurça reproduces a master narrative. In which ways do notions of a "Black" and "gay" coming out differ? Does a Black coming out mean creating a small space for the exotic to exist within German borders, or can it include a politics that means challenging notions of Germanness, that questions the exploitation of outside labor within German borders? Can this identification escape the visual hegemony of national production in which Black bodies are always Other? Can it defeat the violence that people seen as foreign experience in the name of national or European unity?

To have a gay coming out is to call attention to one's difference, or at least to call attention to a process that normalizes heterosexuality. It is as if to say, "I am here, but not as you thought." A Black coming out also challenges a normalizing process that defines German as White, but in a certain sense it cannot move completely outside preconceived borders. Germanness remains a desirable category. Blackness persists as an open signifier, a site of travel, a position from which, in Gayatri Spivak's (1988) terms, "the subaltern cannot speak" or, more precisely, can barely be heard because she is continually being spoken for and being seen. Through this seeing, she is "fixed like dye"—in Frantz Fanon's (1967) words—in her "different" skin.[9] As Judith Butler writes in *Bodies That Matter*, "Although the political discourses that mobilize identity categories tend to cultivate identifications in the service of a political goal, it may be that the persistence of *dis*identification is equally crucial to the rearticulation of democratic contestation" (1993: 4). Where does this *dis*identification, however, leave the body? How does *dis*identification complicate travel?

As a direct articulation of this *dis*identification in process, in my conversations in 1995 and 1996 in the former East Germany with a number of people with at least one African parent, I found resistance to the term *Afro-German* as well as to a discourse of oppression. "I haven't felt so hated. They [the ISD] always feel discriminated against," said Annie, who described herself as a *Misch-masch* (hodgepodge). Apiyo, then thirty-one and a teacher's assistant, called herself a *Mullatin* (female mulatto) and said that she did not feel comfortable in her one and only ISD meeting. "When you grow up as a small colored child [in East Germany], you are something special. When you're with others [colored people] in a room, then you're no longer special."

Marcel Obua refused to identify himself as Afro-German, German, or East German. He remarked, "I have my problems with these categories. I'm simply a human being, first of all. Otherwise, I'm a mixture of African and German." When I asked about his childhood experiences of racism, he said, "My childhood was fine." He added, "I have a slogan. There are three minorities in the world: good sense, intelligence, and humanity." This apparently naive formulation, "I'm simply a human being," actually moves the speaker out of a space in which he is being spoken for without being able to speak himself. Obua rejects my question about how he defines himself, because he doesn't accept the terms of my framing. Nevertheless, it is not clear whether or to what extent he escapes the way he is seen.

In Alaine Locke's introduction to *The New Negro*, an anthology from the Harlem Renaissance in the United States, he writes about "American Negroes": "The chief bond between them has been that of a common condition rather than a common consciousness; a problem in common rather than a life in common" (1992 [1925]: 7).[10] Of course, the "problem" in Germany is framed very differently than the "problem" in the American context. There is no pervasive history of slavery or colonialism that explains the presence or unifies the history of Blackness in Germany. But the image of hypersexuality is pervasive, and in certain sectors violent attack is a serious risk.

Of people of African and German descent, most have fathers who came from Africa and America to Germany, not as former colonial subjects, but as occupying forces, to get an education, to work in East or West Germany, or to claim asylum in West Germany and now in the unified Germany. Germany is imagined as a place of political, economic, and educational opportunity, if not for the fathers, then for the children, although it may not come in the form the fathers had imagined. Furthermore, the "problem" might not always be seen as a problem in the German context. Obua admits his exoticness but says that he uses it to his advantage in relationships initially based on sexual desire:

> When one grows up as a man with a dark complexion in a white society, then one already stands out [and is noticed] by women, of course. Women develop a natural curiosity for the other sex, especially when it looks exotic. For me, there have been more advantages than disadvantages. The question is only how one fulfills this advantage with the right energy and, how should I say, requisite performance/power.

On the other hand, J.B., a woman who grew up in East Germany but then moved to Nigeria, to Jamaica, and ultimately to West Germany with her parents, says that she prefers to be around Black people in her most intimate relationships:

> Consciously and emotionally I have come to a point where I realize that in my closest relationships, I would rather be with Black people, where I [don't] have to deal with this one element. I just don't want to be so vulnerable in such close relationships. It's usually something that I realize afterward, that someone has approached me primarily because I have black skin and because he wants to try it out. In the end, that's how it is.[11]

A diasporic aesthetic, in Stuart Hall's sense (1990), may not be possible outside of the hypersexualized body, a body that represents travel. Remaking Blackness may only be an illusion, promised but never seen. In Germany, the national incorporation of Black bodies seems always to be associated with an image or a fantasy of travel. Hall argues that "we" must understand "identity as a 'production,' which is never complete, always in process, and always constituted within, not outside, representation" (ibid.: 222). Although Hall challenges notions of fixed, essentialized identities, one might question the long-term usefulness of identities at all, particularly if one thinks in terms of citizenship and the production of noncitizen bodies. One might instead understand identities as particular positions used at particular moments to effect certain responses, not as goals, but as organizing techniques that always need to include practices of critical distance and questioning. One needs to focus on the problem of noncitizenship, and not the identity. Hall does talk about the need for identity (defined as positioning), which "makes meaning possible," as a temporary, arbitrary, and strategic position, in much the same way that Gayatri Spivak speaks of strategic essentialism (1988: 129). The problems, however, are the historical inability to get out of this essentialism, and the ways in which it renames those who resist naming.

In the end, conceptions of identity formation may not do enough in terms of assessing the possibilities for social change. It is the site of production, the technologies of exclusion themselves, that need to be analyzed and dismantled.[12] If identification is always within representation, as Stuart Hall claims, then it is the technologies of exclusion that are most critical to the process of producing noncitizen bodies.

If "Germany" remains "Germany," and even allows new identities such as "Afro-German" or "Black German" to enter, to be constructed and recognized, it seems unclear that any political or economic change will result purely as a result of this new framing. Will the contradictions of "foreign" travel be resolved? Can coalitions function in an arena in which relationships between allied technologies of exclusion cannot be seen? In "The First Exchange for This Book" in *Showing Our Colors*, Katharina Oguntoye and May Opitz (later Ayim), enter into this discussion:

> *May: People try to classify me right away: from North Africa, from South Africa, from Argentina or Hawaii or India—depending on where they had just been on vacation, so that they think that I'm typical for that place. . . . Before, I used to think that I didn't belong anywhere, because I stood out everywhere. I thought, I can never be just me; I'm always walking around in this skin color. Then the idea of a country like Brazil, where the population is mixed, consoled me; there, without being particularly conspicuous, I could be accepted. That gave me a feeling of internationality.*
>
> *Katharina: I know that feeling, but it's difficult too: I'm not a Sinti, nor am I from the Philippines or Grenada; I can't pass for one of these nationalities because I don't know what it feels like to be from there. It was clear to me that I feel like a German and feel the closest connections here: to my language, to my growing up here. At a certain point that became what I've identified with. The options for identification offered me from being appropriated by other groups were very confusing to me; sure, it was exciting to feel international, but it also took too much out of me.*

> *May: . . . Another thing that comes with being judged or appropriated is, for*
> *example, Turks complaining to me about their trouble with Germans and not*
> *even seeing me as a German. Even though I can understand their problems, I'm*
> *still not a part of them. Since I've come to understand this conflict, I feel more*
> *conscious of being a German and also recognize the differences that are there,*
> *despite everything we have in common due to discrimination.*
>
> *Katharina: I was always against being equated with Blacks and thereby*
> *being separated from Germans. (1992: 153–154)*

This conversation makes clear that something gets lost in the attempt to make Afro-Germanness a symbol that doesn't travel, but that attempts to locate itself firmly within Germanness, distancing itself from Blackness and from Turks.

Hinting toward transnational pluralism, the East German government had a point in calling for a global brotherhood/sisterhood, but the reaction to this framing when connected to its actual practice has resulted in the opposite. The nation-state was at the center of socialist production, and power organized in this way does not liberate bodies but produces them in its own interest (see Foucault 1991a). One can see this in Obua's response to the explosion of racialized violence: "After the fall of the Wall, the people [in the East] did what they always wanted to do." In Hasselbach's statement:

> Even though most of us had been punks not long before, by 1988 or 1989 we saw punks as pawns of the state—as part of the leftist hegemony that needed to be slammed, scared, and brutalized to make room for us to breathe.
>
> For me, protest became ever more closely associated with the forbidden Nazi past. I'd reached a point where I thought that I've always rejected communism and the idea of the anti-Fascist state: now I would fight the anti-Fascists by being a Fascist. (1996: 41)

Given this reality, how does one strategize for social change? If Durkheim is right when he suggests, "We are the victims of the illusion of having ourselves created that which actually forced itself from without" (1938: 4)—e.g., Afro-German identity—can identificatory regimes ever be adequate?

How does the Black body move in a German society, and what does this movement have to do with power? The Black body symbolizes difference, adventure, and travel. The most striking disavowal of this imaginary is an unwillingness to have sex or an inability to dance. This sentiment is explicitly expressed in J.B.'s withdrawal from a White world while remaining in Germany. How might a politics proceed that wants to make this withdrawal unnecessary? Can emphasizing the relationships between travel and citizenship undo the separation between "natural" citizen and foreigner? Or might hypersexual performance (à la Marcel Obua) be the only means for recognition and survival for certain groups of people, such as asylum seekers or temporary workers? In which ways does Afro-German or Black German identification limit the ability to get out of the nation-state paradigm, which necessarily limits citizenship and produces noncitizens?

THREE

We Were Dancing in the Club, Not on the Berlin Wall: Black Bodies, Street Bureaucrats, and Hypersexual Returns

The production of noncitizens and their exclusionary incorporation take place in part via the emerging bureaucratic and sovereign status of White German women in club scenes and in their intimate relations with Black diasporic men.[1] Intimacy, rights, and residency are negotiated via the (sometimes unwitting) expectation of hypersexual performances on the part of the men and, ultimately, the women's decisions about whether or not to marry noncitizens. These encounters have been shaped by African American military occupation, West German feminism, and transnational eroticized fantasy and tourism.

The historical and contemporary currents that configure these relationships entangle hypersexual performances and rights with residency and consumption. Dance clubs act as key sites of production, as do bedrooms and other familiar spaces. "The state" and state power get reinscribed in these places. Relations of race and desire are shifting as well. In a noteworthy inversion of Fanon's notion of the Black need for "White masks" in European contexts, black skin itself opens up new, though limited, possibilities for incorporation. Although White German women ardently and openly desire, even fetishize, Black men, the terms of Black male noncitizen incorporation remain exclusionary.

From National Socialism to Sexual Liberation?

The imaginary of Black masculinity has a particular history in Germany, linked in part to other European and colonial pasts. Following World War I, Europeans expressed outrage over the occupation of the German Rhineland by

Black French troops. Images and imaginaries of Black men raping White German women circulated widely (see Campt 2004b; El-Tayeb 2001; Opitz et al. 1992). In her book *Sex after Fascism: Memory and Morality in Twentieth-Century Germany*, historian Dagmar Herzog notes: "While racism of any kind has necessarily always been about sex, this was especially true for National Socialism" (2005: 10). She elaborates:

> The Third Reich was an immense venture in reproductive engineering. But no less important than the dual project of prohibiting (through sterilization, abortion, and murder) the reproduction of those deemed "undesirable" and of encouraging and enforcing (through restrictions on contraception and abortion, financial incentives, and propagandistic enticements) the reproduction of those prized as healthy heterosexual "Aryans" . . . [t]hey also drew on profound (and strongly church-fostered) associations between sex and evil—and between sex and Jews—in order to make the disenfranchisement and murder of Jews appear morally legitimate. (ibid.)

Herzog goes on to note that the Nazis made strong links through visual and other media between "sex and Jews" and the supposed threat of rape.

Linking this body politics with an African presence in Europe, historian Heide Fehrenbach writes that in addition to mass murder, Nazi policy also included sterilization campaigns against Germans of African descent: "In 1937, the Nazi regime ordered the sterilization of all black German children fathered by foreign occupation troops of color stationed in Germany after World War I" (2005: 1; see also Campt 2004b). Even after World War II, historian Maria Höhn (2002) notes, conservative commentators, religious leaders, and politicians heavily criticized relations between Black GIs and White German women. In spite of this criticism, however, these relationships became increasingly public and increasingly popular.

An important example can be found in the work of Leni Riefenstahl, a famous filmmaker contracted by the Nazis to make *Triumph of the Will* (1935), which powerfully promotes Hitler and the Nazi Party. In the larger corpus of Riefenstahl's work, one sees a shift in her visual movement (and its popular consumption) from the idealized "Aryan" body to Black bodies such as that of Jesse Owens, who won four Olympic gold medals in Berlin, conquering Hitler's claims of Aryan superiority. Riefenstahl's camera produces Owens's body as a central figure in *Olympia* (2000 [1938]). After this motion picture, Riefenstahl gained popular recognition for her films and photographs of the Nuba (1982, 1997 [1976], 1999; see also Gates 1998; Müller 1995). As Lisa Gates writes, "Leni Riefenstahl left for Africa in 1956, armed with a Leica camera and a vision of the continent culled from the pages of Hemingway's novel *Green Hills of Africa*" (1998: 233). She quotes from Riefenstahl's autobiography (1992 [1987]):

> I was magically drawn by a very specific Africa—the dark, mysterious and still barely explored continent. All this was very impressively conveyed in a photo with which I couldn't part and which shows a black athlete carried on the shoulders of a friend . . . the black man's body looked like a sculpture made by Rodin or Michelangelo and the caption read: "The Nuba of Kordofan." There was no other information. (Gates 1998: 234–235)

In Riefenstahl's own words, there is a connection between her images of Jesse Owens and those of the Nuba, both reflecting her vision of a fantastic African "essence." As Gates notes: "She read the book [*Green Hills of Africa*] in one night, she writes in her autobiography, inspired by the passage: 'All I wanted to do now was to get back to Africa. We had not left it, yet, but when I would wake in the night, I would lie, listening, homesick for it already'" (ibid.: 233).

In the 1960s and 1970s, when Germany's sexual revolution was in high gear, one could see a similar emphasis on sexualized and nude Black bodies in the work of New German Cinema filmmaker Rainer Werner Fassbinder, who also paired Black masculinity with White German female desire. In *The Marriage of Maria Braun* (1986 [1979]), nude sexualized images of a Black GI are central. In *Ali, Fear Eats the Soul* (1989 [1974]), a nude Moroccan immigrant body also has critical visual importance. In both films, the White German women are the primary figures who look (see figures 3.1 and 3.2). In the same period, a group of women writers from an important left-wing Frankfurt paper, *Pflasterstrand*, concluded, "Some women dream of a foreignness that rises to the point of pain and just then into a wild orgy of the mob that then falls apart. . . . Eroticism is a search for the foreign Other."[2]

In *The Imperialist Imagination* (1998), Friedrichsmeyer, Lennox, and Zantop link this type of encounter to a colonial fantasy, which persists in the present and which, I argue, was transformed by the World War II defeat and the postwar reality of "African American" occupation. This occupation made it possible for White German women not only to participate in the colonial imaginary (in many ways, they already had), but also to become normative Germans who participate in regulating national belonging. This participation is simultaneously

Figure 3.1. Scene from *The Marriage of Maria Braun*. [Rainer Fassbinder Foundation]

Figure 3.2. Scene from *Ali, Fear Eats the Soul*. [Rainer Fassbinder Foundation]

fraught with a sense of loss in that they have lost touch with a "purer" form of sexuality. Relationships with Black men offer the possibility of getting back a relationship with this lost self, which is more in touch with its body, in addition to escaping the dominance and "boringness" of White German men. On the other side of the post–Cold War border, although without Black American occupiers, East Germans also desired Black men, first through U.S. films and U.S. music (see Poiger 1998), then through the ways freedom, consumption, and desire became interlinked. Although direct access to Black bodies in East Germany was limited (even though African students and workers and U.S. images did get through—see Piesche 2003; Spennemann 1997), for some White East German women, Black men came to index foreign adventure and were linked directly to expanded possibilities of consumption. Daphne Berdahl explains: "The milk-and-honey promises of the [East German] regime that frustrated consumer desires, combined with the constant and inevitable comparisons to the West, ultimately laid the foundations not only for 1989, but also for the constitutive relationship between political legitimacy and consumption" (2005: 241).

In other words, just as the Wall was falling, and as East and West Germans and the World War II Allies (the United States, the Soviet Union, France, and the United Kingdom) considered reunification, West German political legitimacy became linked to access to consumer goods. Newly consuming subjects compared BMWs, Audis, and Porsches to the East German Trabant, "a little car made of fiberglass and pressed cotton" (Berdahl 2001; see also Berdahl 2005; Borneman 1992; Darnton 1991). As Berdahl describes:

> Immediately after the fall of the Berlin Wall in November 1989, one of the most pervasive media images consisted of East Germans on a frenetic, collective shopping spree. For many western Germans, as well as for much of the world, the "triumph" of capitalism and democracy seemed to be reflected and confirmed in the "consuming frenzy" (*Konsumrausch*) of the "Ossi" [derogatory term for East Germans]. (2005: 235)

However, as the Wall fell and possibilities of consumption began to expand rapidly, new trends toward officially differentiating the newly incorporated Germans from noncitizens coincided with and affirmed new trends toward racialized violence. In this context, the noncitizens' need for recognition became ever more acute. Black clubs and a persistent attraction to Black music provided the social space for this possibility.

Beyond the national context, one should note that contemporary desire for Black bodies is not distinctly German, but part of a European sociocultural matrix established through historical images, diaries, literature, and scientific texts (see Gilman 1985; Friedrichsmeyer, Lennox, and Zantop 1998) in relation to colonialism and European encounters with the African continent. But one should also note a distinct shift from the Europe-wide outrage over the presence of Black French occupying troops, originally from Senegal and North

Africa, in post–World War I Germany (see Campt 2004b; El-Tayeb 2001; Fanon 1967) to the escalating social embrace of African American GIs in West Germany after World War II (see Fehrenbach 2005). In his memoir, Hans Jürgen Massaquoi, the son of a Liberian diplomat and a German nurse who grew up in Hamburg during the Nazi era, recalls that the end of World War II was a turning point for him and other Black men in Germany:

> It was gratifying for me to note that my skin color, which for so long I had regarded as my major liability, had almost overnight turned into an asset. During my previous, mostly clandestine, encounters with German girls, I rarely could escape the feeling of being used as forbidden fruit— quite willingly, I admit, but used nevertheless. Now I had the new, ego bolstering experience of being pursued openly and unabashedly because, as far as the *fräuleins* [unmarried women] of the immediate postwar period were concerned, black was definitely in. (1998: 288)

Elaborating on this experience, Massaquoi describes a trip to Nuremberg in which Black GIs mistake him and his friend for U.S. soldiers and invite them to a dance in their segregated military barracks (former SS quarters):

> The huge hall was jam-packed with hundreds of black GIs and their German dates. Never in my life had I seen so many blacks. And what a wide range of complexions, from white to deep ebony and all the shades in between. It was quite apparent from the choreographed-looking jitter-bug acrobatics put on display by the *fräuleins* and their black GI partners that they had had plenty of practice. Watching rapturous expressions on the young women's perspiring faces as they "jived" to what the Nazis had always derided as *Negermusik* [nigger music], I was sure that if the Führer hadn't blown out his brains, the mere sight of his cherished *Deutsche Mädchen* [German girls] with the "apelike creatures" would have killed him. (ibid.: 323–324)

Because the U.S. forms of racial segregation persisted in the midst of Germany's racial reeducation, Black and White U.S. troops went to different clubs and bars in the decades after World War II. But even the Black clubs were frequented by White German women (see Fehrenbach 1998, 2005; Höhn 2002; Ege 2007). After the Cold War, U.S. troop numbers declined and Germany was no longer officially under U.S. occupation. However, the club scenes continued, now with largely African as opposed to African American men.[3] Although formal legislation makes it nearly impossible for Africans to legally immigrate to Germany, the club scenes undercut that impossibility via the discretionary power of White German women.[4] Men from Africa, the Caribbean, and even the United States who come as refugees, tourists, students, temporary workers, apprentices, or soldiers find possibilities to stay longer than they or the state had imagined.[5] They are empowered by a female gaze that erases their invisibility, giving them a new status as extra-visible subjects.

Germany's Reunification, Personal Discretion, and Street Bureaucrats

> I only married him because he was here illegally. . . . Maybe this is a sign that I take my politics seriously. . . . I was in awe of him, because he is beautiful. . . . The intriguing thing about multiculturalism is the mixing. I am turned on by the unusual. On one hand, I am scared. On the other, I think that I can learn a lot. I have always found Black people fascinating.
> —*German social worker*[6]

Reference to foreign (and particularly African) migration in contemporary Germany is often a reference to an asylum law that the national legislature changed in accordance with EU norms in 1993.[7] These changes occurred amid increasing discussion about the social and economic costs of unification, in which the financial and social support for East Germans and for ethnic German migrants from other parts of Eastern Europe was leveraged against the state's ability to support those thought of as unnatural, economic refugees. The legislation created many more restrictions for the latter, requiring, for example, that refugees leave Germany if the state deems that the situation from which they fled is again safe. Refugees who first land in neighboring countries deemed to be "safe third countries are excluded from the right to political asylum" in Germany (Donle and Kather 1993). These include all countries on Germany's borders.

The possibilities for asylum within Germany thus have become much more limited. "By 1993, about eighty per cent of all applications for political asylum within the EC [European Community] had been filed in Germany. More than ninety per cent of these applications were finally rejected as unfounded" (Donle and Kather 1993: n.p.). At the beginning of the twenty-first century, the number of successful applicants has dropped even further. According to a UN High Commissioner for Refugees report from April 2001, asylum seekers have seen a steady decline in the number of cases the German government officially recognizes or that are filed at all. The numbers went from 23,470 out of 127,940 applicants in 1995 to 10,260 out of 95,110 applicants in 1999 (Hovy 2001: 11–12).

As a result of the 1990 concession to noncitizens with long histories in Germany, many of whom were referred to as *Gastarbeiter,* or guest workers, "German immigration and labor laws make a strict distinction between aliens already living in Germany and aliens having foreign residence. Non-resident aliens generally may not obtain a work permit or residence which exceeds three months" (Donle and Kather 1993: n.p.). There are a number of exceptions, which include study, apprenticeships, temporary work as a chef in a restaurant of the "temporary" resident's nationality, and demonstration of the ability to fill highly skilled positions that cannot be filled by equally qualified EU citizens or Germans. "Exotic" restaurant work becomes like sex work in the case of Black bodies.[8] Just as cooks from China would be given visas to cook in Chinese restaurants, in the informal club arena, Black men gain access and recognition by living up to hypersexual expectations.[9]

"It should be noted, however, that the *alien and labor authorities have discretion about whether to issue such work and residence permits or not.* One of the central factors in exercising this discretionary power will be whether there are a sufficient number of German and/or European applicants, who are equally qualified for *that special job*" (Donle and Kather 1993: n.p.; emphases added). One must read "that special job" not only in terms of the formal economy but also in terms of the economy of national desire.[10] A law went into effect on January 1, 2001, that allows asylum seekers to work, but they come after the above-mentioned groups in their priority as potential employees. Furthermore, even though Germany has moved toward official acknowledgment of the need for immigration, it continues to emphasize highly skilled workers and limited stays. Although the law is changing toward more possibilities for noncitizens' incorporation, this incorporation remains exclusionary.

Who Gets to Stay in Germany and How?

It is critical to recognize how state power and formal law operate through personal discretion, often exercised by low-level bureaucrats. Stefan Senders offers examples:

> One bureaucrat working in the foreigner registration office in Berlin told me that he puts particular pressure on Poles applying for residence permits, offering them shorter residence periods and demanding more evidence of secure income from them than from other foreigners. Another bureaucrat, I am told, prefers Poles to other foreigners when granting work permits. (1996: 156)[11]

In the German club scenes I encountered, this official form of discretion is configured informally as a preference for Black male bodies because of the way they move in both public and intimate spaces. Attention to this type of discretion is critical to understanding White German women's relationships with Black men as a form of street-level bureaucracy. But in his analysis of "street bureaucrats" who "implicitly mediate aspects of the constitutional relationship of citizens to the state," Michael Lipsky (1980: 4) does not have these types of encounters in mind. In their official functions, Lipsky's bureaucrats "hold the keys to a dimension of citizenship" (ibid.); in my analysis, the informal street bureaucrats hold the keys to the *possibility* of citizenship or legal residency at all. They have the sovereign power—in Carl Schmitt's language, emphasized by Giorgio Agamben—to decide when and how *not* to implement the law.[12]

Agamben is concerned with the ways noncitizens are excluded from universal belonging, even while professional politicians claim that universal belonging is in operation (often via discourses of human rights and humanitarianism; see Ticktin 2006). I am concerned, however, with the exceptions to the rule of exclusion. That is, I assume that noncitizens and people of color are usually perceived as not belonging and are actively excluded in everyday life, on the street, and at the border. But White German women have the power to make noncitizens into legal residents, exercising their ability to make an exception to the rule of exclusion. Black men obtain legal status not just because they have been seen, but because they are desired and are willing to perform, and because White German women, taking on the mantle of national sovereigns, ultimately decide to marry them.

In this expansion of the bureaucratic field, everyday citizens unwittingly become bureaucrats, and formal laws accumulate interests and criteria beyond what they explicitly articulate. The discretionary power exercised by White German women in their relationships with Black men illustrates how desire and rights become entangled. In these instances, the discretionary power of the state falls into the hands of unofficial actors, and the law is ultimately constituted through informal, everyday decision making or personal discretion. White German women exercise state power through their intimate engagements. For Black noncitizen men, staying in Germany becomes contingent on being seen as beautiful and becoming hypersexual.[13]

Encounters and Entanglements

In *Bodies That Matter*, Judith Butler argues that the "exclusionary matrix by which subjects are formed . . . requires the simultaneous production of a domain of

Figure 3.3. This image launched *Amica,* a popular German women's magazine, in Berlin in 1995–1996. The initial advertising campaign cost 12 million German marks (approximately US$8.3 million; see Süddeutsche Zeitung 1996). According to the Associated Press Worldstream: German (1996), "Die erste Ausgabe habe sich knapp 300,000 Mal verkauft. Die Haelfte hatte man sich erhofft" (The first issue sold more than 300,000 copies. The initial hope was that half this number would be sold).

abject beings, those who are not yet 'subjects,' but who form the constitutive out-side of the domain of the subject" (1993: 3; see Ewing 2008, who also relies on an analysis of abjection).[14] In my analysis, those subjects being formed through their encounters with a "constitutive outside" are German subjects.[15] Moving beyond an explicitly inside-outside, self-Other dichotomy (see Agamben 1998; Stoler 1995), I invert Butler's opposition of subjects and abject beings to point to exclusionary incorporation. What previously would have been abject beings become subjects, but in a way that preserves and even depends on their position as outsiders. In the contemporary German context, Black male bodies can be incorporated if White women see them as beautiful and if they successfully perform hypersexually. The process is not one of normalization, but of hypersexualization.[16]

I began to recognize this process in the mid-1990s when I visited, observed, and danced in a number of clubs, including Abraxas, the Plantation Club, Fu Na Na, Mandingo, Havana, the Salsathek, and the Strike Club. Despite having entered Berlin with my anthropological lens focused on citizenship and racial inclusion, I was nevertheless surprised by the prominently displayed billboards, magazine covers, late-night sex shows, and multiple club scenes all featuring Black bodies (see figures 3.3 and 3.4). Almost completely naked Black men

Figure 3.4. The cover of *Unicum,* a "university magazine," which I found at a travel agency across from the main building at Humboldt University in Berlin's center. In a mixture of English and German, the text on the man's chest reads: "Body & Soul: Sport makes [one] sexy." The Black body stands in for "sportiness" and "sexiness," confirmed not by nudity or by actually playing sports, but by his mere presence. Germanness and Whiteness are brought into the picture through the apparently heterosexual White German women. Via either sex or sports, the Black body is a site of visual and erotic pleasure. It can also entice White Germans to buy magazines.

danced on floats year after year in the now world-famous Love Parade (a then annual, formerly Berlin-based, daylong, pan-European, open-air, summer techno party with an attendance that approached one million at its peak), at the Carnival of Cultures, and at Berlin's Christopher Street Day gay pride parade. In one instance an erotic float was sponsored by the *Partei des Demokratischen Sozialismus* (Party of Democratic Socialism), the post-Wall successor party to the official East German Socialist Unity Party (see figure 3.5). Often, Black bodies were the only nude bodies on display.[17]

In my interviews, White German women described their attraction to Black men as based on the possibility of adventure, spontaneity, the exotic, and travel. They commented on what they perceived as an aesthetic of Black beauty and the ability of Black men to inhabit their bodies fully (as opposed to being "stiff" like White German men). They linked their desire to movie images from childhood, to music they heard in their formative years, or to the fact that their parents always had foreign friends, opening them up to a world outside of the nation. I saw more of these images when I visited my female interlocutors at home. Images of Black men were in their bedrooms and on their walls, from Marvin Gaye to anonymous beauties. Some also had books filled with images of Black men. When I asked one White German friend who grew up in an East German town why she liked Black men, she said that she liked the way they move. She

Figure 3.5. Men on top of a PDS (reformed East German socialist party) float at the annual Christopher Street Day parade in celebration of gay rights.

said that she liked their buttocks. Films and popular culture consistently were at the center of framing the desire for and production of Black bodies.

Abraxas, 1996

Abraxas, a Berlin club, is packed on a Saturday night at 1 AM. You have to push a doorbell on the outside that flashes a red light on the inside. Usually a bouncer of African descent lets you in. There is a bar to the left, a seating area to the right, a DJ behind a glass window, and a dance floor. The entranceway is crowded, mostly with men with Afro complexions and White women in groups or, as on the dance floor, with the Black men. The music is amazing: funk, acid jazz, hip-hop, soul, rhythm and blues, and salsa. When it slows down, and as it gets later, grinding becomes more common.

I often find the gaze of older White women fixed on me. At about 4 AM one night, my African American friend Charles and I are about to leave. An older woman with curly blonde hair grabs my hand as she sees me making my exit from the dance floor and says in English, "See you again soon?" I nod and smile, but leave. We haven't danced or talked all evening. Should I be flattered?

Sexual Emancipations

In February 2000, I attended a screening of the film *Fremd Gehen: Gespräche mit meiner Freundin* (Heldmann 1999) at the Berlin International Film Festival. *Fremd Gehen* means "having an affair while already in a committed relationship." In this case, it also references the phrase's literal meaning: "going foreign." I translate the full title as *Having Affairs/Going Foreign: Conversations with My Friend*. The film is a pseudo-documentary about a White German woman writing her dissertation while being sexually intimate with a series of African American GIs she meets at a U.S. military base in West Germany. In the subsequent session with the film's producer, the audience broke into a heated discussion. One White German woman said the film confirmed that "Black men are sex machines." A man from Frankfurt said that the film reminded him of his daughter's contention that "Black guys fuck better than Whites." "I was jealous," he admitted. To this discussion, the moderator added: "When I was sixteen, I was really intrigued by the army base. . . . I also did it. I slept with a Black soldier. But I never talked about it. This film was emancipatory for me."[18]

References to the emancipatory effect of relationships with Black men recurred in my discussions with White German women. Some sought and found a particular kind of physicality. Others found pleasure in resisting family norms of sexual behavior. A woman I met through a group called Eltern Schwarzer Kinder (Parents of Black Children) described her experience this way:

> *I purposefully went into a club where they play Black music, where Black people come. . . . At the time, it was a club where there were mostly Black Americans. There weren't so many Africans, just a few. And, yes, it was fun for me. I liked the music. I liked the way things happened. I liked the way [they] danced. And so it was fun for me. . . . I didn't like German clubs . . . they were not very fun for me, because the music was different. The people were different. I liked this [aspect in the other clubs]. There was a certain . . . I can't put it into words. . . .*
>
> *Okay, so I was recently, for example, just on Friday, in a German club. From work, a woman organized a singles party. Not that I'm single, but I went because a female colleague also went. I went just for fun. It was, yeah, hip-hop music. And it was, yeah, a German club. It was totally boring. I thought, "No." In an African club, I know that I belong there. I feel more comfortable. Because . . . Black men approach you. White men don't do anything. They just stand around with their beer. [I start laughing, and she speaks louder with emphasis.] Yeah, it's true, they just stand there with their beer and gawk at you dancing.*

Anna, a woman I got to know in another context, offered a similar analysis. Comparing her relationship with an African man to an earlier one with a White German boyfriend, she told me: "He was a little boring . . . sex was boring. Of course, that doesn't have anything to do with nationality. . . . That's what I think of as Brazilian . . . knowing how to move with one's body. With sex . . . as a German, you don't learn that . . . to move freely with your body. I find it fascinating. That's Brazilian."[19]

In yet another context, Emma, who is married to a Nigerian man, compared her relationships with German and "foreign" men:

> *In comparison to German men, the relationships . . . always have something new to offer, always something unfamiliar. . . . I think that what moved me in those circles had something to do with the idea of something far away, [of] another culture.*
>
> *But the German man . . . expects the German housewife. The German men want something traditional.*
>
> *T. (my husband) is a man who cleans up around the house. But I don't think that has anything to do with the fact that he's African. That's just how he is.*

Another woman, Silke, an advanced university student who had been dating a young "Afro-Brazilian" man, admitted: "I am more attracted to Black men than to White men. [White] American men don't do anything for me. [White] German men don't either. . . . They are rigid. It takes a certain fluidity. . . . German men . . . they don't know how to live in their bodies." She went on to associate her desire for Brazil (and Brazilian men) to the film *Orfeu Negro*, which she first saw when she was twelve. More recently, Silke has become more critical of the film, partially because of her Brazilian friends' critiques, but she admits that her love of Brazil is connected to the film and the fact that "my father listened to lots of [foreign] music. . . . He always brought music back from his trips. He was also in Africa, for example."

Erika, a social worker originally from West Germany who had married a Senegalese man, revealed the formation of her desire for Black men:

> *I have always been interested in Africa and Black people. I have been to Africa six times, and the country [sic] was great. . . . I have always thought that Black people were great. . . . [When] I was a kid, I became interested in Africa. It was all so colorful. And they were always laughing in the films. . . . As a child, Africa was always something for me that was far away and very big, but not in the sense of being exotic . . . but big and real. . . . The first thing I wanted to do was to meet real Africans. That was a childhood dream for me. In comparison to other children, I wasn't scared. I was interested.[20]*

Julia, a White East German student from a small town on the border with Poland, added another dimension, explaining how her family's reaction to her Nigerian boyfriend fueled her interest:

> That he was from Africa (or his skin color) was a problem for my aunt and grandmother. I wanted to show them that they couldn't control me. I knew from the beginning that he wasn't the one. It was a little bit of adventure. When I realized that I was being confronted by my family, then I wanted to show them: "If you have something against it, then I'll do it out of my own pride." That was a reason for staying in the relationship. Otherwise, I might have ended it earlier.

Later in our conversation, Julia noted that her boyfriend was an asylum seeker. She didn't find his claim convincing, however, insisting, "He wasn't being politically persecuted."[21] Even though he asked, she decided not to marry him.

Confinement, Racialized Violence, and the Stakes of Recognition

I was scared as I drove past the West Berlin border into the former East German state of Brandenburg.[22] I had rented a car and bought a map, but I couldn't find anyone who was willing to go with me and I had considered hiring bodyguards. Through my work with the Anti-Racism Initiative in Berlin, I had learned of what would soon become a public document, in which asylum seekers demanded that they be removed from a town, Rathenow, and a federal state, Brandenburg, where they were under constant threat of skinhead attack:

Honourable Statesmen:

We the asylum seekers in Rathenow have the honour most respectful to present our claims. We have thought it very wise that the silent scribble of the pen is stronger than the thunderous sound of the gun. We believe strongly in the power of argument and not the argument of power. Our claims have reduced us to the level of second-class citizens and have made some Germans to consider us as valueless to the extent of always beating us mercilessly. From these racist attacks we incur serious body injuries to the extent of death. We consider these attacks racist because of the words that always come out from the mouth of the aggressors. Exemple [sic]: "Foreigner, what do you want here, we hate you becouse [sic] you are a foreigner, we are fighting for our land, you should go back to your land and fight all the foreigners there."[23]

Asylum seekers in Germany are sent from their original point of entry (or the place where they request asylum) to a central distribution center where they are fingerprinted and receive a meal card that allows them entrance into the camp (the term they use) and daily meals. From there, weeks or months later, they are taken on a bus and dropped off at various locations throughout Germany. When the asylum seekers arrive in their new residences, their movement is restricted to the county lines. In the case of Rathenow, this is a fifty-kilometer radius. It is illegal for them to cross this border without explicit permission from the local "foreigner administration office." Berlin is thirty-five or forty minutes away by train. (I didn't take the train, because I didn't want to run into any skinheads.) According to John, a resident of the Rathenow camp:

If you go beyond, then you are caught by the police, you are going to pay a penalty between 60 and 120 marks [approximately US$36–72]. At times, when the police find you in a situation, in a place more than one time, they formulate a crime and put it on you, and say they caught you in this crime, and they take you to court and they judge you in court and you are punished.

According to another of the camp residents, whether or not one gains permission to leave depends on the mood of the official and, even more important, on which official you ask. For personal trips or to see friends, according to the residents, permission is almost always refused.

I arrived in the town as school was letting out, and I saw a skinhead leaving the school grounds with two of his friends. As John later told me, "We are scared of being attacked. Because it happens just like that. You don't know when it is coming. Always we have developed this attitude of moving in a group, because when we move in a group, we feel a little bit secure. It's very difficult to see a foreigner here moving alone. It's very difficult." John also told me about life in an asylum camp, explaining:

According to the law, the asylum seekers are entitled to a space of 6 square meter[s]. . . . That is what I have as a right. In this room [which he shares with three other men], if you calculate it mathematically, it's going to give you 24 square meters. And it is not even up to 24 square meters. And meanwhile a German shepherd dog is entitled, according to the law of Germany, to 8.3 square meters. So the German shepherd dogs are considered more [important] than the asylum seekers here in Germany.

The evening I arrived, I sat with the residents as they ate dinner. They were all men, almost all from sub-Saharan Africa, and they would be identified in

Germany and the United States as Black. After dinner, we talked about the situation of asylum seekers in Rathenow and Brandenburg. John insisted:

> *Marriage is the only way to get out of this mess. You see so many people get-*
> *ting married and coming out of this mess, because there is no other situation.*
> *If you are waiting until your asylum case will be recognized, then it is just*
> *like somebody waiting to see God. [One of his friends and I laugh.] If you can*
> *imagine that out of 90,000 people who are coming to Germany per year, they*
> *are just recognizing 3 percent or 2.5 percent.*

Almost all of the men with whom I spoke in the Rathenow asylum camps had been to the local *Diskothek* (dance club), and almost all of them had been attacked there. One man lost some of his teeth one night at the club, and ran away when he saw my camera. White German women in Rathenow, John told me, do not have the "civil courage" to sit down with a Black man in a club or talk to him unless they are much older. When the Black men enter the club, White men throw cigarette butts down their clothes, or people spit on them. In one incident, several of the men were kicked out for responding to one of these attacks, only to find a group of skinheads outside waiting for them. They ran all the way back to their asylum camp.

In this region, the only significant possibility of meeting German women is in Berlin, where there are ample club scenes with Black men and White German women.

Jason

Jason, who is from sub-Saharan West Africa, has lived in Berlin for a number of years and was studying business when I first met him in the mid-1990s. He wears Gucci and Versace and is generally obsessed with his look. He is always clean-shaven and tells me that he has to have a particular style of Armani glasses that no one else has. On one occasion, he makes a trip to Amsterdam with me, to send money to his brother in West Africa through a family acquaintance, but also to buy a style of leather boots unavailable in Berlin. I meet up with him year after year on my trips to Berlin. He contrasts his current style with his earlier years in Germany as a student who was subjected to hard and undesirable physical labor. He did this type of work in spite of the fact that his parents are former diplomats. His access to economic capital, however, shifted as he learned to move in new ways. He frequently talks about his encounters with White German women, and says that he prefers dating law or medical students, who seem to have more money and often come from wealthy families. He claims that he can tell if women are law or medical students by looking at the way they dress. As if to prove that this isn't pure fantasy, on one occasion he stops a young White German woman at Bahnhof Zoo (then, the main West Berlin train station), gets her phone number, and plans a future date.

On one of my summer visits to Berlin, Jason takes me to his girlfriend's apartment near Savignyplatz (an upscale neighborhood in West Berlin). She is, in fact, a medical student. Her parents own the high-ceilinged, hardwood-floored, courtyard-facing, modernized turn-of-the-century apartment. Jason is already married to another White German woman who lives in the same neighborhood, and we see her as we sit in a café. But he tells me that his new girlfriend's parents are very wealthy and have agreed to give him a loan to pay for tuition at Harvard Law School. He asks me to help him with the application. He has already transferred from Berlin and been accepted to a top law program at a university in England, but his ultimate goal is the United States.

Needing More Than Mere Attraction

Although Black masculinity carries with it a certain cachet in these scenes, asylum status does not. In my conversations with White German women and African diasporic men, I have repeatedly heard about relationships broken or never pursued when a woman suspects that her potential partner is an asylum seeker. One acquaintance, for example, describes his experience as follows:

> I never lied to any women. I say that I am a poor refugee. . . . [But] I have realized . . . after three [relationships], it has become clear to me that the women are unsure and insecure, because my legal status is unsure and insecure. . . .
>
> After three weeks, we were going out. She knew that I lived in an asylum Heim [camp/hostel], but she wasn't interested in the specific conditions. After a concert, she said, "P., what status do you have?" I said, "I have asylum." She was in shock. She suddenly changed. She didn't say anything. I was allowed to accompany her [home]. . . .
>
> Or another woman. She had a daughter. She was five years older than me, but very, very pretty—my ideal female body type. I met her in a club. I was hitting on her. I was a little drunk and thought, "I need to hit on her. I want to be with her." . . .
>
> We loved it. It was great. . . .

Out of the blue, I got a letter.

She knew that I was living in exile. My asylum case had not yet been decided. She wrote a letter: "P., if you think that you can marry me one day for the papers, it's out of the question." I was extremely angry. I had bought two tickets on that day to go to the movies.

One of her relatives had been disappointed [about our relationship]. She apologized, but I was hurt. Someone says, "I love you," and then has such ideas.

After three times, it has become clear to me. . . . For that reason, I've decided not to get married in Germany.

Clearly, attraction, or even love, alone does not suffice. When we spoke, P. was experiencing the strain of imminent deportation. The *Ausländerbehörde* (the agency responsible for foreigners in Germany) had recently sent a letter telling him to arrange his return to a situation he still believed was life-threatening. His hair had grown long, and he was not clean-shaven. Furthermore, he had a chronic cold and headaches. At one point in our conversation, he said that it was up to the German government to decide whether or not he was in need of protection. He had already been denied intimate recognition.[24]

Marriage Effects

Importantly, "[m]arriage has no longer any immediate effect on nationality under German law" (Krajewski and Rittstieg 1996). The five years of marriage (three years before residency) that are required before citizenship is even considered puts German citizens married to non-EU citizens in the position of unofficial state regulators with their partners under constant surveillance. As one German woman noted, some German wives use the threat of deportation to get their husbands to do what they want, such as cleaning up around the house.

Inversions, Retrenchments

Another deep source of the contemporary appeal of *Black Skin, White Masks* is the association it establishes between racism and what has come to be called the scopic drive—the eroticisation of the pleasure in looking and the primary place given in Fanon's text to the "look" from the place of the "Other." It is the exercise of power through the dialectic of the "look"—race in the field of vision, to paraphrase Jacqueline Rose—which fixes the Negro from the outside (Fanon's word, which I will use in this context) by the fantasmatic binary of absolute difference. "Sealed into that crushing objecthood." . . . "Overdetermined from without." . . . Not only is Fanon's Negro caught, transfixed, emptied and exploded in the fetishistic and stereotypical dialectics of the "look" from the place of the Other; but he/she becomes—has no other self than—this self-as-Othered. (Hall 1996: 16–17)

In contrast to contemporary Berlin club scenes, in the colonial context that Frantz Fanon describes in *Black Skin, White Masks*, recognition (what Butler [1993], reading Hegel, calls a type of negation) requires approximating Whiteness: "I wish to be acknowledged not as *black* but as *white*. Now—and this is a form of recognition that Hegel had not envisaged—who but a white woman can do this for me? By loving me she proves that I am worthy of white love. I am loved like a white man" (Fanon 1967: 63).

The scenes of contemporary Germany invert this matrix. The realities of patriarchy, Nazi genocide, German guilt, African American military occupation, and the success of African American popular culture have led to a situation in which White German women openly desire Black men. Many of these women experience the consummation of this desire as liberating. Many express concern about racial violence and other forms of political exclusion while expressing their desire for the exotic and while asserting their discretionary power. Their desire can determine opportunities for their Black partners, as it shapes the conditions for the Black partner's incorporation. The politics of consumption-as-liberation drives this process while reinscribing an opposition between what is German and what is not. It is in this context that exclusionary incorporation operates. The successful performance of beautiful, hypersexualized Black masculinity in contemporary Germany means limited access to national rights while it augments the space of national desire.

Love (Im)possibilities: Berlin, 2010

When I arrive at Anna's house, I am surprised that the table is set for three. I slowly realize that we will be eating dinner with her ex-husband. I wonder how I am going to conduct the interview if he is going to be sitting there. But after dinner and a delicious dessert, he retreats to the living room to watch the winter Olympics. I notice that before he leaves, he carefully picks up all of the dishes and takes them away. He also makes a comment that she shouldn't pick her teeth at the table.

To begin the interview, I talk about the fact that there is a link between the formal law and the relationships between Germans and noncitizens. I am a bit cautious about making this point, not wanting to imply that their relationship was only instrumental, but she understands and quickly agrees: "Yes, why does one marry? A German and a German marry, in the best case, because they love each other and say: 'We want to stay together forever.'" (She sounds skeptical about this position. In the past, she has purposefully left the love marriage out of the equation completely.) She continues from the hypothetical perspective of the normalized "ideal couple":

> "We want to formalize it somehow." Of course, there are also others who say: "We want to save on our taxes." But the important thing for J. and me . . . I felt responsible. . . . I felt I was responsible, "if something happens . . ." I had this internal sense of responsibility. When you marry, of course, there's this mixture, and you can never really keep things clearly separated, or I'm not able to keep them separated: "What just happened? Would we have married if this situation didn't exist?" or "Would we have stayed together?" The reasons one gets married are such a mixture. And I think that J. also briefly considered, "Should I not find another woman for a sham marriage?" . . .
>
> Me: You didn't want that.
>
> Anna: . . . First of all, to find someone. And then the money. And then I thought it was odd, somehow, the thought, "He's married to someone else." . . . What already occurred to me is that, "Okay, we will get married because after two years he will need a residency permit [Aufenthaltsgenehmigung] so that he can work, to have a reasonable life here." . . . [It was clear that we were getting married] "for legal reasons," but nevertheless, as I was leaving the Civil Registry Office, I did have the feel[ing] . . . "I am married now and not just for legal reasons."[25] I also felt an emotional bond with him, even though in the back of my head I was always thinking, "We're going ultimately [to] separate."
>
> Me: Why?
>
> Anna: Because it was clear that he was [much] younger. But also because he had married due to the legal situation. . . .
>
> Me: Had he made this clear?
>
> Anna: No, I just had a feeling. And the crazy thing is that now that we're [legally divorced], everything works much better. I have the feeling that J. felt obliged. And the feelings were simply not clear. As a result, as long as we were married and living together, things were difficult. Strangely, now that he has

a German passport[26]—*he has a German passport now*—*I find things very uncomplicated. Now that he has a normal legal status, everything is okay. . . .*
Me: *Do you mean at an emotional level?*
Anna: *Yes.*

After their divorce, J. had actually left Germany to go back to Brazil *für immer* (forever), but he couldn't manage financially, and now he is back.

Anna: *And now he has registered for Hartz IV [welfare] to tide him over. He doesn't get very much. There is no way that he can live off that amount of money, but someone came here to inspect.*
Me: *What were they inspecting?*
Anna: *They were checking to see if we, that is, if the ex-wife . . . "Are they together again?" If we were in a* Lebensgemeinschaft *[life partnership], then I would be financially responsible for him. Then he wouldn't get Hartz IV.*

Fortunately, she says, on the day when the welfare agent came to check whether or not they had resumed their relationship, J.'s things were being stored in another room. She told the inspector that it was her ex-husband's room and that the inspector could look through it and leave. He seemed convinced that they were no longer a couple and went away.

When they were formally married, she would push him to get a job. In their relationship as it stands now, she says that she doesn't mind such things. He doesn't have to pay rent, and she doesn't force him to try to get a job.

Over the course of our conversation, she goes back and forth about the status of love in their relationship, in their marriage, and now. She says that he will eventually leave her, but she won't be hurt. She says that all along, even after they were divorced, he kept coming back to her. Now she enjoys the sound of someone snoring next to her. She says that she "must admit" that she likes being with an "exotic" man. She doesn't like the men in her age group. He is twenty years younger. They go together on vacations and she pays. She makes dinner. They eat together. She says that she was never lonely, but now she is less alone.

Anna and J.'s relationship has served multiple needs, desires, and wants at once. It links intimacy and a negotiation with nation-state regulations, including legal and economic support and the possibility of less restricted transnational mobility. (He went to Brazil, but he could come back without worrying about being stopped at the border.) His German passport, however, does not guarantee or secure him a job, and he is not cut out to be a successful entrepreneur. Anna says that J. couldn't make it in Brazil, because he always gives everything away to his friends. The fact that he is not able to obey the tenets of neoliberal capitalism, which more tightly regulate the noncitizen even if he has a European passport, means that he still may need to perform in other ways.

In his relationship, however, his legal status does make a difference. In this conversation, one can see the ways in which Anna's role as a street bureaucrat shifts. As he gains formal citizenship, she is able to focus her energies less on the bureaucratic and more on the intimate. Even though the "exotic" dimension remains, as do questions about J.'s economic security, the negotiation of power and sovereignty seems less extreme. This does not, however, mean that her partner has achieved the status of a normal citizen. Though possessing a German passport, he remains a Black man and, in this sense, a noncitizen.

FOUR

The Progeny of Guest Workers as Leftover Bodies: Post-Wall West German Schools and the Administration of Failure

What does one do with these people? One has to force them to learn German . . . to speak German. . . . This is the critical basis for employment success. Lots of mistakes were made . . . because [the politicians] were thinking humanistically. In some Oriental ways of thinking this can't be understood. People, we are now here! There are laws here! For the past two years, there's been an attempt to catch up. Even [Otto] Schily [the minister of the interior at the time] is trying to catch up. It's too late. One can't get them there. The third generation speaks much worse German than the first and second generations. The school has to have space for different ways. It has to have the financial ability. . . . One has to build new schools that are more practice-oriented . . . ones that emphasize working with one's head much less. Lots of these kids aren't in the position to do cognitive work. They have to learn through practice.

—*Kreuzberg elementary school principal who had recently left his job for a school in a different neighborhood with a different student population*

Alongside hypersexuality, another way to examine noncitizenship and processes of exclusionary incorporation is to investigate the position of Muslim, Turkish German, and Turkish youth. In Germany and Europe, the rights of a citizen are intimately connected to expectations of protection and care. While one might assume, as Soysal (1994) does, that Turkish students in German schools are being protected and cared for based on their universal humanity, the ambivalence and resignation of German teachers, administrators, and the broader public about the futures of Turkish and Muslim students reveal something quite the contrary.

95

The apparent post-Wall and post-unification possibility of the naturalization of people of Turkish descent in Germany, a perceived inclusion, is undercut by substandard schools that reinforce the centrality of speaking perfect German, the official and unofficial disapproval of women and girls wearing headscarves, and an institutionalized neglect of the children. They are not desired subjects, but the progeny and reproduction of leftover bodies.[1] Most of these students end up in the lowest level of the three-tiered school system, where the possibility of obtaining skilled jobs is severely limited. Their bodies represent both an extra unskilled labor force and an undesired presence, but primarily the latter.

In conversations at a Kreuzberg secondary school (*Haupt/Realschule*), where 80 percent of the students are from Turkish- and Arabic-speaking families, one teacher tells me that these are the *Restkinder*—leftover children. Another says that he isn't sure for what purpose he is training his students. A number of teachers are explicit about the fact that they are preparing students for unemployment. One teacher smiles ironically as he tells me that I have come to the center of *Elend*—distress, misery, and poverty. Most of the teachers, who are White Germans and do not speak Turkish, express concern for the "German" students, who are a "minority" in the school.

The parents of most of the students are unemployed, or they work as cleaning people or in factories. Many Turkish and Muslim children were born in this district or have lived here most of their lives. The teachers are from other parts of Germany, and a few are from Turkey; they used to be very active in advocating a politics of social transformation, but they are tired now, waiting for retirement, not sure about their purpose, teaching old syllabi, hanging on.

The Berlin government has opted to increase the numbers of *Gesamtschulen* (mixed-level schools), but to keep many of the distinguishing features of separated schooling in place. Even though Kreuzberg is almost universally hip when one is in his/her twenties or early thirties, White Germans who have kids change neighborhoods in order to put their children into less "troubled" schools, which happen (perhaps not coincidentally) to also be less diverse. Mitte and Prenzlauer Berg, formerly districts in East Berlin, have become particularly trendy for young parents, many of whom have only recently moved to Berlin. The teachers who couldn't get jobs elsewhere came to Kreuzberg, without any special training, maybe with ideas that turned into frustration, then with other ideas, but without the power or the resources to implement them. They have been left to administer failure.

I initially pick the secondary school in Kreuzberg to study because members of the Anti-Racism Initiative told me that the teachers had recently held a meeting to talk about the possibility of making the school a German-only zone, where students would have to speak German while on school grounds, including during breaks. After several months at the school, no one will admit to me that this was the purpose of the meeting, but it is clear that there is a great deal of frustration. A number of teachers tell me that their pupils (described as the second, third, and fourth generations of Turkish immigrants) speak worse German than the parents. The newspapers and some teachers blame the influx of Turkish TV (via satellite), Turkish stores, Turkish banks, and Turkish doctors. Many argue that although these people are in Germany, they are living as if it were an extension of Turkey. They are not "integrating."

At a mainstream political conference, someone calls this a "parallel society," but that term misses the ways that Turkish articulations in Germany are a response to modes of exclusion and to contemporary Turkish German history. Like the satellite dishes protruding in great numbers from the windows and balconies of the Berlin apartment buildings, the headscarf is another visible symbol of *dis*identification (Butler 1993), much like speaking Turkish (a number of teachers say it is actually not even good Turkish). Students call it a mixture of Turkish and German—*gemischt*.

My First Visit to the Kreuzberg Secondary School

When I enter the school for the first time, I am surprised by how clean it is and how nice it looks. It is a red brick building, tucked away from traffic. Inside, everything is in good order. I have counseled students in a low-income school in West Oakland, where the schoolyard is covered in blacktop. The physical plant of the Berlin school is nothing like that. This one has trees and a beautifully laid-out basketball court that looks as if it never gets used.

I go to the principal's office to find out whether I can do research in this school. Behind the counter, a secretary is disciplining the speech of a young student. I think she is telling him to say "Please," or "Thank you," or "May I."

The principal is a tall, gray-haired, slender man. He gives me the impression that they have had problems with researchers in the past, but I assure him that I won't behave like previous investigators. I will not be handing out any surveys that the students "won't understand." We set a date for me to come back.

When I return, the principal calls in a ninth-grade teacher, who takes me to her first class, computer science. In the class, they don't actually use the computers, but instead fill out a simple worksheet. The teacher makes a point of having the students raise their hands to show me that most of them do not speak German as their first language even if they are from Berlin.

Perspectives on and from Teaching

On my first day with the tenth-grade class with which I will spend most of my time, two young women invite me to sit next to them in the front of the classroom. One wears a headscarf. She is of Turkish descent and is adorned with makeup. The math teacher, who has been at this school for twenty-five years, tells me later that my presence has intrigued his students:

> *I was three-quarters unemployed. I was supposed to work in a* Gymnasium *[college-preparatory high school] at first. But it didn't work out. The process went on for half a year. One side said it would work. The other said it wouldn't. . . . I was already in the classroom in the* Gymnasium.
>
> *I would have had to go back to the university . . . because I only had the training for* Hauptschule *[the lowest-level high school].*
>
> *Then the final decision came from the Cultural Ministry: "It won't work."*
>
> *I decided right away that I wanted to teach in Kreuzberg. At the time, there were almost only* Hauptschulen *here.*
>
> *[In] Zehlendorf [a district many have historically thought of as one of the wealthiest in West Berlin] . . . only the kids who have completely messed up land in the* Hauptschule. *In Kreuzberg, I thought, there are teachers and parents [who haven't had a chance]. . . .*
>
> *At the time it was different in Kreuzberg though. Not because of the foreigner population. At the time, that wasn't noticeable. They were fully integrated, [but] . . . there was a very raw climate here.*

Deciding that he wanted to have an impact, the teacher moved into a working-class district, primarily made up of working-class White Germans:

> *The principal resigned as a result of a major argument. Then there was an interim principal. The first thing he told me was not to stand next to the [outside] walls. "When you go to the school, a chair or desk might fall." And that's the way it was. It was a very raw climate.*
>
> *One could walk through locked doors [because the centers had been kicked out]. [During instruction], sandwiches would land on the blackboard.*
>
> *I thought, okay, I just have to get through this. Two other teachers had already left the school. After a half year, [my students and I] were good friends.*

[The next year . . . the administrators asked], "Who wants the two entirely Turkish classes?" [Teachers stay with the same group of students for the students' entire career at the school.] They also said that two teachers would have to leave the school. . . . I thought about it and realized that [my job] would be safest if I took [one of] the class[es]. Then it happened, I had one of the first completely Turkish classes in Berlin. I couldn't speak Turkish. I had never been to Turkey for vacation. . . . Before, I never realized that I had Turkish kids . . . [except for] the names and dark hair. . . .

Then I began with a half year of Turkish instruction. I worked with the Turkish teacher at the school. The students couldn't speak German. Even less than they can now. The parents could barely speak German. . . . They were supposed to be integrated in a mixed class. That was purely theoretical.

Lots of students danced during the breaks. Kids from the mixed classes, they had something to do with everyone.

Then, German families began leaving. Families moved away from Kreuzberg. They actually moved, German families. . . . The parents said: "In Kreuzberg they're teaching German for foreigners."

Then we said, we have to draw the line. More and more [Turkish] families are coming.

We wanted to have a school that was interesting for all families, what was missing in Kreuzberg at the time. . . . [There were] six Hauptschulen, *one* Realschule *[mid-level school], one* Gesamtschule *[literally "mixed school"— all levels mixed together].*

[This is] SO 36 and behind was Kreuzberg 61 [the old postal codes for two Berlin districts that were joined as Kreuzberg]. The Realschule *was very small. The* Gesamtschule *filled up very quickly with students from 61 [the more wealthy of the two former districts]. There were also students from other districts in that school.*

And then there were also three Gymnasien *here. They were pretty exclusive. At the* Gymnasium, *most of the people were children of academics. Schoolchildren are what [they] inherit. One [is] born into it. The kids of nobility . . . become nobility.*

The SPD [Social Democratic Party] government [wanted to send] kids from working-class families to better schools. Berlin had a relatively large number of Gesamtschulen. *Berlin was pretty progressive. But here in Kreuzberg, there was only one. There was no chance of getting into the* Gymnasium. *It was mostly for the Bohemians. A lot of them lived here. Lots of kids from these families went to the* Gymnasium.

Then there was the new proletariat, the Turks. Almost 100 percent of these kids were sent to the Hauptschule. *They didn't have any chance of going to a better school. The* Gymnasien *didn't want to have anything to do with Turkish kids. The* Gesamtschulen *weren't allowed to take more than 40 or 30 percent. The* Gymnasien *fought against admitting Turkish students.*

Our idea was that we had to make the schools more interesting. We wanted to build a Gesamtschule *on this site. [That] was sixteen years ago.*

Then we started with the plans. That was just when there was a new election in Berlin. The SPD-Liberal government came into power. They stopped all plans for new Gesamtschulen. *That's socialist [they said].*[2] *[He laughs.] Imagine. All of the other schools in Western Europe are socialist.*

Then we bargained pretty hard. Then things were quiet. We had to become a bit more diplomatic. [We decided on something] like a Gesamtschule, *but we would call it something else. We would also offer a real* Realschule *degree. . . . [We called it] a city-oriented school. Then, with a bad taste in our mouths, we limited the number of Turkish students. Even though it hurt, we decided on a 50 percent quota. Then we said, we would even allow 60 percent foreign students.*

Then it actually came into being. Things worked perfectly.

However, [as] the result of a falsely understood hospitality, the [new] Green/ Red [Green Party and SPD] government said: "There aren't any foreigners."

Then there was only a differentiation made along the lines of the mother tongue. However, this wasn't relevant for quotas. Then, what we had tried for one class was gone.

Now, in the class that we're going to have after the summer semester, there will be two classes [with only Turkish students]. [There will be a total of] six German students.

I ask why he thinks things have gotten worse in terms of integration. Why does he think people speak worse German in the third generation compared to the first and the second?

I think that the fall of the Wall is partially responsible. [In] Treptower Park [a park and district in East Berlin, bordering Kreuzberg] . . . [people said to the Turkish residents]: "What are you doing here? We are in Germany."

Then asylum hostels started burning. In West Germany too. . . . People were killed on the S-Bahn. [In] Alexanderplatz [central East Berlin] . . . [Turkish people still think], "I could be killed." That is an exaggeration, but . . .

At the time, Turkish fathers told me, "We aren't [just] allowing our kids [to carry weapons], . . . we are giving our kids a weapon." Why were kids coming to school with knives? One student was killed.

*[The Turkish residents were saying]: "Germans are racists, . . . Germans
are Nazis, . . . the German language is the Nazi language."*
I ask if he thinks things will get better.
*It will take a hundred years. Then there's no other option than to get to
that point. I don't think it's possible to really have an impact any longer.*

In the initial conceptualization of the new school, quotas operated as a
technology of exclusionary incorporation, dooming the school to failure, given
the changing political circumstances and the support the school would receive.
Using quotas to limit the number of Turkish students, however, correlated
directly with the majority of the teachers' backgrounds and training. Teachers
are not required to learn Turkish or to take additional training on teaching
German as a second language, nor do they receive enough resources to teach
the students who speak German as a second language. While Americans might
suggest busing (a number of teachers asked me how I would resolve the situation), the formal organization of school districts in terms of residential districts
leads to the isolation of these students. Teachers aren't given, and don't seek,
the right resources to address the actual circumstances in their classrooms,
only the resources and technologies to accommodate a working-class, White
German–centered classroom. Thus the possibilities of student success—if one
views success as getting a job after graduation—are limited.
A tenth-grade science teacher had a number of good ideas about how to
change the situation, but argued that there was a lack of political will:

*The schools should offer single-language instruction for Turkish students. It's
completely uncovered. It isn't even mentioned any more politically . . . to give
these students instruction in Turkish. They're not learning English any more as
their first foreign language, but German.*
Why doesn't single-language instruction in Turkish exist?
*Because people are scared that a particular group will be too strong . . . not
integrable . . . [so] with all of the power possible, German is forced into them. . . .*
*Then there's also a UN program for the Sorbs [an ethnic group in eastern
Germany]. They have rights from the UN. They are taken care of. . . . Or South
Tyrol. . . . [But] the same crap [continues to exist for Turkish students]: "You all
should integrate. You should be exactly like us."*

Because integration is the main rhetorical emphasis, it is clear that the best
interests of the students are not being considered. Perceived national interests
(which require caring for the national population) are really at the center of local

education. The science teacher admitted that he was burnt out, even though he is only forty-five. He has to teach for another twenty years before he can retire.

Actually, I wanted to teach in an elementary school . . . with young children. It would be much more fun for me than with teenagers.

I ask how much longer he's going to stay in the school.

Probably until I retire . . . even though . . . many teachers don't make it to retirement. The last teacher [who left the school] . . . she was sick . . . cancer . . . heart problems. . . . The last few teachers had to go. . . . One has diabetes that was diagnosed too late. . . . [He's] a nice person, but he doesn't want to see anyone any more. He doesn't like people. It's terrible. I mean, the teachers have to deal with so much here. They have lots of vacation, but they are exposed to a lot [of] stress.

Where can [the teacher] put all of his anger? It all goes into his body. Most colleagues aren't able to put up a thick wall.

Why does one stay then?

The question is, What would one do otherwise? I have invested a lot. . . . I have experience. . . . I mean, I can do things as a teacher.

Is it fun?

Yeah, sometimes it's fun . . . seldom . . . seldom. . . . These euphoric feelings come very seldom.

I was never good at chemistry, for example. I worked hard . . . tried to do something new. I had to learn things again from the beginning. [He takes a sip of his coffee.]

How old are you?

Forty-five.

Then you have another twenty years. It's hard to imagine.

Yeah . . . it is hard. . . . I don't think I will be able to give it my full effort in the future.

The teacher's reluctant role as an administrator of national interests is impacting his own body. He smokes heavily and drinks a lot of coffee. He tells me that the last few teachers who left the school didn't make it to *Rente* (retirement). They left sick, their bodies defeated.

It became clear that teachers in this situation are really managers of the leftovers and that whole schools get designated for this job. It is not the same job as teaching White German children to become citizens and to enter the *Arbeitsmarkt* (workforce).

The science teacher continues:

The language proficiency [is a problem]. . . . Over the past twelve years, I've constantly scaled back what I teach . . . [because of] the technical language. I used to work a lot with formulas. You don't just say, "The apple falls down."

It was a failure of mine. I set my expectations too high. Over time, I've scaled back. I am open to the possibility that they could understand, but they tune out. They tune this subject out. They don't develop any interest in this subject . . . in the material . . . normally. . . . I don't know if it makes any sense, but I study in order to do my work. . . . That doesn't happen in this school. . . . I [would normally] begin with the assumption that students will open a textbook.

I teach them to learn sentences by heart. I've had the experience that the students can't speak in full sentences. I think that they also have this feeling: "I can learn something. I'm stupid, but I can learn something nevertheless."

In the beginning, I was often depressed. In the meantime, I've realized that I'm not the only one who is depressed. The grades . . . when I see the scores . . . the level of achievement is horrible. . . . I have real crises. I don't know where to go, where I can file a complaint.

My own observations in the classrooms of the school confirm this teacher's experience. Students do tune out. There are problems with language, except in subjects where language is not as critical or where students can teach other students. In general, the teachers seem resigned.

This is managing failure produced by structural inadequacies. It is the process of producing noncitizens. The schools themselves function as national warehouses, the means for exclusionary incorporation. The science teacher goes on:

Lots of students end up in the service sector, cleaning. . . . When the students arrive at this school, some of them want to become doctors . . . [but] there's a big need for people who can clean. Our students will get the jobs that don't pay very well. In Germany, it used to be the case that you [went] to [the Hauptschule] *and learn[ed] a trade. It won't be like that any more.*

Should the *Hauptschule* still exist then?

The Hauptschule *will continue to exist, because there will always be people who require this type of school. . . . [In fact, the trend is toward combining Haupt- and Realschulen.]*

In the past, lots of colleagues came to the schools . . . [and] a number of teachers came from Turkey. They were the second teacher in the classroom. Now they have to take a test in order to [be fully credentialed in the German system]. It's a stupid situation. The Turkish colleagues were translators . . . translation machines. [He laughs, I laugh.] They were also unhappy about having this role.

The German state imported Turkish teachers essentially to translate in German schools. They do not have the same authority as the German teachers and are not completely credentialed, but they take on, possibly against their will, an administrative function. Most of the Turkish teachers still don't have full teaching roles or permanent positions. This is part of the administration of failure. I ask a teacher who came as part of this program about the role of the Turkish teachers and why things haven't worked in spite of their presence.

> *It has something to do with the fact that Turkish teachers weren't hired for pedagogical reasons.*
>
> *It was the case that Turkish parents brought their children to Germany very quickly. And it was very difficult, because they couldn't speak any German. It was also very difficult for the German colleagues to teach these students. The [Turkish teachers] were supposed to play sheriff aides. . . . They were supposed to play the role of police. . . . [It hasn't worked] because that's how things were originally structured.*

Other organizations, such as German mosques, have taken up the role of caring for Muslim youth that German schools as national institutions have refused.

In an anti-racism group meeting, one of the founders says that teachers act as if they have traditional German pupils. Their models have changed slowly, but the classroom population has changed rapidly. In the school one day, watching students discuss a film about the Second World War from the perspective of young German soldiers, I notice the history teacher's conviction and her attempt to show the dangers of fascism and the ways in which (from her perspective) everyday Germans got used to carrying out German nationalistic ideology on the battlefield. But this type of teaching about the Second World War cannot have the same meaning for students whose parents and grandparents didn't participate in the war, who have no direct connection to the war, and who have no possibility of identifying as White Germans or with the guilt of a Nazi past.

In the Kreuzberg secondary school, many of the teachers are former 1968-era activists who have not been able to figure out how to make their politics relevant to the present. The reasons that a student is becoming a neo-Nazi today are clearly different from what those reasons might have been in the 1930s. In fact, many of these teachers sympathize with such a student. They understand that this mode of belonging may be the only way he can find community in his isolation as one of very few White Germans at the school.

Teachers and activists complain that in Turkey there is a fascist group called the Grey Wolves. Some students tell me that one of the students in a class I am observing is a Grey Wolf. She makes outrageous comments when the history teacher shows the film about the Second World War. I know that this is mostly for effect. A skinhead group in Germany wouldn't accept her, but this is where she is now. Perhaps her turn to Turkish nationalism is linked to her rejection in Germany. The teachers, however, don't reach the same conclusion. They count this as yet another example of failed integration into modern Europe, which, having accounted for genocide and overcome war (at least internally), has achieved a different moral standard. This conclusion, which entails an air of cultural superiority, serves to drive more distance between the student and the teachers. They don't reach her and they don't reach other students either.

Student Perspectives

It seems that my proximity in age, my non-Germanness, and my American-ness make it easier for me to engage the students. I speak with a number in the tenth grade about their experiences in the school. Jan has Polish parents and immigrated to Berlin, while Marie and Franziska identify as German and were born in Germany.

> Jan: *We used to have a young teacher, but he's gone now.*
> Why?
> Marie: *He was doing practical training.*
> Jan: *He was doing practical training.*
> Marie: *And he was a really good teacher. With him, we learned a lot, [but] he had to go. He wasn't allowed to stay.*
> Jan: *He fit in . . . he was right for us.*
> Marie: *We got along well with him. We could come to him with problems. . . . For example, he told some people, "You can address me with* du" *[the familiar form of address].*
> With some people, or with everyone?
> Marie: *No, only with some people.*
> Jan: *He did things in the afternoons. Lots of things . . .*
> Marie: *Or he had a movie night at his home. . . . One could understand the instruction much better with him. . . . He explained things better.*
> Jan: *He explained . . .*
> Marie: *Because . . . he was younger. . . . He was twenty or something like that.*
> Jan: *Twenty-four.*
> Marie: *Twenty-four or something.*

Franziska: He was much more active. He did things in a much more playful way. He had a better understanding.

This teacher was unfamiliar with his role as a manager of failure, and apparently had hope, which the other teachers must also have had originally. He was aware of the school's composition before he arrived.

> What did he teach?
> *Franziska: History and social studies . . . and German.*
> *Marie: And German.*
> *Jan: And German. [Almost simultaneously]*
> *Marie: With him . . . I had a 2 [B] in his history class. With Mrs. P., I got a 4 [D] or something like that.*
> *Jan: What did you get with Mrs. . . . ?*
> *Marie: A 3 [C], I think. I'm not sure. [She laughs.]*
> *Jan: He made posters with us . . . painted.*
> *Marie: I still remember the things I learned from him. The things I learned from Mrs. P., [I don't know]. . . . She had a new topic every day. I don't remember anything any more.*
> *[I laugh.]*
> *Marie: I mean, every day, we got a new piece of paper.*
> Did the Turkish students also understand more?
> *Marie: Yes, they also understood more.*
> *Jan: Yes, they also understood more.*

I think that I could be a teacher here. I am young. I like the same music. I dance. I am from California. And the headscarf doesn't bother me. I would be most interested in teaching them to think critically and to learn the skills they need. Perhaps language, not speaking perfect German, isn't the problem, but rather the absence of financial resources and young teachers, and the general willingness to let certain schools fail.

Leaving the School

Toward the end of my stay, I talk to the physical education teacher to get her perspective on the school. While I have not been in regular communication with her, she nevertheless agrees to offer her perspective:

> *There are reasons that I've stayed at the school. They were looking for a gym and English teacher. I was intrigued by the possibility of staying at the school.*

I was allowed to decide how the gym would be built. It was lots of fun with the students.

Today, it's a good model school. . . . We are doing things just as we had planned, but we have lost 25 percent of the positions, because money is supposed to be saved . . . but there are consequences.

I think that the student body has become more difficult to manage . . . that Germans and higher-income Turks have moved away. . . . There is a student body with parents who aren't interested in school at all.

The other point is that when one is twenty years younger, one has more energy.

Kreuzberg used to be the model district, where Germans [and foreigners lived well together]. That also has to do with the fact that German is spoken much less now.

Turkish students used to be disciplined. They came directly from Turkey.

The lower-middle and lower classes, who were generally adversely affected by or experienced no benefits from the economic and political presence of the West, had a different perspective on the colonizer's culture and ways than did the upper classes and the new middle-class intellectuals trained in Western ways, whose interests were advanced by affiliation with Western culture and who benefited economically from the British presence. Just as the latter group was disposed by economic interests as well as training to be receptive to Western culture, the less prosperous classes were disposed, also on economic grounds, to reject and feel hostile toward it. (Ahmed 1992: 174)

It is not clear why Muslim and Turkish parents with children in German schools would actively support a system that is not educating their children. They came as laborers, and the nation-state and national industries benefited from their bodies, but the society refuses to care for their progeny. Islam works against this backdrop as a form of both discipline and care, but it is not allowed to operate fully. The "return of the veil" and the "return of Turkish" are about the failure of enthusiastic inclusion. No one imagines that inclusion would liberate Muslim people in Germany, but it could give them access to the German labor market in a form that would make it possible for them to more successfully compete with their White German counterparts. It is not as if everyone is without jobs, in jail, or forced into an informal economy, but the treatment of these children in the schools shows that they are seen as leftovers. In this context, on top of hip-hop and gangsta rap, Islam provides a different outlook.

FIVE

Why Can't You Just Remove Your Headscarf So We Can See You? Reappropriating "Foreign" Bodies in the New Germany

On one occasion, the principal at the secondary school in Berlin-Kreuzberg noted:

I think our city is much too tolerant. . . . For example, here is a situation in which . . . we allow students to wear headscarves during academic instruction.

[I say to the young Turkish male students,] "Your women are so beautiful and they have to walk around with veils. And you ugly guys, you're allowed to walk around without anything."

After a brief pause without laughter, the principal added: "It's just a joke."

Is the principal's sentiment really "just a joke," or is he indicating one of the principal tensions underlying debates about "integration" into Europe? Is accessibility to noncitizen bodies what is really at stake? Are headscarves, speaking Turkish, and other noncitizen articulations part of a noncitizen response to national and transnational technologies of exclusion? Are they part of the process through which noncitizen bodies get produced?

In Germany today, one finds a simultaneous disdain and desire for Turkish and Muslim bodies, particularly female bodies.[1] The headscarf disrupts the visual field in a national and increasingly European context in which men and women, boys and girls, expect to see these bodies (see Fanon 1965; Partridge 2003; Scott 2007; Ewing 2008). Billboards, advertisements, and late-night sex shows on widely accessible private television stations advertise the accessibility of women's bodies and link them to sex. In the public landscape, particularly when the weather gets hot, White Germans wear significantly less clothing. Their bodies become symbols of sex, accessibility, and reproduction.

In an early twenty-first-century training video for the Dutch "civil integration test," immigrants—U.S. and European citizens exempted—are exposed to
nude women sunbathing as a sign of Dutch culture (Christian Science Monitor
2006; see also Ewing 2008). In a German naturalization test administered
by the federal state of Baden-Württemberg, also apparently aimed at Muslim
immigrants, would-be citizens were asked (before the country implemented a
national test that went into effect on September 1, 2008) if they would—given
that "sport and swim classes are part of the normal school curriculum"—allow
their daughters to participate in swimming lessons (implicitly, wearing appropriate swimwear). The test also asked what potential (male) citizens would do
if their "adult daughter or . . . wife wants to dress like other German women"
(see Spiegel Online 2006; also cited in Ewing 2008).

Further revealing the contest over the management of all women's bodies, in
the German workplace, where it is not legal to ask about partners or plans for
children, a number of female friends and acquaintances told me that employers
usually find not-so-subtle ways of asking about these issues. These employers
see long-guaranteed maternity leaves as a liability. In addition, although fully
subsidized day care programs exist in the East, they are largely absent in the
West. An American friend who works for a large multinational company in
Berlin told me in the early 2000s that she thought about getting married and
raising a family, but imagined that she would put her career on hold when
she had kids. In the same period, an issue of *Der Spiegel* insisted: "Der neue
Mutterstolz: Kinder staat Karriere" (The New Mother-Pride: Kids Instead of
Careers; Der Spiegel 2001).[2] The cover showed a business suit, briefcase, and
high-heeled business shoes in the faded background of a much larger picture of
a woman in a purple halter top and unbuttoned jeans, holding her protruding
stomach. Also in the same period, Steffi Graf moved from being a national
symbol of tennis greatness to a national symbol of maternity.

Earlier, in the mid- to late 1990s, *Der Spiegel* featured a number of issues
with nude White female bodies on the front cover. Katherine Pratt Ewing
traces the public display of nudity to a regime of "hygiene, racial purity, and
bodily perfection" (2008: 193) that began with the nineteenth-century "back-
to-nature" response to industrialization (ibid.; see also Krüger, Krüger, and
Tretau 2002, quoted in Ewing 2008; Linke 1999). More recently, in 2006, the
Christian Democratic Union, the leading center-right party, prominently used
a campaign poster that featured a blond, blue-eyed baby and the words "Secure
Germany's Future."[3]

Figure 5.1. "Coming Soon . . . Carnival of Cultures 2006." Poster at the city-financed Workshop of Cultures, the organizers of the annual Karneval der Kulturen in Berlin. The balloons behind the woman are blown-up condoms, and she is a member of Meeting Point and Counseling for Prostitutes.

In contrast to this national and European move to rearticulate women's bodies, not in the image of German or European feminism, but in the image of accessibility and reproduction, speaking Turkish and wearing headscarves have become sounds and sites/sights perceived as the production of a dangerously unsurveillable counter-home. The Muslim/Turkish body becomes the site of a counter-articulation, just as citizenship makes demands for transparent belonging. National accessibility would guarantee a tangible alternative, a way that Turkish/Muslim women's bodies could potentially find a place in Europe and, in this case, in Germany. Multiculturalism, to the extent that it still has any resonance left, demands recognition and access (see Taylor 1994), as the popularity of the annual city-sponsored Carnival of Cultures demonstrates—advertised via the image of a semi-nude, and thus accessible, Black woman's body (see figure 5.1).[4] Produced precisely through discourses and technologies of exclusion alongside what Saba Mahmood (2005) refers to as a "politics of piety," covering the head and speaking Turkish operate in a complex negotiation with German and European body politics. The normative national response has been to try to unveil Muslim women or, if that fails, to push them out of public space.

The popular national television series *Türkisch für Anfänger* (Turkish for Beginners), shown on Germany's publicly financed and most watched channel, begins as a kind of *Brady Bunch* remake when a White German psychologist moves in with her Turkish German lover and they each bring their two kids to live under the same roof in an "immigrant" neighborhood in Berlin. While the young Turkish German daughter (whose mother is apparently dead) follows her mother's example and holds on to her religion, including wearing a headscarf and observing Ramadan, the White German stepmother encourages her and the girl's father to "enjoy life" and not miss out on her teenage years.

By the sixth episode, the daughter starts eating during the fast (once even unwittingly eating the stepmother's organic pork), and she also removes her headscarf. Her new sister breaks her "call to prayer" alarm clock one morning because she wants to continue sleeping.

Confirming the social politics of this television series in the German and European contexts, covered Muslim bodies are not only unpleasing, but also suspicious (Ewing 2003). They cannot be consumed with pleasure because they are inaccessible and potentially dangerous. In the immediate aftermath of September 11, headscarves were seen as visual proof of an enemy within. Pictures of women on Berlin streets wearing them appeared repeatedly in news reports alongside discussions of Islamic sleeper cells and images of people jumping from the burning towers of the World Trade Center. Like the TV show, these reports appeared not just on sensationalistic private networks, but also on ARD (channel 1, the main publicly financed channel).

In the battle to produce transparency—to see these bodies clearly—even before September 11, Muslim women's bodies had become a site of contestation, and they continue to be, as evidenced in local school politics and in national and supranational politics about headscarves and women's liberation. As anyone who follows the international news knows, this is the case not just in Germany, but also in places such as Turkey, France, the United States, and Egypt (see, for example, Abu-Lughod 2002; Ewing 2003, 2008; Çinar 2005; Shively 2005; Keaton 2006; Scott 2007; Bowen 2008). While there are national, European, and American claims about the need to liberate Muslim women, the meanings of Muslim women's bodily articulations as they perceive and represent them have not been taken seriously, nor has the success of the headscarf as a counter-politics to noncitizenship. Instead, the normative German public views the headscarf as a sign that counters the production of real (and "really liberated") German bodies.

In a speech on May 12, 2000, that claimed to promote integration, then German president Johannes Rau (SPD) said: "When we talk about immigration and integration, then it is not only legitimate, but important that we consider our own interests" (Rau 2000). These interests include not just export markets, but also national pleasure and the confirmation of national desire.[5] President Rau continued, "An important example is the question of the rights and role of women in the society. Everyone should know that we won't tolerate it when a woman, as a result of tradition or culture, is supposed to have fewer rights" (ibid.). One of the primary referents in this speech is the headscarf. The threat is to German women and national citizenship. *Duldung,* or tolerance (in Germany, this is also an official legal status for noncitizens without any other legal residency status), operates as a form of exclusionary incorporation not only in the arena of asylum politics, but it is also seen in the words "we won't tolerate it when a woman . . . is supposed to have fewer rights," and wearing the headscarf symbolizes "having fewer rights." It is intolerable because it is, the argument goes, a sign of Muslim men's domination (implicitly, an assertion of noncitizen sovereignty), i.e., their perceived control of Muslim women's bodies is in opposition to national ideals and national interests.

Opposition to the headscarf and to other articulations of Muslim bodies is part of not only national political rhetoric, but also local administration. This is a conflict over citizenship and the production of Muslim bodies between local official and unofficial state agents, and Islamic institutions including families, mosques, and imams.

One should note not only the persistent conflict about the use of the veil, but also the way that Muslim women's bodies are used, and the ways in which they themselves use them, as sites of cultural production, where debates about belonging and practices that determine citizenship take place. What is the process through which women's bodies become sites of contestation for and against transparency? How do women who wear headscarves attempt to renegotiate a politics of liberation?

I begin with a personal encounter, a visit to an imam I first met during the public discussions about Islam in Berlin, greater Germany, and Europe. Although I could recount many others, I use this example because it is compact but representative of the central tensions concerning Muslim women's bodies and Muslim life in Germany and Europe.

Visit to an Imam

It no longer seems as if I am in Berlin. The road leading to the converted mosque is at first dirt and then turns into a narrow brick path. As I approach the two-story house, it feels more like I am in a suburb.

I see men sitting on the lawn and I am immediately conscious of my short sleeves. I am not sure whether my arms are supposed to be covered. I remember someone telling me something about Muslim men always covering their arms in public, especially in the mosque.

Just after I arrive, sweaty, on my bike with lots of recording equipment, one man brings soft drinks, and the imam asks him to pour me a glass. We are all men, of varying ages. The man pouring drinks and I seem to be the youngest. He is a student at the Technical University. He and the imam are both from Pakistan. The imam, however, has lived in Europe for thirty-five years.

We sit outside as planes land just on the other side of the fence, often interrupting our conversation. We are so close to the planes that they would hit us if they veered even slightly to the right. When a plane is landing, the imam pauses until the noise has subsided.

It is mid-August. There are two men visiting from England, but they decide to go for a walk when I arrive. The imam asks me first to listen and understand what he is saying before I write anything down. (While I had originally planned on recording, I find it awkward to set up and use the equipment.) After he speaks, he repeats what he has said so I can write it down. After each point, he asks me whether or not I understand. The imam tells me what he sees as the three main points of contestation concerning Muslim life in Europe:

1. When Muslims come to Europe, they have to understand and justify all the rituals and laws. For example: Why should I believe in God? Why should I pray five times a day? Why should I fast? These questions were never asked in the homeland. In my homeland—I'm from Pakistan—I never asked these questions. We simply believed, but here, I have to ask: Why?
2. When people come from their homeland to Europe, they are influenced in the sense that they give up everything that they used to do. In the beginning, they pray . . . five times a day, and then they only pray . . . once a day, and then they [give] up completely. They are moving toward evil. They begin to drink alcohol, and sometimes they don't know when Ramadan has started and when it is already over. . . . Most of the people who have fled to Germany are in search of a better standard of living. They want to earn money. In the homeland, there is poverty and corruption. The Muslims here are gradually coming under the influence of Europe. They are distancing themselves from their belief.
3. At issue are the relationships between men and women. Here, relationships are open and free. In Islam, relationships are very formal. Here, there is free sex. In Islam, the woman shouldn't show her beauty. Here, we have

the problem, for example, of swimming lessons [in public schools][6] . . . after twelve years of age. . . . Here, [Muslim] girls are raised very strictly in some families. Other families are Europeanized. . . . When [Muslim girls] are twelve years old, they don't go to swimming lessons. There are problems in the school. People write letters.

The second problem is the headscarf.

The third problem is the class trip. The youth drink and dance and trouble the girls. The teachers don't have a clue. When a boy kisses my daughter, the teachers say, "This is normal." For me, it's not normal. It is an insult.

Unlike the majority of the normative German public, the imam doesn't question whether there has been integration. This is clear to him. His concern revolves around what happens to Muslim bodies and Muslim bodily practices as a result of this integration. As an imam, he is supposed to explain and help articulate the practices of Muslim bodies (e.g., no consumption of pork and alcohol, wearing headscarves, not taking swimming lessons, etc.). These practices, however, are at odds with normative German expectations. Schools, as a principal site of subject making, are thus a primary site for the intensification of this conflict between articulations of Islamic practice and German citizenship. Islam takes over to care[7] for the bodies the German nation-state has now "left over." Women's bodies are a primary site over which this conflict takes place, sometimes erasing Muslim women's voices in the process, at other times accentuating the possibilities of their speech. But even when they speak, can they be heard?

In Schools

In the *Haupt/Realschule,* where 80 percent of the students are of Turkish and Arab descent, many of the young women wear headscarves. A sixteen-year-old of Turkish ancestry remarks that she can't wear spaghetti-strap shirts in school because she would be ridiculed. A young White German student tells me that Turkish boys see her as available. She adds that Turkish girls look down on her for wearing shirts that show her breasts. "But if people want to look, then let them," she tells me.[8] This is a prerequisite for gaining normative recognition. The headscarf disrupts this visual and potentially sexual availability, while it also disturbs the national and European gazes. It is a reaction against accessibility and visibility. Accessibility, read also as the possibility to consume (see Partridge 2003; Berdahl 2005), represents freedom (at least, the freedom of the normative citizen), whereas the veil seems, to many White non-Muslim

German men and women, to represent a rhetorical wall and the domination of Muslim men.

Both for progressive left-wing and for right-wing non-Muslim White Germans, the headscarf is a symbol of male repression, men keeping women from expressing their own desire and from being seen. This covering up, however, produces a pronounced visibility (Partridge 2003; Scott 2007). In an elementary school in Kreuzberg with a large proportion of Turkish German pupils, I interview a group of fourth-grade boys after spending several months in their classroom; they say that they are annoyed by headscarves because they "can't see the women." These youths, raised and educated in Germany, sound like the national subconscious speaking. Even if the nation sees many of these boys as foreigners (their parents are from all over the world, particularly non-European places), the articulation of their desire is a German production. Some of the boys in the class were intrigued by an image in the newspaper of a nude woman, who was trying to get some relief from the heat. The teacher had actually brought in the newspaper because at least one of his students was in it. Thinking of yet another context, it occurred to me that bringing a paper with a nude woman in it to school could be grounds for a teacher getting fired in the United States.

Describing normative conceptions of gender in European and U.S. contexts, Judith Butler argues, "This conception of gender presupposes not only a causal relation among sex, gender, and desire, but suggests as well that desire reflects or expresses gender and that gender reflects or expresses desire" (1990: 23). In Germany, this causal relationship has become part of the framework for national belonging. While women's desire is not discounted, if popular culture is any guide, women are there to be seen. The headscarf disrupts this logic and implies the hidden hand of other men—the Muslim fathers, husbands, and brothers who are keeping their daughters, wives, and sisters from being put on display. The women themselves are never believed by White Germans to be agents in the decision to wear a headscarf. This is about a network of symbolic men in an economy of sex, where women become currency. I use the term *symbolic men* because German women do play a role in this economy, emphasizing and critiquing the presence of Turkish and Muslim men and the limited availability of Muslim women.

A history teacher at the secondary school where I did extensive research in 1999–2000 talks about Turkish men. She argues:

> The man is the pasha,[9] regardless of how dumb he is. Yes. He is the pasha and he is in charge. And that is to some extent the religion, when it is practiced

in its traditional form. And this is the crux of the story. The society . . . the
people who march through these neighborhoods . . . [are] from the Middle
Ages. They want to have everything modern, but the religious structures are
from the Middle Ages. They have not been adapted to a modern culture.

In 1932, Atatürk wanted to end this. He got rid of the headscarf, because
it wasn't in the Qur'an. He didn't get rid of the Muslim religion. No no. He
said that [the headscarf] is tradition. That is not religion. One has to carefully
distinguish between the two. Yes.

This teacher, who tells students not to wear their headscarves, mixes state
agency and subject making with feminist inflections, saying implicitly, "We
as women have a right to desire and will not have our desire obfuscated by a
male-centered politics." Being modern means, in this sense, being feminist.
An unintended consequence of this economy, the supposed liberation, is in
fact re-objectification, inasmuch as freedom means being seen, which makes
invisible Muslim women's own desire to wear headscarves. Furthermore, this
opposition between modernity and tradition obscures the fact that wearing
the headscarf is a modern phenomenon, a response to a contemporary condition, a bodily political articulation in the field of body politics. The opposition
between tradition and modernity and the crediting of Turkish men with the
sole power to determine how women practice their belief indicate a refusal to
let these women speak and to recognize their agency. Much more important
to this teacher and other street bureaucrats[10] is fashioning bodies that are recognizable or, at the very least, accessible in the ways in which she and others
conceive the nation. The history teacher continues:

What we mean [is] a reasonable integration . . . and that is what we all find
exciting. It is not at all as if we are against it [integration]. I want to get
to know the people who I am involved with. And when can I get to know
someone? When we speak the same language. Otherwise, it's not possible for
me to get to know the other person. If you [she speaks to me] didn't speak Ger-
man, then I would have to speak with you in English. You would be lucky,
. . . because lots of people here speak English. But otherwise, communication
would not be possible. I can only get to know the culture when we have the
same language.

Again, one can see the desire for transparency, visibility, and availability.
This discussion began with the teacher telling me about her attempts to learn
Turkish. "But we are in Germany," she concluded. She told me that learning

Turkish wouldn't get her further in her career. Perhaps English, she said, but not Turkish. Other teachers say similar things about attempts to learn Turkish. All of these teachers are White Germans.

The history teacher's argument is consistent with the broader normative response to the headscarf in Germany. Speaking the same language should also be understood as having normative if not identical national bodily articulations. Alternatively, if a woman is exotic, her bodily presence creates frustration when it is walled off. Taking off the headscarf would mean erasure, but on the other hand, it would mean "getting to know them," as the history teacher puts it, fulfilling the White desire for access to the exotic (getting to know "them" not as they actually are, but "them" as an exoticized German production). What appears as a contradiction—how can one have access if one is erasing that which one claims to want to know?—is central to modes of exclusionary incorporation in which noncitizen bodies must in some way be useful or desirable to the nation or risk expulsion, at least from public life. The headscarf is both a symbolic and a material form of inaccessibility, of the supposed failure to transform, of some forms of domination, and also of resistance.

Patriarchy, Feminism, and the Headscarf

> Whether in the hands of patriarchal men or feminists, the ideas of Western feminism essentially functioned to morally justify the attack on native societies and to support the notion of the comprehensive superiority of Europe.
>
> —*Ahmed 1992*

Women everywhere are consciously challenging patronizing and patriarchal acts, whether men or other women articulate these acts. On the other hand, even within patriarchal systems, women find ways to participate in "valuable forms of human flourishing," even if these are "outside the bounds of a liberal progressive imaginary" (Mahmood 2005: 155).

A young woman, one of the two I met in the first class on my first day in the school, agrees to be interviewed at the end of the school year. We sit in an empty student lounge with a pool table in the center. She talks to me from across the table:

Have you had problems in school because you wear the headscarf?
No. I won't put up with very much.
What do you mean?

For example, when they provoke me, then I don't just stand there. I also speak.
What do they say?
*"Why do we wear [headscarves]?" "We don't have to wear headscarves," and
so on. . . . "Why do you believe in such a thing?"*
Who asks you these questions?
Do I have to give names?
No, no names. Are they teachers or students?
Yeah, teachers too. . . . I don't really care. . . . Do you know what the Qur'an is?
Yeah, of course.
*They say, "That's not in there." I mean, we Muslims know better than her
[a teacher in the school], because she's a Christian. She says, "You don't have to
wear that." I say, "That's not true." But she doesn't understand. One cannot
discuss it with her, because she keeps the same opinion and she'll never change
it. No one can convince her. Even if you told her a thousand times, she would
never understand. So I don't discuss it with her. I just tell her, "You're right."
Then I drop the topic.*
What do you think of that?
*I think it's okay. . . . Her religion is Christianity, and I don't say anything.
If she's a Christian, that's okay. If she does something, I don't tell her that she's
doing it the wrong way. But she makes so many commentaries. I don't like that.
Everyone should have their own religion. And no one [else] should criticize it.
When someone believes in something, then they should be able to believe. That's it.*

*When I believe in something, then I stick to that belief. And no one can stop
me. I am not ashamed. When I want to do something, then I'll do it. When
people say something, that doesn't make me change my mind. They provoke me,
and then I'm even more likely to do it. Do you understand?*

From this young woman's perspective, it is clear that whether women wear
headscarves has something to do with their social encounters. Because of the
constant objections, their decision cannot just be an automatic act. It is at least
partially in response to others—a process of negotiation.[11]

Even more interesting than the fact that so many young women in certain
parts of Berlin wear headscarves is the way they wear them. In 1999–2000,
long-sleeve shirts and long skirts that hug the body had become hip. Young
women in these tight-fitting clothes emphasized the curves of their bodies,
even while wearing headscarves. As one young blond German male student in
the same school put it, "I don't see the headscarves any more." To him, they
had become normal.

Figure 5.2. This *Der Spiegel* cover reads: "Foreigners and Germans: Dangerously Foreign. The Failure of the Multicultural Society."

Choices about which parts of women's bodies to fetishize or to hide are arbitrary social choices. Battles over this negotiation, however, are not arbitrary, and meanings change in new contexts. What a number of teachers call a worsening of German-language skills in public schools with predominantly people of non-German descent, and an increased presence of the veil coincided with both the two Germanys' unification and an abandonment of certain districts by White German inhabitants. The post-unification threats of racialized violence, the increasing resistance to moves toward multiculturalism (see figure 5.2), and the transnational politics of piety (see Mahmood 2005) have all led to new uses and meanings of the headscarf in the German context.

Özcan Mutlu went to school in and represents the same district where I do my school research. He was born in Turkey but grew up in Berlin. Now, he is a Green Party politician and has been instrumental in advocating and promoting the group ImmiGrünen (Immigrant Greens) in Berlin. He says: *"Wenn man in einem Land lebt, und immer ausgegrenzt wird, immer diskriminiert wird, dann . . ."* (When one lives in a country where one is always excluded, and discriminated against, then . . .). He switches to English: "People turn back to their roots. . . . They are not accepted, so they say, 'Forget about your culture, forget about your religion, forget about everything. I have everything

Figure 5.3. This image appeared at multiple Berlin U-Bahn stations when it came out.

I need. I don't care about your language. The Turkish language is much better than yours.'"

Moving from the use of language to the politics of the veil, wearing the headscarf is a sharp contrast to the centrality of female nudity and accessibility, the images posted in public spaces, the sex shows on television that emphasize the hypersexuality of Afro-German female moderators, and the accessibility of women's sexuality through eroticized nudity (see figure 5.3). What brings together oppositional movements—German nation building and articulations of Islam—are women's bodies as sites of contestation. The same Turkish Muslim female student who wears a headscarf notes:

> *There are lots of Turkish girls who get married right away. Did you know that? I don't have any plans to get married. I want to work. I don't want to just sit at home. I want to have something tangible. I want to earn my own money. I don't want to just get money from my parents. I don't want to be dependent on someone else. I want to be independent.*

What does your mother say to that?

> *[She laughs.] The Turkish generation has a very different opinion. The woman isn't allowed to have her own apartment. . . . Either marriage or nothing—living with the parents. But that's not what I want. The thoughts in my head go in a completely different direction.*

What does your mother say to that?

She doesn't agree.

And your father?

He doesn't agree either.

How are you going to do it then?

I don't know.

Abitur?[12]

Yes, my mother wants me to get an Abitur. *My father too. They say that I should have a career, a good career. "Don't just sit around."*

Actually, I don't plan on getting married. Not at all.

Within this context, acts claiming to liberate Muslim women seem to be more about using Muslim women's bodies to articulate national selves (and even collective selves that are resistant to this local and national articulation). The older Turkish generation has different desires and uses for the headscarf than the several generations born in Germany, who are confronted with exclusionary technologies in all aspects of their existence.

The Case of Fereshta Ludin

One night, on the way back from Rathenow, the town with an asylum hostel I had just visited in the middle of the former German Democratic Republic, Fereshta Ludin calls on my cell phone in response to a note I left at her school the day before. A friend told me that she was teaching at the private Islamic school in Berlin-Kreuzberg, near where I used to live. Her case had been all over the national media. She had been refused a teaching position in a public school because she wears a headscarf. Both left- and right-wing politicians thought that this was the correct reaction, arguing against the oppression of women. In the summer of 1998, I had been shocked when I saw the active leftist leader of the Social Democratic Party (later, a leader of the Left Party) nod in agreement when the head of the Christian Democrats gave a monologue about foreigners and guests and made a case against Muslim men for the oppression of "their women." He cited women wearing headscarves in Germany as evidence for the validity of his position.

Winter 2001

I arrive late, but Ludin is waiting for me outside the school. She is the same age as I am (twenty-eight) and has brought something for me to eat and drink. She takes me through the courtyard, behind the building, and into her classroom, where miniature chairs encircle large tables. I sit down and set up my equipment. She insists that I have something to drink and eat.

As we begin, the director of the school comes by. She assures him that I am not a journalist: *Er ist kein Journalist. Er ist ein Doktorand aus Amerika und schreibt über Diskriminierung* (He is not a journalist. He is a doctoral student from America and is writing about discrimination). I hadn't actually used the word *discrimination,* but this is how she articulates it. The school director, it turns out, knows someone in California. He has been to San Francisco and has fond memories.

I ask Ludin very general questions, telling her simply to recount how she was ultimately banned from teaching in public schools.

> *First, a week before I had planned to begin [a teaching internship], the instructor asked me if I really wanted to go "like that" into the classroom. She said: "Do you really plan to work like that?"*
>
> *I said: "Of course I'm going to go in like this. You've seen me this way all along. Now, just because I'm going into the classroom, I'm not going to take off my headscarf. This has something to do with my belief, and I don't want to take it off."*
>
> *Then this was discussed back and forth. They went behind my back and discussed it with the Teachers College. . . . They said that they simply had to tolerate me. They tolerated me, so to say. It was a shock for me. I couldn't find any explanation other than the headscarf.*
>
> *I wrote a letter to the Cultural Ministry as a result of this form of discrimination. They wrote back: "In the future, we won't be able to make any guarantees." . . .*
>
> *I finished my studies . . . and was supposed to begin a year as a student teacher.*
>
> *The director called all over the place [to find me a position] and said that I wear a headscarf. . . . Then he tried in other schools. . . . The other school directors said: "We don't want to have this woman . . . because then we won't be able to tell our students that they can't wear a headscarf. . . . If you come, then it is possible that everyone will start coming to school with headscarves."*
>
> *I told them that I can't just operate from some assertion. I'm going to challenge this. [She sighs.] And then, . . . they told me that I [would] have to reorient myself. They said that I should simply consider whether or not I could do something else. After four years, I should think about doing something else, maybe like becoming a cleaning lady. They didn't say that directly, but that was my impression.*[13]

Then I went to get advice from other instructors at the college. There were a number who had studied human rights.

And then I contacted a journalist I knew. He wrote a very fact-oriented article about the situation. Then everything became clear. I didn't have to do anything else. Since then, this has been very heavily discussed. They also got a lot of calls at the Cultural Ministry. Then, two weeks later, they allowed me to begin my practical training.

One constantly has the feeling that one can't be normal. One must continually prove that one is normal. This plurality doesn't exist. . . . That was the most difficult time in my life. As a child, I survived the death of my father, but . . .

I didn't want to convert anyone to Islam. To the contrary, I just wanted to be a teacher. Period. It never played a role for me whether or not a teacher wore a headscarf. I thought that this was clear.

Just before my student teaching was supposed to begin, I was called to the Cultural Ministry. They wanted to know about my position in terms of swimming instruction, what my position was in terms of sex education. They were shocked that there wasn't a problem. I often experience their surprise. But the decision came nevertheless.

I am not suitable because I wear a headscarf, because this is a sign of oppression. They accused me of that which I am fighting against myself. This had a powerful effect on me. That was really something . . . that women are oppressed. . . . I had the feeling that they didn't want to accept that I am who I am. Then, of course, I had to challenge this. They said that their decision was not generalizable, but they spoke so universally.

Where should I be tolerant? Where should the other be tolerant? They accused me of being intolerant. . . . I want to be seen as a human being and not a human being with a headscarf.

A number of issues are at work in this story. Ludin's desire to "be normal" can be read as her desire not to be excluded. To be *nicht normal* (not normal) in Germany is to be asocial. In this case, the bodily articulations of a Muslim woman mean that she cannot teach in public school and that she cannot belong to the national polity in the same way as her "normal" peers. Being a teacher in public schools in Germany, an official bureaucratic position with guaranteed career-long employment, requires formal German citizenship, but Ludin's choice to wear the headscarf means that her and others' citizenship is being put into question in spite of their official status. When I ask how she feels about teaching in a private Muslim school, she explains, "In the past, I actually never wanted to be a private school teacher, but it has happened this way. It took me a long time to feel comfortable. I still don't feel completely at ease." In Germany, Islam is tolerable, as long as it remains private (see Brown 2006 on the politics of tolerance).

Beyond the official realm, a famous West German feminist magazine, *Emma,* attacked Ludin for wearing a headscarf. A representative of the magazine called her on the phone, pretending to be someone else. An article followed in 1999:

Fereshta Ludin was born in Afghanistan in 1972 and has German citizenship, *because she is married to a German man.* At the time of her birth, her father was the minister of the interior in Kabul and then a diplomat in Bonn [the former West German capital]. Her mother was a teacher and has never worn a headscarf. Fereshta came to Bonn as a little girl and did her *Abitur* [pre-university high school degree] in Schwäbisch Gmünd. (1999: 63, col. 3; my emphasis).

The article puts Ludin's belonging, her Germanness, into question, but it gets the facts wrong. Ludin and her parents were refugees. The state accepted their claim for asylum and she was granted formal citizenship long before her marriage. The fact that her mother doesn't wear a headscarf actually makes a better case for Ludin's independence, but *Emma's* editors are convinced that her bodily articulations are a result of an outside influence:

[In] April 1997, when *Emma* (under another name) called Fereshta Ludin, *the Afghani by birth,* and asked her about her opinion on the oppression of women in her homeland, she answered, "I would not like to respond to that question." When *Emma* asked the active Muslim woman what she thinks of the sharia law in fundamentalist countries (according to the sharia, "God's law," polygamy, among other things, is accepted and the death penalty is enforced for women who break up their marriages), the teacher answered the question again: "I would not like to give any comment." As *Emma* pressed her, she explained, "As a state official, I would not like to answer such questions." Would Ludin's answer go against her position as a state official, because it is not in sync with the constitution? (ibid.: 64, col. 3; my emphasis)

The links between the positions of this feminist magazine and the state are apparent. As a Muslim woman who wears a headscarf, Ludin's citizenship is repeatedly called into question. She is not really German, the magazine suggests, on the basis that her beliefs are in opposition to the German constitution.

The article's authors even question her husband's citizenship, suggesting that his body is also a site of un-German articulation: "At age 18 Fereshta Ludin married the five-year-older Raimund Prochaska in Schwäbisch Gmünd. He is a full-beard-wearing, to Islam converted, unemployed German teacher. The TV program *Mona Lisa* explained that the couple prays five times a day, beginning every morning at 5 AM. Raimund Prochaska even says good-bye to his parents with the words 'As-Salaam Alaikum'" (ibid.: 63, col. 1).[14]

The *Emma* authors attempt to make the case for the nation-state, arguing that Ludin is not a naive woman (as other journalists have labeled her), but a political operator, a fundamentalist Islamist, who uses her headscarf as a political symbol. Again, the body is a site where citizenship is put into question: "At present, Fereshta Ludin is unemployed and pregnant. The child is expected at the end of the year. Since even with a child and with the permission of the husband, as long as the child's care can be guaranteed, even under the orthodox law women are allowed to be employed, Ludin is still fighting for a position as a teacher" (ibid.: 64, col. 3).

The authors claim to understand her religious and bodily practices. But they use her refusal to engage in speech as a form of speech, as a sign of the truth behind the decision to wear a headscarf: an underlying fundamentalism and the impossibility of Ludin's being or becoming German. Ludin went on to use the German courts to claim what she perceives as her rights. But even there her body is reinterpreted and re-excluded. The headscarf is evidence of a trend, a sign of an unwanted transformation:

> Cornelia Hein-Behrens, a teacher at the Dortmund Anne-Frank-*Gesamtschule* where every second student is Muslim, explains, "The behavior of girls over the past six to ten years has completely changed. It was a gradual process. They used to take off their headscarves at the corner before they got to school and then put them on again when the school day was over. Today students come with the full religious gear: headscarf, a long coat and long pants. In the secondary school, it's even more extreme. Some girls have even refused to shake male colleagues' hands when they receive their *Abiturs*."
> . . . It can only get worse. Now the Islamists are even starting to demand "Islamic religious instruction." (ibid.: 67, col. 1)

Interestingly, as seen in the teacher's testimony, the increased use of the headscarf corresponds with the Germanys' unification and the violence that ensued, including chants of *Ausländer raus* and *Deutschland den Deutschen*

("Foreigners get out" and "Germany for the Germans"). The mainstream media, however, miss this connection. Furthermore, there is a refusal to see Muslim women as acting in their own right. National media regimes see them as group members of a fundamentalist Islam and glaringly refuse to recognize the voices of actual women who wear headscarves. Because their bodies have been "instrumentalized," as *Emma* claims through the words of a German politician, they are not the real actors in their own articulations. Their bodies are only links between competing discourses, competing body politics.

But what is so disturbing in the teacher's claim that Ludin and other Muslim women have refused to shake men's hands? Ludin notes:

For me, up until that point, I had always thought that Emma *or that type of magazine . . . that they were part of emancipatory movements . . . that they should also advocate for Muslim women who felt as if they were being discriminated against. One shouldn't allow oneself to limit the religions for which one will advocate, to demonize one and deify the other. In contrast, one must fight for the rights of all women. That really shocked me, especially that that group would be so negative and so aggressive, and so hostile, that they would attack me personally because of this whole situation with the headscarf.*

To some extent, they reported incorrect information and defamed my husband. They suggested that he is a macho. He is German and has converted to Islam. I'm sure that he's not a macho, because if he were [she laughs], I'm sure that he wouldn't be my husband. I'm completely against machos.

I ask how she understands feminism.

Feminism . . . how I understand it. . . . When it means that one should advocate for women, then I'm completely in agreement. But when feminism means that I should be involved in a movement against men, then I'm against it. I think that men should also be seen as equal partners, not as monsters.

Sometimes I'm not sure what is meant here by the term feminism. *I can say though that I see myself as an emancipated woman . . . of course [I deserve] my rights as well. . . . I want to do something for the society.*

How do you understand the headscarf in relation to equality?

The woman doesn't wear the headscarf because she's of less value. The sites of attraction for a woman are different from the sites of attraction for a man. . . . [For the woman], these are the hair, the breasts . . . I'm convinced of this, without forcing others to have the same belief. . . . I don't demand of any other woman that she has the same belief. I leave this up to every woman to decide for herself. *This is an issue between God and me. I am convinced of exactly this.*

Equality . . . that is a matter of existence, not a matter of how one looks, . . . the relationship between man and woman, that one is protected from particular acts and thoughts. No one has ever asked me that, for example. . . . If I were really so oppressed, then I would never be able to open my mouth.

[We both laugh.]

One should be happy that one can fight for one's rights . . . scream for my rights. We have the same topic in Afghanistan. [But] this question hasn't really been addressed in Afghanistan.[15]

Both media and legal regimes produce a national response, and in so doing mimic the nation as exclusionary enterprises.

The Court's Response

On September 24, 2003, the German Constitutional Court, the highest German court, decided Ludin's case:

1. There is no sufficiently definite statutory basis in the current law of the *Land* [state] Baden-Württemberg for a prohibition on teachers wearing a headscarf at school and in lessons.
2. Social change, which is associated with increasing religious plurality, may be the occasion for the legislature to redefine the admissible degree of religious references permitted at school. (Bundesverfassungsgericht 2003)

While this initially seems to be a statement that suggests opening a legal space that reflects the country's and the federal state of Baden-Württemberg's diversity, the second item modifies the first in a significant way that ultimately reduces plural possibilities. Later in the decision, while the court finds that the state's determination that Ludin lacks the "aptitude for the office of a teacher" was false at the time, it qualifies this statement. The court determines, however, that Ludin's right to wear a headscarf is protected. It finds that explicit exclusion cannot persist "without the necessary, sufficiently definite statutory basis for this being satisfied at present." The qualification "at present," however, suggests the possibility of satisfying the requirement through changes in the basic law in the future.

Interestingly, while the court recognizes that Ludin is a German citizen and apparently decides in her favor, it nonetheless helps to articulate the legal basis for her exclusionary incorporation. It constructs the framework for how Ludin can legally be excluded from the position of teacher, without excluding her completely from citizenship or the national polity. Furthermore, in this case we see the persistent link between being German and being a citizen: "The basic law grants every *German*, in accordance with his or her aptitude, qualifications and professional achievement, equal access to every public office" (Bundesverfassungsgericht 2003: par. 32; my emphasis).

While the court denies that Ludin, as a result of her decision to wear a headscarf while teaching, lacks the aptitude to teach in public schools (as the federal state of Baden-Württemberg claims), the court renders this rejection of the state's argument a technical issue and not ultimately an issue of fundamental rights. Rights are designated for certain people, the court reveals. In the argument, being German represents a particular legal status. The word *citizen*, however, does not follow. (While citizenship is an implicit dimension of Germanness, the opposite is not true. As the group of people who constitute legal citizens becomes more diverse, the court reactively suggests protecting Germanness and German rights over the rights of a citizen—what one might call a "paper citizen" as opposed to a "biological German," or what activists in Germany have taken to calling *bio-Deutsch*.) Germanness is potentially defined separately from a generalizable legal status, in terms of certain types of bodily comportment. However, after the court's decision, this cultural dimension of citizenship ultimately determined who has the right to teach.

Qualifying "fundamental rights," the court continues: "Even for those with the status of civil servants, the fundamental rights apply, although the civil servant's sphere of responsibilities under Article 33.5 of the basic law restricts the civil servant's legal possibility of relying on fundamental rights (cf. BVerfGE 39, 334, 366–367)" (Bundesverfassungsgericht 2003: par. 34). The court thus finds that there is a conflict for the civil servant as to whether to uphold her duty as a civil servant or her duty as a religious believer.

The decision ultimately outlines the legal grounds upon which the state of Baden-Württemberg (and, implicitly, other federal states) can ban the headscarf, at least for public servants, who are, implicitly, already German (paper) citizens: "The refusal to admit her to public office . . . would be compatible with . . . the basic law if the intended exercise of freedom of faith conflicted with the objects of legal protection" (Bundesverfassungsgericht 2003: par. 41). The court offers its own example: "Interests that are protected by the constitution that conflict with freedom of faith here may be the state's duty to provide education, . . . which is to be carried out having regard to the duty of ideological and religious neutrality, the parents' right of education, . . . and the negative freedom of faith of schoolchildren" (ibid.).[16]

While the court argues that the state "may not identify with a particular religious community," this doctrine of "negative freedom" is nevertheless a decision against Islam in particular. The decision about that from which one should be negatively free is an arbitrary choice. In its finding, the court refers to the basic law's openness toward a "variety of ideological and religious convictions"; however, it does not acknowledge the extent to which certain ideological positions which are considered normal in the German context might also offend a potentially negative right. In determining a school curriculum, the state is potentially taking ideological positions that might offend.

Revealingly, openness, which might otherwise be read as tolerance, is directly linked to neutrality: "Christian references are not absolutely forbidden in the organization of state schools; however, schools must also be open to other ideological and religious content and values. . . . In this openness, the free state of the basic law preserves its religious and ideological neutrality" (Bundesverfassungsgericht 2003: par. 44). The decision continues: "For the tensions that are unavoidable when children of different ideological and religious beliefs are taught together, it is necessary [to give] consideration to the requirement of tolerance as the expression of human dignity, to see a balance for more detail" (ibid.). In this context, education is a natural right. Parents are primarily responsible for religious and ideological instruction. They also, according to the court, have "the right to keep the children away from religious convictions that appear to the parents to be wrong or harmful" (ibid.: par. 45).

The court argues that because the state creates schooling as a compulsory situation, it has special duties to protect pupils in this context. A states' rights argument follows: "*Länder* [federal states] are to a large extent independent and within the limits of their sovereignty in education matters. . . . [The] requirement of tolerance is inevitably sometimes strained, and it is the duty of the democratic *Land* legislature to resolve this tension" (Bundesverfassungsgericht 2003: par. 47). Again, the court outlines how this tension can be resolved in laws made by state legislatures—in fact, it is the duty of state legislatures to resolve it. The court finds that an individual state can make different provisions that account for "school traditions, the composition of the population by religion, and whether it is more or less strongly rooted in religion" (ibid.). It argues further that if the state wants to restrict the teacher's fundamental right based solely on her appearance, to declare that her appearance represents a lack of aptitude or "an infringement of duties under civil service law," the state must outline a "sufficiently specific statutory basis." "This," the court finds, "is lacking in the present case"; however, with this decision, the court makes the conditions clear for a future ban.

Drawing from an expert witness report, the court concludes, "It is not possible to make any statements that are representative of all Muslim women living in Germany" (Bundesverfassungsgericht 2003: par. 52). It also admits, "[T]he headscarf may not be reduced to a symbol of the social repression of women" (ibid.).[17]

Perhaps in order to protect from future lawsuits any federal states that might decide to allow the headscarf, the court explicitly links the decision to allow the wearing of the religiously motivated headscarf to individuals, as opposed to states. The court finds, "The state that accepts the religious statement of an individual teacher associated with wearing a headscarf does not in so doing make this statement its own and is not obliged to have this statement attributed to it as intended by it" (Bundesverfassungsgericht 2003: par. 54). This initial protection, both of female teachers who wear headscarves and of states that allow this, is followed, however, by a critique: "The effect of a headscarf worn by the teacher for religious reasons may, however, become particularly intense because the pupils are confronted with the teacher, who is the focal point of the lessons, for the whole time when they are at school without possibility of escape" (ibid.). The court concludes that the teacher who wears the headscarf can "weaken its effect" by "differentiat[ing] when explaining to the pupils the religious statement made by the garment" (ibid.). In this decision, the court suggests that the headscarf wields power and how that power can and potentially should be tempered.

In the end, the ultimate decision moved from the court back to state legislatures, which, in most cases, decided to ban the headscarf. In the opinion, neutrality comes into conflict with what the court calls "tradition"; an emphasis on demography; and the language of tolerance—which makes permission to wear the headscarf an exception. Headscarves can be accepted or tolerated, but the decision to wear them is never forthrightly respected: "It is therefore conceivable that there could also be statutory restrictions of the freedom of faith, in compliance with the constitutional requirements. If it is apparent from the outset that an applicant will not comply with such rules of conduct, this can be stated to the applicant as a lack of aptitude" (64).

Broader Significance

The headscarf can be legally banned in French schools, because the French state purports to make a strict separation between church and state. But this is not the case in Germany.

Citizenship can be seen through the body, its contradictions and affirmations, its violence and liberation. Few protest the presence of nude African, African American, African Caribbean, or African German women's bodies. The absence of this protest, however, does not mean that these women are likely to belong fully to the German nation or to Europe.

On a trip to India, three pairs of women's eyes shifted with my movements on the beach in Bombay. Their bodies, with the exception of their eyes, were completely covered in black fabric, suggesting that desire is not precluded by the veil: "unsurveiled [sic], she is able to claim the right of scrutiny. Haleh Afshar has pointed out the 'gaze reversal' implied in the practice of veiling" (Franks 2000: 918).

Critiquing gender roles as a form of power provides moral justification for the implementation of exclusionary technologies. National interests, however, including the production of proper national bodies or accessible exotic ones, are what is really at stake. It is a false move to link Islam with tradition (see, for example, Mahmood 2005, who argues that an analytic of resistance and domination obscures the ways in which women actually practice their piety). To use women's liberation as a justification for Muslim exclusion means not to liberate women. To support the articulations of recognizable European bodies against those perceived as non-European means, in effect, to make claims of European superiority which are not commensurate with the possibility of rights, nor with expectations of protection or care.[18]

The debate over the headscarf in Germany and in other contemporary and historical contexts reveals that opposing the veil is not a position in favor of women's rights, but a debate that uses women's bodies as a site of competition over norms, sovereignty, interests, and the conditions for citizenship and belonging. Within the debate, the meanings of the headscarf are transformed. Neither theological conservatism nor cultural particularism can tell the whole story. The ways in which real women's voices are discounted say a great deal about how the debate operates. As Leila Ahmed argues:

[T]he veil itself and whether it is worn are about as relevant to substantive matters of women's rights as the social prescription of one or another item of clothing is. . . . When items of clothing—be it bloomers or bras—have briefly figured as focuses of contention and symbols of feminist struggle in Western societies, it was at least Western feminist women who were responsible for identifying the item in question as significant and defining it as a site of struggle. (1992: 166)

Of course, as one sees in the case of Ayaan Hirsi Ali (2008), even those raised as Muslim women can be used to tell a normative story. This is also part of the process of exclusionary incorporation. A truly liberatory debate would do something other than make the articulations of Muslim women's bodies the central focus of power and citizenship. On the other hand, as Saba Mahmood suggests in *Politics of Piety* (2005), perhaps the genealogy and politics of liberation need to be examined more closely and more carefully, and in relation to nonliberal practices. Since national (and European) interests are at stake in the definition and production of noncitizen bodies, questions of liberation and freedom are important directions for the debate to take.

In the end, if you took off your headscarf so that "we" could see you, would you remain you? The act of removing the headscarf would require a dissolution of at least some aspects of you. Wearing the headscarf is both a counter-act to a normative social body and a productive act in relation to Islam, as "the state"—a population, institutions, daily practices, and the national social imaginary—dreams in relation to its own interests and expresses in relation to its own desires.

Conclusion: Intervening at the Sites of Exclusionary Production

*Jeder fremde Klang, jeder fremde Blick und jeder fremde Geschmack wirkten
unangenehm auf den Körper, so lange, bis der Körper sich veränderte. . . .*

*Die meisten Wörter, die aus meinem Mund herauskamen, entsprachen nicht
meinem Gefühl. Dabei stellte ich fest, daß es auch in meiner Muttersprache
kein Wort gab, das meinem Gefühl entsprach.*

Every foreign sound, every foreign look, and every foreign taste worked
uncomfortably on the body until the body itself changed. . . .

Most of the words that came out of my mouth didn't fit the way I
felt. Thereby, it became clear to me that even in my mother tongue there
was no word that precisely matched my emotion.

—*Tawada 1996*

For I have reason to conclude, that he who would get me into his power
without my consent, would use me as he pleased, when he had got me
there, and destroy me too when he had a fancy to it: for no body can
desire to *have me in his Absolute Power,* unless it be to compel me by force
to that, which is against the Right of my Freedom, i.e., make me a Slave.

—*Locke 1988 [1690]*

The pleasure and utility of human bodies are not just produced through individual desire, but through technologies that shape individuals into populations, and populations into nations with particular interests. These technologies are the means for managing and producing nation-states and also for creating modes through which noncitizen bodies get produced. They include media regimes, laws, scientific instruments, and industrial designs. One's relationship to the national or European population is determined by the ways in which one can fit in, or cannot. In national and supranational contexts, technologies of exclusion and associated processes of exclusionary incorporation may give one's body a completely different shape and mobility (or lack of mobility) than one might have at first predicted. In Germany, Black bodies become hypersexual while also gaining recognition. Covered Muslim bodies are seen as sites of danger, while Muslim women may be trying to protect themselves.

Attempts to conform to normative standards of citizenship or human rights reveal impossibilities. No one has adequately produced humans in general who think of each other as belonging to the other in the way that human rights as a political theory ideally suggests. It follows that norms, as national ideals (and as modes of incorporating national subjects), may be unachievable for noncitizens. An analysis based solely on the network of norms and the production of the national population may lose sight of how technologies of exclusion operate, as noncitizen subjects are not guaranteed (and often are not even promised) the same type of social contract that citizens in social welfare states are. Even while citizenship is claimed to be universal, exclusionary regimes work differently to produce noncitizens. Although it is not the sole purpose of these regimes to produce noncitizens, even an expanded citizenship law or a more open immigration policy might inadvertently contribute to the differential production and incorporation, and exclusion, of noncitizens. To think of noncitizens as universally belonging to a separate universe, in "a state of exception" to the rule of law (see Agamben 2005), however, misses the range of articulations and specific forms through which noncitizen bodies are made.

In the articulations and production of noncitizen bodies, national sovereignty is at stake, as are national and supranational interests (as expressed, for example, in the reality of Fortress Europe). Investigating and analyzing governmental rationality (see Foucault 1991a) have been important not only because governance involves managing a national population, but also because it involves managing and producing noncitizens. As it relates to governance, sovereignty can be thought of in terms such as "he who decides on the state of exception" (Agamben 1998: 11; Schmitt 2006 [1922]). I have pushed this definition further to argue that sovereignty is diffuse in contemporary democratic life and that social technologies in the hands of national producers, including people who do not identify with the government or with the nation-state, are critical to processes of noncitizen production and incorporation.

Although biopolitics emphasizes the management of life and its uses (see Foucault 1990), seeking to maximize the potential contribution of citizen bodies as they relate to the national economy, technologies of exclusion necessarily contribute to different outcomes. Beyond emphasizing the utility of noncitizens, I have shown how noncitizen bodies may serve as a reserve labor force, or potential added pleasure, or focal points for concentrated frustration.

In this context, the power to determine states of exception, while representing a sovereign position is part of a continuum that includes a range of forms of exclusion and exclusionary incorporation; the power is not solely in the decision to kill, to deport, or to put into concentration camps.[1] The figure of Auschwitz in twenty-first-century European life regulates the forms through which contemporary sovereigns can articulate themselves and regulate others.[2] Highlighting the incorporation and management of leftover bodies, in addition to those who have been racialized or have a refugee status, emphasizes this. The processes of management and incorporation involve obvious sites (such as schools and refugee camps) as well as intimate locations (such as dance clubs and bedrooms).

While the managers of German life—schoolteachers, politicians, women on dance floors, police, and other people who constitute the "we" in national governance (even if unwittingly)—argue that there has been a failure in the integration[3] of the so-called leftovers, integration has been occurring the entire time. One is always in relation to forms of sovereign power and governance, to the technologies of bodily production, and, in varying degrees, to technologies of exclusion. The confrontation with national sovereignty, however, does not mean that noncitizen subjects end up without agency. As we see in the production of hypersexualized Black bodies, one's own agency may also contribute to one's production as a noncitizen, who can only be included in the national polity under exceptional terms and conditions.

Integration—also referred to as incorporation (Soysal 1994) or exclusionary incorporation, the term I have been using—produces hypersexual Black bodies, leftovers, and social exteriority, while it also reveals the frame for normative desire. In other words, integration politics in contemporary Europe is producing precisely those forms of so-called culture that its supporters then call *fremd* (foreign or strange)—or even see as repugnant. The process of incorporation into the national polity suggests the impossibility that noncitizen subjects will or can ever become ideal (read: normal) citizens, unless they undergo physical surgery. The violence of this example is on par with that of the castration of the intersex newborn, whom doctors (with the parents' consent) make look like a girl. Protecting themselves from this outcome, noncitizens' integration produces the seeming necessity for headscarves (to offset hypersexualization) and private Muslim schools. In this sense, integration is an analytical lens through which to assess the processes of exclusionary incorporation at work; it is the mode through which excluded subjects are incorporated into the national polity, but it also clearly reveals the limits of this incorporation.

Multiculturalism is exposed as a dubious analytical trajectory, inasmuch as it operates under the illusion that there could be discrete cultures in the same sovereign sphere, that recognition (see Taylor 1994) would not also produce noncitizens. I agree, in this sense, with Talal Asad, who sees "diversity as an *effect* of modern government" (1993: 260).

The degree to which one approaches becoming normal (the ideal average subject) is the degree to which one's sovereignty can be realized, as long as it conforms to broader national interests. Sovereignty, then, is never completely individual or personal, but is an individual practice with normative and exclusionary outcomes. Official government agencies are not the only sites of sovereign practice; it is everywhere that decisions about the state of exception,[4] not only from the law, but also from the normal decision to exclude completely, are being made, i.e., in dance clubs, in school classrooms, in advertising agencies, on factory floors. I understand the state of exception in less absolute terms than Agamben. It is not only constituted through the death camp (symbolized historically through Auschwitz), but also via the forms of politics in which the Other gets produced. It is realized in the instances in which being recognized as a citizen (either nationally or globally) becomes an impossibility but does not necessarily result in total exclusion. The state of exception is not necessarily a suspension of the rules or an increasingly permanent state of emergency (in the Benjaminian sense). It is often the insistence on the rules at the expense of the Other. The counter to this is not a technical problem of returning to the rule of law. The counter is a negotiation of the sovereignty inherent in the rules and the exceptions.

In my research, I talked to a number of former contract workers who continually asserted their desire to "go back" home, even if only in retirement. *Heimat ist Heimat* (homeland is homeland), one woman remarked. In a high school in Kreuzberg, one young Turkish student said that she might end up in Turkey, while her friend who wears a headscarf said that she would like to live in New York or Los Angeles. She asked how Californians perceive people who wear headscarves. The possibility of migration is a way to negotiate sovereignty and bodily production, as are private schools and alternative religious and social articulations. Even these forms of negotiation, however, have constraints.

While Agamben argues against Foucault's form of liberation via "bodies and pleasures" (Foucault 1990: 157), suggesting instead, "[l]ike concepts of sex and sexuality, the concept of the 'body' too is always already caught in a deployment of power" (Agamben 1998: 187), one should note that Foucault does not advocate pleasure outside of power, but pleasure as "the art of not being governed quite so much" (Foucault 2007 [1997]: 45). It is not at the site of the body, but at the site of technologies that one might most successfully contest the deployment of power. Pleasure is inadequate to liberate the excluded, who might, in fact, experience new forms of governance through pleasure—e.g., Black bodies that must become hypersexual in order to belong and gain residency within the national polity, or Vietnamese contract workers in the German Democratic Republic to whom authorities offered condoms while refusing them the right to have children. It is at the site of production where the tools of bodily production can most effectively be countered. These technologies, after all, are the means through which national production and exclusion take place.

Although Agamben argues for a distinction between bare life and political life,[5] I question whether there is any outside to political life. Modes of exclusion are relative and relational. They exist within and without national boundaries, as they exist materially and within the social imaginary.

In my second year-long research visit to Germany, in 1999–2000, as I moved from Berkeley to Bonn and then to Berlin, what had been anticipated as an introduction, meant to set the stage for a year of intense research, in fact thrust me directly into my project on citizenship and the body in post-unification Germany. From former and current government officials, politicians, and professors from the CDU (Christian Democratic Union), SPD (Social Democratic Party), FDP (Free Democratic Party), and Greens, I learned that Europe was Christian, Turkey was not ready to join Europe, and Islam was the main threat to NATO and European security. I was surprised by the words of a Defense Ministry official who said that he could understand the position of a Spanish general who had asserted that he would start shooting if Muslims were to march into Spain en masse from North Africa. The ministry official showed maps on threats to NATO security with all of the countries on the other side of the Mediterranean highlighted. It is only a twenty-minute speedboat ride from North Africa to southern Italy, he said. He added that development aid was a defense strategy meant to keep poverty at bay in Asia and Africa so that the "population time bomb" did not spill over into Europe. He expressed displeasure at the thought of gay men in the military and said that women could be incorporated into the military through administrative duties, after they had finished raising their children.

The politics of constructing Germany and Europe are clearly related to a politics of regulating Africa. Africans are outside of Germany, but they are not outside of German politics. Death camps are the extreme of exclusionary articulation. While Europeans do sell arms to Africans, the European universal human rights discourse and the reality of genocide in European history make it more difficult for Europeans to kill directly. While the Spanish general can imagine mass shootings, such an explicit act of exclusion would surely result in a national or even international trial, since the human rights discourse incorporates the world into the political life and regulation of persons, groups, and nation-states. It is no accident that the location of the International Criminal Court is in Europe. Although there has been a division historically, there is no longer a neat split between expendable human life and political human life, as the sending of troops to Somalia, Rwanda, Iraq, the former Yugoslavia, and Libya, among other nations, attests. There are, however, different modes of inclusion and exclusion.

Technologies of exclusion and processes of exclusionary incorporation are the most apt terms for sociopolitical analysis, both in the case of "humanitarian" military intervention and in the case of the contemporary German nation. The ways that access to and the ability to reside within national and supranational territories (e.g., Europe) get regulated are important to understand.

As I rode a train back to Berlin from meetings with EU and NATO officials in Brussels, I was selected as a target for passport control on the train within Germany after having already crossed the Belgian-German border. We had just been repeatedly told that the borders were now open (i.e., there would no longer be any regular passport controls). The border guards, however, said that they had specific criteria that they used to select people on the train. They controlled (requested passports from) 30 out of 120 people, they said. They had arrested a man who said he was from Albania. They were sending him back to Belgium to get his papers. There were a lot of people from Kosovo *unterwegs* (under way), they told me. In a hypothetical example, they added that it was their job to keep such people from moving through Germany on their way to Great Britain. "They don't want them there either," one guard told me.[6]

As they declined to give me their criteria for selecting me and the others, I thought of a short documentary film I had seen in my work with the Anti-Racism Initiative in Berlin. The film ends with a man from South Asia, with German citizenship and with whom I had happened to live, running after taxis that are collectively driving away, without passengers, from a taxi stand. It seems humorous, as if the taxis are scared that this man will enter and ask to be taken somewhere. For the taxi drivers, his dark-skinned body represents danger, not in the sense of New York taxi drivers who refuse to pick up Black men, but in the sense that they could go to jail for "helping someone illegally enter the country." Here, the taxi drivers become border guards within Germany. Citizenship is immediately marked by the body, regardless of the passport. Before the scene showing the drivers deserting the taxi stand, the police had asked the same man for his papers after he refused to show a taxi driver his ID. The driver saw it as his job to establish whether or not the man was legally in Germany. The police come and eventually the man shows them his German identity card. When questioned about why he was stopped, one of the officers says, "He doesn't look European." At another point in the film, a high-level border guard says that when riding a train, he can tell who is a "foreigner," "and the likelihood that I'm wrong is very small."

In the process of regulation, noncitizen bodies and noncitizen bodily articulations result, and it is this differentiation that is the source of so much national anxiety, particularly when these subjects begin to make demands on the nation-state, such as the right to wear headscarves or to stay indefinitely.

Citizenship, Biology, and Universality

In order to understand what persists as nation-state and supranational practices (and not just as universal biomedical ones; see Rose 2001), one has to look at the systematic processes of differentiation that take place in everyday life to produce noncitizen bodies. In this sense, neither citizenship nor the body nor biology is universal. They continue to be the products of interests and power. These relationships do not inevitably lead to the death camp, but they do lead to differentiated modes of belonging and qualified access to national and transnational forms of biomedical care and universal citizenship. These modes of differentiation, exclusion, and exclusionary incorporation are not only taking place in the West, but have begun to define the relationship to "Western" modes of universality in Europe, the United States, and beyond.

In *Against Race* (2000), Paul Gilroy suggests that with the Human Genome Project, there is a movement away from biopolitics toward nano-politics—a politics that is centered on the subcellular level as opposed to biology in its immediately visible form. This move, however, does not guarantee that humanity will be proven to be truly universal (see Rabinow 1996).[7]

Anthropologist Henrietta Moore suggests a simultaneous emphasis on universality and particularity: "the discipline [of anthropology] has to engage with theories that are about the commonalities—and not just the differences—

between all human beings" (1999: 17). In my work, questions of citizenship and human rights engage questions of difference and similarity, care and biology in their everyday practice. At the various sites of national and supranational sovereignty and production, processes of differentiation have real material effects. While one might be tempted to distinguish these from processes of differentiation at the genetic level, we should see the Human Genome Project, for example, as part of a continuum as we consider the ways in which differentiation is regulated and managed, not universally, but in particular locations and with particular (often national or supranational) interests at stake.

This study on the production of noncitizen bodies in the extended moment of post-Wall euphoria (reemphasized with the 2011 notion of an "Arab spring") has shown the contradictions between universal pronouncements and everyday realities. If politics is oppositional, as Carl Schmitt (1996 [1932]) argues, then citizenship also has to be understood in this light, particularly given the fact that its universal guarantees are managed and regulated in local, national, supranational, transnational, and multinational contexts. Furthermore, after the initial encounter with or imagination of the exotic noncitizen, a process of transformation takes place, not only in terms of representations, but also in terms of biological and bodily articulations. Hypersexuality is not only a performance, but also a shift one feels in the body insofar as the mind and body are linked—and as representations are related to desire, and as the success of a performance is judged by normative expectations. We could say the same for the displeasure at seeing a headscarf, which cuts off accessibility and potentially heightens desire. These processes, which manufacture noncitizens, are very different from the processes by which normative bodies are imagined and produced. The technologies of exclusion are different from the technologies that help produce the mad, the sexually disturbed, and the socially deviant, which are not in opposition to national bodies but are expressions of a continuum of national forms or even normative mutations.

I have not described a process of being controlled by the state, but rather a process of acting and being imagined, of being excluded and being desired, of resistance and exclusionary incorporation. These are the stakes and the articulations of citizenship, of politics, and of governance. Michel Foucault relates the art of government to "a power we can call 'pastoral,' whose role is to constantly ensure, sustain, and improve the lives of each and every one" (1980: 235). Balibar modifies this statement by pointing out the ways in which these guarantees are ethnicized and racialized: "it is not the modern state which is 'egalitarian' but the modern (nationalist) nation-state, this equality having as its internal and external limits the national community" (Balibar and Wallerstein 1991 [1988]: 49).

I have offered a critical analysis of the present condition of noncitizenship and the noncitizen's bodily production. I have also tried to offer understandings of the modes through which what I have found might successfully be contested. Though there may not be a universal mode for challenging the present situation, it is critical to understand and invent specific ways to think about and act on transformative possibilities.

I am concerned with the implications of my analysis of technologies of exclusion for present and future politics. A recognition of the technologies of exclusion suggests the limits of a politics that relies solely on strategies of identification like "Black is beautiful" or "I'm Black and I'm proud." An approach that takes into account the modes through which technologies of exclusion operate suggests that intervention at the sites of bodily production could be more effective. Finally, while one might counter technologies of exclusion with oppositional technologies in particular contexts and circumstances, this countering will never be outside of relations of power or interests.

Epilogue: Triangulated (Non)Citizenship: Memories and Futures of Racialized Production

In 2009, I returned to Berlin with my family for a year of additional research on new projects and to complete this book. In that year, I began to notice a new state interest in a topic that had already emerged in my research: I had observed that students of non-German descent didn't show up for a tour of a concentration camp, and that a history teacher had complained about her students' lack of interest in the Second World War. It had come up indirectly when an anti-racism activist at a weekly meeting I regularly attended pointed out that the curriculum of German public schools still assumed the idealized, normal, White German student as its principal subject. It also came up in my emerging critique of the insistence on the perpetrator discourse, in which to be a German citizen also means accounting for one's responsibility for the Nazi Holocaust. This is advanced as the only way to teach about that genocide, leading many teachers and politicians to speak about the Holocaust and the Armenian genocide as parts of a related perpetrator dynamic. The lack of apology and the lack of recognition for the Armenian genocide have become a central trope among American and European governments and also in the politics of Turkey's accession talks, related to its admission into the European Union. My point is not that one shouldn't speak of these mass murders, but what can one learn when one asks: Why is this emphasis occurring now?

As part of a governmental turn toward an emphasis on the "immigrant's relation to German history" and to the history of Nazi genocide in particular, there seems to be something akin to a civilizing mission at work. Street-level intellectuals and government officials are increasingly holding immigrant and noncitizen youth and immigrant and noncitizen mothers accountable for this history (as if the fathers are already a lost cause). In this context, Muslim anti-Semitism seems to have become a new national site of interest that is then retroactively linked to the Shoah, perhaps replacing the need for German guilt or deflecting accountability for contemporary racism. This new emphasis then becomes a teaching moment of incomparable import, a secure space for a universalized moral education. In a sense, a normative national mastering of Germany's past becomes a way to simultaneously manage its image and put it on the right side of the global order, now in a position of moral superiority, having learned and having the ability to teach about the dangers of other people's extremism as opposed to its own.

It was in this context that I began observing and participating in a project sponsored by a prominent anti-racism organization with federal funding to help Palestinian/Palestinian German and Turkish/Turkish German youth address their own anti-Semitism via a more focused engagement (than they apparently had in school) with German history. This project would ultimately end in a trip to Auschwitz (see Partridge 2010).

At the conclusion of this project, the principal organizer and I, still traumatized by the experience in Auschwitz and the responses of these youths to it, worried about the youths' future. In particular, the organizer worried that he had engaged them in a project in which thinking about broader social outcomes had not been central. While the government funders of this project write explicitly about democratic education, there is no language of democratic accountability—that is, to what extent the state should be responsible for the social, economic, and political success of these youths, whom they were teaching (successfully) to be less anti-Semitic. When I spoke to the group's social worker about the same issue several months later, she pointed out that one could only set short-term goals for their future. Ultimately, the young people who came to the youth center four to five times a week and who seemed to function like a family (many were in fact related) would have to make way for the next generation of youths who would start coming to the center. But to what end? To be left over? To fade into the background of everyday life on the margins? To become criminalized? To become noncitizens?

Just as I was getting ready to leave Berlin at the end of August 2009, a controversy erupted along the same lines as the youths' temporary reeducation program. This provided another opportunity to begin to understand the politics of post-genocide citizenship, in which the national community can only be legitimately formed through mastering the past and becoming the pedagogues of the practices of and responsibilities for genocidal perpetration, as if teaching others what not to do would make the (normative German) self whole again. The only problem has been that teaching others has not generally become a two-way conversation, but a positioning that leads to absolution on one side and a sustained charge of anti-Semitism lodged against the Muslim Other, making it impossible for those Others to make demands (particularly moral ones) about changing their social, political, or economic position. Seen by the normative public as an anti-Semite, the Muslim Other proves that she/he is morally and, by extension, socially and politically inferior. Muslims need to be civilized first, before they can become citizens. Inasmuch as the Muslim subjects resist these lessons or the teacher, however, becoming civilized (becoming modern moral subjects who know the difference between right and wrong) would be impossible. In this sense, they not only remain noncitizens, but also are reproduced as such. Their claims of unfair treatment or discrimination are dismissed as the distracting cries of resistant pupils, carrying no moral weight against the recall of the horror of genocide.

People of Color in the Second World War and the Workshop of Cultures in Berlin-Neukölln

When I began writing this book, my purpose was to analyze the forms and technologies of exclusion that came into existence after the horror of Auschwitz, which were intensified but hidden beneath the universal claims of freedom made by a seemingly global public when the Berlin Wall fell. I also sought to understand and explain the types of subjects who would emerge from these forms of exclusion and from the simultaneous partial avenues of incorporation that would educate, police, and produce noncitizens.

The controversey which surrounded Phillipa Ebéné (the Afro-German director of the Werkstatt der Kulturen [Workshop of Cultures] in Berlin) erupted as I was getting ready to leave Berlin in the late summer of 2009; it is just one instance of the post-Holocaust and "post-racist" dynamic that simultaneously moves normative Germany to the superior position and makes normative citizens no longer accountable for the persistent acts of exclusionary incorporation.

Ebéné had ordered and agreed to display an exhibit on the Second World War from the perspective of people of color from the rest of the world. Seemingly at the last minute, Ebéné rejected the exhibit and refused to show it in any part of her institution. "This is not the exhibit I ordered," she told me several months later in an interview. The sticking point came when she realized that the exhibit would also include a section on "Third World collaborators." (Collaborators, in this instance, referred to those who had worked with the Nazis, the Italian fascists, or the Japanese regime.)

When word got out—fueled in part by the White German curator Karl Rössel's publicity machine—that Ebéné had refused to allow the exhibit to be shown at the Workshop of Cultures, she was accused in public of being anti-Semitic and undemocratic, and was called a censor. Someone went so far as to send her an e-mail that told her to go back where she came from. (The writer was most likely not referring to Ebéné's origins in southern Germany.) In one account in a popular Berlin tabloid, the Social Democratic mayor of Neukölln—the district of Berlin in which Ebéné's Werkstatt der Kulturen is located—speculated that Ebéné's hand was being forced by an "arabischer 'Platzhirsche'" (an Arab "top dog") (BZ 2009).

As these events were unfolding, I had time only to collect press releases, rush between packing and press conferences, and take notes. At the time, it was not immediately clear to me why she felt that banning the exhibit was necessary. Why couldn't collaboration also be part of the story about people of color's involvement in the Second World War (even if I did find the exhibit title's use of the term "Third World" problematic)? Only much later, as I was completing this book, was I able to return to this incident, which is significant and symptomatic of the larger and longer processes I have described.

First Press Conference: Amadeu Antonio Foundation[1]

The press conference takes place a day after the official opening of the exhibit in its new location in another part of Berlin. When the conference begins, I can see the stress on Phillipa Ebéné's face. A friend has made me aware of the press accusations. Berlin's mainstream newspaper *Tagesspiegel* (*Daily Mirror*) has run an editorial on its first page, now referring to the Workshop of Cultures' popular annual parade as the "Carnival of the Degenerate Cultures," implying that the groups that normally participate in the parade (called the Carnival of Cultures) are also responsible for Ebéné's decision. Given this stress, Ebéné looks as if she hasn't slept, tortured perhaps by allegations and miscommunication. For her sake, I wish that she had a media advisor or a press team. The audience of journalists and recognizable community activists is a mix of support and accusation.

After introducing the other panelists (including the historian Götz Aly and the English professor Susan Arndt), Anetta Kahane, the director of the Ama-

deu Antonio Foundation, notes that Ebéné "sits here today not as the director
of the Workshop of Cultures—there will be a press conference there tomorrow.
She is here as a person of color [Kahane uses the English phrase] who lives in
Berlin." Kahane then asks her why the exhibition was canceled.

Ebéné responds: "In my experience, a commemoration is a commemoration,
and the theme of collaboration must, from my perspective, at the very least
be contextualized."

One woman says that she doesn't understand. Someone else speaks the word
aloud slowly, emphasizing each syllable: "con-tex-tu-al-ized."

Kahane asks: "Was there a problem with the title [of the exhibition]?" (The
official title was "The Third World in the Second World War.") Ebéné answers:

> No, that was also a problem, but I could have stomached that. "The Third
> World in the Second World War" [is] a, how should we say, difficult title. But
> I was of the opinion that one could still talk, must talk. . . . [The title] wasn't
> completely understandable to me. But at the end of the day, the partnership
> broke down because I didn't think that the millions of relevant people were
> being honored. It's not just about the people who died here or [who were] on
> their way [to Europe], but [in addition] the families at home who were also
> affected. I didn't understand how one would really be honoring these people if,
> in the end, everything was relativized, if at the end of the exhibit, where the
> final impression is made, one sees the collaborators.

Kahane then talks about the mufti of Jerusalem, who was a Palestinian collaborator. The exhibit points this out, showing that he moved to Berlin and
joined the SS, and displaying an archival photograph of him sitting down for
a meeting with Adolf Hitler.

> Kahane: What about the mufti? Why did he achieve . . . such a prominent
> position? [Much of the media attention had focused on Ebéné's refusal to have
> him, in particular, mentioned in the exhibit, thus the mayor's claim that she
> must have been forced by an Arab "top dog."]
> Ebéné: I also asked myself that question. [Laughter] Why does the mufti have
> such an elevated position? Just to make things clear . . . the mufti was no friend
> of ours. The mufti was a Nazi sympathizer. And . . . it's not the case that one
> can't do something on the topic of collaboration at the Workshop of Cultures.
> Kahane: You could also do that.
> Ebéné: We can also do that. We could say, "Let's talk about collabora-
> tion." Yes. Then we also need to talk about Ukraine, about Lithuania, about

Hungary, about the IRA, about France, about the mufti, about everyone. Yes. That's the context.

Kahane: About the Indians.

Ebéné: About the Indians. About all those who collaborated. Lots of people collaborated. In order to kill so many people during the Second World War, a lot of people had to have participated. Yes. We have to all be clear about that. For this exhibition, our point was to say: "There are people here who have not been honored for seventy years, who fundamentally, in the media landscape, either never come up or who are always portrayed as illegal immigrants or, very willingly [implicitly, from the perspective of the German mainstream], as the recipients of development aid." We are talking about the people who did not, as a rule, receive any recognition. As a rule, they were sent back to their homelands, in which there was no autonomy [because of colonial authority].

Kahane: Understood. You wanted a homage.

Ebéné: Yes, exactly.

Kahane [to Arndt, who has written on representations of Africa in Germany and on Whiteness]: Why did this result in such a fiasco? Why is this room now so full?

Arndt: Colonialism is rarely mentioned in schools. . . . This is the very first exhibition.

Susan Arndt's point seems to be that as the first exhibit of its kind, a lot is at stake, including recognition for the curator and the expectations of the potential audience, which, in this case, includes people with personal connections to the colonial histories being remembered. Kahane continues, "Anti-Semitism also became a part of this discussion." Arndt says that racism, colonialism, and anti-Semitism need to be thought of together. The discussion proceeds:

Kahane: I found the exhibit incredibly interesting. [There were] lots of things that I didn't know.

Aly [historian]: In an exhibit, one can do what one wants. . . . In general, I think it's good that these first steps were made. . . . [A] homage to colored troops, good. . . . That the mufti was a collaborator, okay, but the main collaborators were the Bosnian Muslims who went into the SS. We don't like to hear that. That the mufti was bad, we know that. Just as pronounced a friend of Nazi Germany was Mahatma Gandhi. [Aly has this wrong. The exhibit reports on collaboration by the Indian freedom fighter Subhas Chandra Bose.] . . . It's very clear that this falls under the rubric of "An enemy of my enemy is also my friend." It was about British colonialism. That is how this German-Indian collaboration came into existence, not because Indians were Hitler Aryans. That did not play any role. . . . War is not pretty. It is horrifying. Of course, horrifying things happen on all sides.

Afterward Götz Aly goes on to talk about the history of "Rhineland bastards" (he insists on this term) and why streets such as Mohrenstraße (Moor Street), a name many Afro-Germans see as racist, should keep its name. Kahane eventually cuts him off: "Sometimes, historians answer questions they weren't asked." Later in the conference, perhaps realizing the increasing animosity from a large contingent of the audience, Aly gets up, bangs his fist on the table, and leaves.

In the question-and-answer session that follows the panel, a woman who worked on the exhibit accuses Ebéné of having known about the contents of the whole exhibit in advance. She asks why she "censored it" at the last minute. Ebéné says that she only found out about the collaborator portion in the final stages. Another woman, who identifies herself as a "person of color," says that although she worked on the project, she hadn't heard anything about the collaborators. That portion wasn't part of the press release.[2]

The reporter from the *Jerusalem Post,* who speaks with an American accent, calls Ebéné an anti-Semite. Shermin Langhoff, the director of a highly successful "post-migrant"[3] theater in Kreuzberg, says that the way Ebéné is being attacked in the news media is unacceptable. A representative from the Initiative for Blacks in Germany reads a letter in support of Ebéné from an African American former soldier who had been stationed in Germany for twenty years.

After the conference, Ebéné, whom I already know from an interview I conducted for the article "Citizenship and the Obama Moment in Berlin," says, "I'm getting slaughtered."

Second Press Conference: Werkstatt der Kulturen

This second press conference, sponsored by the Workshop of Cultures itself, is less crowded than the first. Ebéné sits at a table with an older White German man, Rainer B. Giesel, the acting head of the Workshop of Cultures' board. This time, he is the principal speaker, and says that he stands fully behind the director.

He explains, "[It is not about] three panels [the initial controversy centered on the three exhibition panels concerning "Arab collaboration" and "the mufti from Jerusalem"], but eighteen. . . . In Europe, the question[s] of victims of the Third Reich and [of] collaborators have been separated. . . . A reduced form of the exhibit is now hanging in th[is] seminar room, based on a vote by the board."

Phillipa Ebéné speaks infrequently. I am a bit confused because Giesel has just said that he fully supports Ebéné, but in the room where the press conference is taking place, parts of the exhibit are already on the wall. Specifically, there are panels with the word *Collaborators* written in large blue letters down the sides of each one. I see a panel about Indians' collaboration with the SS. It ultimately becomes clear to me that in spite of the support from the board, Ebéné has been overruled.

Press Release from the Werkstatt der Kulturen

The Exhibition shown here is a smaller version of the original exhibit that opened on September 30, 2009, at the Uferhallen in Wedding [Berlin], where a wide-ranging accompanying program is also on display.

As a result of the different conceptions concerning the goals and the content of the original exhibition between the exhibit curators and the House of World Cultures, our institute declined to have the exhibit on display here.

Through public disclosures from some of the already named participants, the theme of this exhibition and the position of the Workshop of Cultures has unfortunately resulted in factually inaccurate reporting in the Berlin and supraregional press.

Through the mediation of the Berlin Senate's commissioner for Integration and Migration, the board of the Workshop of Cultures voted to show the exhibition in this optically reduced form, without the planned accompanying program. In this way, a discussion about the exhibition can take place.

The Aftermath

Nearly eight months later, Ebéné told me that amid all of the press attention and the accusations of anti-Semitism, she wanted to quit her position. Talking about the lack of diversity among the German press corps, she said, "I find that the press landscape in Germany . . . that it's Hitler's wet dream. They all wrote the same thing. Whether left or right, it didn't matter." She went on to argue, "Only White Germans wanted the mufti from Jerusalem to be responsible for Auschwitz." They had, according to her, "incorporated Jewish people into the 'we' group, so that [White non-Jewish Germans] could be even more racist. . . . I wanted to go. My mother called and said, 'I heard you on the radio.' Speaking in a southern German dialect, she told me: 'You're staying put. . . . One doesn't quit at such moments.'"

In a subsequent article, after the initial barrage of accusations, Berlin's *Tagesspiegel* concluded: "In the fight over the world war show, two different memory cultures came crashing into each other. In this process, Neukölln became the test field for establishing a new global understanding of history.[4] In hindsight, this experiment was even, perhaps, successful" (Tagesspiegel 2009b). In this context, the paper argued, the fight itself became the appropriate mode for a culture of memory, implicitly ensuring that there is no one dominant or hegemonic culture. This is reminiscent of the argument concerning Berlin's Holocaust memorial. Some suggested, "The discussion is the *Mahnmal* [memorial]!" (Till 2005) before the organizers, the architect, and the German parliament agreed on which form the memorial would take and before the physical memorial actually materialized.

But these tidy concluding remarks cover over the conditions under which the fight took place and how it ended. The Afro-German director was forced to show the exhibit in her center and lost control over how it was shown. Furthermore, she was accused of being anti-Semitic and anti-democratic, and told to go back where she came from. There was no media-led vindication. She retained her position as director but only in a compromised sense. The exhibit was not only shown in her center but also in another, larger forum (with lots of media attention), and there was a plan for its future use as a tool for public school education around the country.

In the midst of the controversy, in his remarks at the opening at the alternative location, before it was decided that the exhibit would also be shown in the smaller format at the Werkstatt der Kulturen, the main curator, Rössel, argued (seemingly as a bona fide anti-racist): "To finally change the Eurocentric and therefore racist discourse of history in this country, to finally give it a global perspective, a changing of consciousness is needed among the white majority society, just as with their dominant historical research, and the lessons taught in schools and universities" (Rössel 2009).

Earlier in his remarks, he said that his role and the role of his associates in creating this project were to be both "translators and intermediaries." In the context of "the fight," the self-assigned role of translation and mediation takes on hierarchical dimensions: in asserting his role in terms of translation and mediation, he pushes out people of color, such as Ebéné. In his speech, one can observe a linguistic shift. Rössel moves from the term *Third World* to *MigrantInnen* (migrants), to people *mit Migrationshitergrund* (with migrant backgrounds), to *people of color,* the most contemporary term and the term that Ebéné's supporters (including those from ADEFRA, a Black women's organization; and ISD, the Initiative for Blacks in Germany) used in their press releases and public discussions. Rössel asserts:

> Also among people of color, to use this blanket term for people of different backgrounds and dispositions, there were not only anti-fascist heroes, but also supporters, fascists, and collaborators. Whoever attempts to ignore or suppress these facts disregards the victims of these collaborators. In the end, this is not just about a few individual cases. . . . Ten thousand people freely volunteered to work in the arms industry for the aspiring powers. Hundreds of thousands volunteered to fight on their behalf. And millions celebrated their victories. (ibid.)

Here, Rössel implicitly pits slain Jews against people of color, insisting that they are also responsible for genocide and putting people such as Ebéné on the side of Holocaust denial, a serious charge in Germany. In this process, Rössel, advocating for the importance of his exhibition, adopts a position of moral superiority in relation to his detractors, many of whom define themselves as people of color.

This is a critical part of the process that I want to label *triangulated citizenship,* in which (1) one atones for Germany's past through a strong condemnation of the Nazi-era politics (Rössel does this via his condemnation of the "Third World collaborators"); (2) one comes out strongly against contemporary racism (Rössel does this by arguing against the absence of a "Third World narrative" in the public discussion of history); and (3) one presents oneself as the ideal translator/interpreter of contemporary and past racism. In pushing people of color out of the discussion, however, this triangulated citizenship also produces noncitizens.

Rössel concludes:

> The list goes on and the exhibition recalls very deliberately the victims, who would not have existed as such without the collaborators in the Third World.
>
> As a result of the public controversy concerning this topic, we are sponsoring an additional event on the topic of Nazi collaborators from the Near East and their German apologists, [and] in this case, one should note that there are also female apologists. (ibid.)

In the exhibit and in his remarks, Rössel links the mufti from Jerusalem to Yasser Arafat, and argues that after the controversy he realized that the accompanying film and video program, if anything, gave too positive a representation of people from the Middle East: "As a whole, the accompanying program is actually too Arabophilic" (ibid.).

In this context, it becomes clear that Rössel has a bone to pick with the particular memory of "Arab collaboration." While Ebéné emphasizes all eighteen panels of the exhibit (*Um diese achtzehn Tafeln geht das*), in his public comments Rössel always mentions only three—the ones that involve "Arab collaborators." In his extended interview with the self-proclaimed anti-fascist journal *Jungle World*, he insisted, "Either the exhibition appears in its entirety or not at all."

Rössel's position is part of a broader trend in contemporary Germany that targets, in particular, Muslim anti-Semitism. This trend can also be seen in the programs for *Stadtteilmütter* (city district mothers), which are federally funded and specifically attempt to incorporate immigrant women into the delivery of local social services. One program with the mothers in Neukölln was oriented toward local and national Holocaust memory and involved a trip to Auschwitz. The women, it turns out, were very moved, but in the media reports and public forums, they were accused of being anti-Semitic.

Normative representations of racism in Germany have a bifurcated position (see Bunzl 2005, 2007; Özyürek 2009). They look simultaneously to the Nazi anti-Semitic past and to the violent neo-Nazi present, but not to racism's institutionalized everyday persistence or to the relevance of Germany's own colonial past. If the mainstream public, especially public intellectuals, were to look critically at continuity, including that of colonialism, they would find that they were also implicated in racism's contemporary manifestations, including but not fully explainable in terms of neo-Nazi violence. That is partially what is at stake in this triangulated debate between histories and the present situation of anti-Semitism, racism, and perpetration.

In his press releases and self-advocacy, Rössel refuses to make these links, and instead looks for an implicit personal/national vindication in the history of the Other. He simultaneously shows that he is an anti-racist, while insisting on the permanent continuity of Arab anti-Semitism, to which he successfully links Ebéné in her rejection of his exhibit. With the help of the broader media landscape, he makes Arab anti-Semitism into the main issue. Talking about the representation of Arabs in the exhibit, particularly as it relates to Arabs helping Jewish residents in the context of the Second World War, Ebéné argues: "Only one single Arab is represented in the context of Yad Vashem [the Israeli Holocaust memorial]."

Fortunately, other voices are emerging. However, the situation has become more difficult for Arab and Muslim Germans concerning accusations of anti-Semitism, as well as for those who want to call attention to German colonialism as a means of exploring a broader history of racism (and noncitizenship). Responding to some of these issues as part of a federally funded and locally run project concerning German history and the *Stadtteilmütter*, in *Unsere Geschichten—eure Geschichte? Neuköllner Stadtteilmütter und ihre Auseinandersetzung mit der Geschichte des Nationalsozialismus (Our Stories—Your History? Neukölln City Quarter Mothers and Their Confrontation with the History of National Socialism)*, Havva Jürgensen wrote:

> For me there is a human interest that I have in the topic of National Socialism. We often hear that the topic of National Socialism is not for us, because we are migrants. Just as frequently, it is assumed without a doubt that we are too anti-Semitic to be interested in this topic. Of course there are anti-Semites among the immigrants, but it hurts that we are so often confronted with this blanket accusation. We live in this country and want to grapple with the history. How did anti-Semitism come into being? Why did so many people vote for Hitler and support the Nazis? Why did the perpetrators behave so horribly? How did Hitler function? Why wasn't there more resistance against the Nazis? Why was there supposed to be a pure Germany? In addition, we also wanted to know more about the relationships between Judaism, Christianity, and Islam. In the pursuit of questions about National Socialism, there are also related questions that are important to us: How are minorities dealt with today in Germany? With which values should we raise our kids? How can we achieve solidarity [with] each other? (2010: 54)

Voices like this are rarely heard in the German mainstream. They appear in small booklets where only the truly interested uncover them. The more likely scenario is the one that arose around the "Third World in the Second World War" exhibit and the controversy that followed. Perhaps emerging transnational possibilities will create new opportunities for a reformulation of citizenship. Perhaps by our continuing to examine the lives of noncitizens, new theories of possibility will materialize.

Notes

Prologue

1. I have used the form "re"unification here because, as other scholars have also pointed out, Germany did not return to its pre-1945 borders after the fall of the Berlin Wall. The notions of unification and reunification are persistently caught up in the production of imagined community. See Anderson 1991.

2. For an example of this type of claim, see Garton Ash 2009.

3. Mandel 2008 provides a detailed analysis and critique of the claim that Kreuzberg is an "immigrant neighborhood."

4. While the conversation took place in German, I have translated it to English here.

5. While formally understood to be an isolated incident, in 2009 a pregnant Egyptian pharmacist was killed in a courtroom:

> Just before the knife attack on the Egyptian woman, Marwa el S. [Marwa al-Sheribini], in the Dresden Regional Court, the perpetrator made known his sympathies for the NPD, according to *Tagesspiegel*'s information. Next, Alex W. [the defendant] asked the Egyptian woman in the courtroom, "Do you even have the right to be in Germany?" Then he added, "You don't have the right to say anything here." The Russian German became louder and threatened, "When the NPD comes to power, that will be the end. I voted for the NPD." Just after that he toppled Marwa el S. and her husband and began stabbing them. (Tagesspiegel 2009a; my translation)

6. Although I was hired as an associate producer and directed some key scenes, my name does not appear in the credits.

7. This text is from the film. I have added some visual explanations.

8. Here, the Nazis cite Rosa Luxemburg.

Introduction

1. Following Aihwa Ong's (1996) definition of citizenship as a process of "self making and being made within webs of power," I understand noncitizenship in similar

terms, although the noncitizen is being made and is making herself along a different trajectory than that of a citizen.

2. These numbers are drawn from a discussion with the Berlin senator Özcan Mutlu in 2008. While not differentiated by specific family background and somewhat obscured by the fact that people can be legally "German" without being understood as German by their teachers or the normative public, according to the official Berlin website, "Deutliche Unterschiede zeigen sich in den Schulabschlüssen von deutschen und nicht-deutschen Schüler/innen. Gingen in Berlin im Schuljahr 2003/04 unter den Schüler/innen deutscher Staatsangehörigkeit 9,2 Prozent der Schule ab, so waren es unter den nicht-deutschen Staatsangehörigen 20,5 Prozent." (There are noticeable differences between the types of school degrees received by German and non-German students. In the school year 2003–2004 9.2 percent of pupils with German citizenship left school [without a degree], whereas 20.5 percent of students without German citizenship left school [without a degree].) http://www.berlin.de/lb/intmig/statistik/aus_bildung/schulabgaenger.html?_=print, accessed January 15, 2009.

3. In this book, I capitalize Black and White, because I see them as political terms that are associated with discourses of belonging, but that are also potentially reductive discourses of social scientific analysis. In Germany, "White" is not frequently used as a social marker (see Eggers et al. 2005; Tißberger et al. 2006). I use it in this text as a way to mark the unmarked. "Whiteness" is both a historical and a situated production. As Michelle Wright points out:

> [R]ecalling Gobineau's dizzyingly complex hierarchy of categories of whiteness (beginning with different types of Aryans and moving down in purity and superiority), as well as Hegel's location of Germany as the most superior of all Western nations, we can understand how white Germans do not read themselves as racially [the] selfsame with other white Western Europeans but rather as a distinct *Volk* with a specific cultural and *racial* heritage. (2004: 184)

I would add that the term *race* in the German context is not used without some self-consciousness. With the exception of the extreme right or discussions about dog breeds, it is usually avoided. On the other hand, there are still racial effects of the contemporary politics of belonging. These effects are, of course, not just in Germany. On a visit to France as part of a Fulbright seminar for American university faculty, "Muslim Minorities in France and Germany," I found the denial of racism in France to be pronounced. In Austria in the 2008 elections, around 30 percent of the population voted for extreme right-wing parties.

4. The ban on dual citizenship does have exceptions, but they are notably not for Turkish Germans.

5. In his essay "Citizenship and Social Class" (1992 [1950]), sociologist T. H. Marshall assigns citizenship to three different categories: civil, political, and social. He further assigns these differentiated aspects of citizenship to different eras in English history. In short, *civil* refers to the law and courts, *political* refers to political parties, and *social* refers to both social class and economic distribution. The contradiction inherent in the social aspect of citizenship has to do with the differentiation between legal and

economic equality. Does equality of opportunity suffice? My analysis goes further to ask how, within these differentiated fields of citizenship, noncitizens might be taken into account.

6. Ruth Mandel writes about the "biopolitical division between people and citizens" (2008: 211). Giorgio Agamben (1998) distinguishes between bare life and political life. In writing about governmentality (governmental rationality) and biopolitics, Michel Foucault (2003, 1991a, 1990, 1980) writes about the contemporary nation-state in terms of its attention to simultaneously producing, protecting, and regulating the lives of the (implicitly, national) population. In my work, I see noncitizens as political subjects who reside within the nation-state, but who are nevertheless differentiated from the national population. This has effects not only on their legal, political, and socioeconomic status (see Marshall 1992 [1950]), but also directly on their physical bodies.

7. I was a member of a local foreign advisory committee in 1999–2000 in Berlin, and was astounded at the relative ineffectiveness of the committee and the dominance of the German citizen members.

8. See also Fikes (2009) on the relationship between the turn toward "European modernity" and the articulation of the "citizen-migrant" distinction in Portugal.

9. I refer to bodies here and not simply to noncitizens, because I want to emphasize the materiality of the processes I describe. The process of becoming a noncitizen has bodily effects.

10. My point is that normalization is a social process that includes the physical. This is also Foucault's point inasmuch as the biopolitical includes biology, which is both social and physical (see also Butler 1993). In this sense, both citizenship and the process of becoming a noncitizen act on the body. The example of the intersex child who is made to undergo a possibly unnecessary surgical procedure reveals the stakes quite explicitly. In this case, future pleasure, mental health, and biological functions are sacrificed for the sake of being perceived socially and physically as normal. Even worse, as Agamben's account in *Homo Sacer* (1998) suggests, normalizing institutions operate on the "non-political" body (bare life) without acknowledging these operations as sacrifices. In the case of the intersex person, the doctor suggests that he/she is, in fact, helping the child.

11. Benedict Anderson (1991) has interestingly pointed to the problematic use of the term *naturalize* as it relates to national belonging, as if national belonging were a natural state of being.

12. Before the Haitian revolution, Haiti was part of France.

1. Ethno-patriarchal Returns

1. One should note that other countries in Western Europe had similar policies of family unification (see, for example, Fikes 2009).

2. Workers from China, Cuba, and North Korea were recalled to their countries by their national governments when these governments realized that the end of European socialism was imminent.

3. This information is from a presentation that Bui gave at the Bundeskanzler Fellows alumni meeting, Providence, Rhode Island, 2005 (see also Bui 2004).

4. This refers to the districts on the outskirts of many East German cities with prefabricated high-rise and low-rise housing complexes.

5. Of course, we should remember that "rights" are always a bit tainted (see Brown 1995 and the introduction to this volume). In order to gain access to them, the political subject must give up parts of his/her own potential self, inasmuch as he/she submits to the collective or governing will, even shaping his/her body and desire around it. For non-citizens, this may mean gaining the right to stay in the country without the expectation of the same safety or care as the normal citizen. Indeed, in the moments immediately following the fall of the Wall, and even now in certain parts of the new country, one could expect to be attacked, and it was/is not clear whether the police would/will show up.

6. It is not clear that she would define herself in this way. Many people with one African and one German parent do not. Some refuse any sort of identification. But she has been active in the Afro-German movement.

7. "The Party" here refers to the SED, the East German Socialist Unity Party.

8. These were the demonstrations that began the "peaceful revolution" in East Germany.

9. Except where otherwise credited, translations in this text are my own.

10. This is the former West German currency.

11. A math teacher at a *Haupt/Realschule* in Kreuzberg talked in an interview about unification as the moment when the success of schools with students of primarily Turkish descent started to turn. Drama and other programs were suddenly cut.

12. Even with the expression *das Volk,* there is a sense in which a national (ethno-racial) community is being invoked.

13. The East German government at times sold its own citizens to the West German government in order to get much-needed West German currency. Those sold were usually East German dissidents or those who wanted to leave the East.

14. A friend in her early twenties who had grown up in East Germany told me about her disappointment after buying her first McDonald's burger. "They looked so big on television," she complained. Another friend, in his fifties, who had been a committed socialist before and after the fall of the Wall, for years had told me that he was happy driving his small Honda. Through his emphasis on simplicity, he seemed to be commenting on the surrounding environment that overvalued excess. One summer, I learned that he had bought a BMW, although he still had the Honda. His son had started driving a BMW as well.

15. This might explain how the Social Democrats defeated the Christian Democrats in the 1998 national election.

16. In German:

> Die Unterbringug der vietnamesischen Vertragsarbeiter erfolgt in Gemeineschaftsunterkünften mit einer Belegung von höchstens vier Personene je Wohnraum, wobei die Wohnfläche je Person mindesten 5 m² betragen soll. Die Entfernung zum einsatzbetrieb sollte eine Fahrzeit von 40 Minuten nicht überschreiten Außerdem wurde festgeschrieben, was einem Vertragsarbeiter an Gegenständen zusteht: 1 Liege mit Bettkasten, 1 Steppdecke, 1

Kopfkissen, 2 Handtücher hell, 2 Handtücher dunkel, Geschirr (1 Tasse, 1 Unterasse, 1 Teller flach, 1 Teller tief usw). (Spennemann 1997: 11)

17. This was the East German currency.

18. Much of this information is from two interviews with East German activist Tamara Hentschel in the summer of 1998. Hentschel is the founder of Reistrommel, a group that advocates for the rights of Vietnamese people in East Germany and defends them from police and skinhead attacks.

2. Travel as an Analytic of Exclusion

1. For me, "Black" means "of African descent" and sometimes simply Other. I am aware of the problematic in which people who are seen as Other also want to distance themselves from Blackness. I want to leave the category of Blackness open, while recognizing the ways in which it is often closed.

2. While Poles now have full rights to move throughout the EU, the hierarchy of the relationship to movement is nevertheless made clear via this example.

3. Mecklenburg-Vorpommern, in Germany's northeast, is a region that includes major tourist destinations on the Baltic Sea. It was also the location of the 2007 G8 meetings.

4. Access to German-language courses is a major issue.

5. As opposed to a positive right to asylum, the *kleines Asyl* (small or little asylum) expresses a *Verbot* (ban) against deportation. On its website, the Bavarian Ministry of the Interior lists asylum in terms of three levels: *großes Asyl* (large asylum), *kleines Asyl*, and *subsidärer Schutz* (subsidiary protection). See http://www.stmi.bayern.de/buerger/auslaender/asyl/detail/06477/index.php, accessed February 1, 2008. The main ground for the "large asylum" is political persecution.

6. Explaining "time-space compression," David Harvey writes: "The time horizons of both private and public decision-making have shrunk, while satellite communication and declining transport costs have made it increasingly possible to spread those decisions immediately over an ever wider variegated space" (1990: 147).

7. Except where otherwise noted, all interviews in this chapter were conducted in German. I have translated them into English.

8. Rostock is an infamous port city on the Baltic Sea. After the fall of the Wall, the West German government sent many asylum seekers there, and they ended up fearing for their lives because of instances of severe violence in which hundreds of youths threw Molotov cocktails and entered the homes of "foreign" residents, shouting "Foreigners get out."

9. The *subaltern* is defined here as outside the binary oppositions of self and Other, East and West, or Black and White. These oppositions problematize what the subaltern would say, in effect, silencing the possibility of her speech.

10. Michelle M. Wright has written about "'Blackness' as a unity of diversity" (2004: 5–6).

11. In analyzing the play *Keloglan in Alamania* by Turkish German playwright and author Emine Sevgi Özdamar, Katrin Sieg concludes, very similarly to J.B., "In this

play, there *is* no ethnicity outside of its performance; like Joan Riviere's famous essay, which theorized the same about femininity and the masquerade, Özdamar's dramaturgical thesis, that ethnicity and masquerade are the same thing, is both novel and consonant with orientalist presumptions" (2002: 244).

12. By *technologies of exclusion*, I do not mean only physical technologies such as border fences or surveillance cameras, but also social technologies such as immigration laws, asylum laws, and the German *Aufenthaltzgesetz* (residency law). They are not just exclusionary, but also productive, in that they produce the foreign subject as a noncitizen.

3. We Were Dancing in the Club, Not on the Berlin Wall

1. In writing about White German women in this context, I am selecting only one aspect of White female subjectivity. "Whiteness" here points to the fact that all Germans are not White, and also to the ways in which Whiteness works in relationship to German citizenship and sovereignty. The category "White German women" is not a static one, but is always in relationship to and in negotiation with normative understandings of German history, including the Nazi era, the 1968 resistance, and feminist movements. In this chapter I focus in particular on the relationships between this nexus and the subjectivity of and possibilities for Black diasporic men. For more on Whiteness, see Tißberger et al. 2006; Eggers et al. 2005; Rasmussen et al. 2001; Frankenberg 1993.

2. Quoted in Tageszeitung 2002; my translation.

3. This represents a shift from occupiers to potential immigrants (which should not obscure the fact that some African Americans have become German residents). As I argue elsewhere, the fact that Germany has a history of Black GI clubs also opens up regularized space for other Black subjects to enter into the clubs and into relationships with White German women. As the historical circumstances change (away from occupation and toward an increasingly Fortress European mentality), however, the meanings and possibilities of these other relationships also change.

4. My point is not to condemn these relationships, but to examine the conditions under which they take place. There is no innocent sex here, even if one imagined that one were having it.

5. I write about a range of Black men, those with and without a status that allows them to stay in Germany. African Americans, for example, have a different status than men who are from Togo and living in asylum camps in hostile neo-Nazi territory. I point to both African Americans and asylum seekers, though, to illustrate their different relations to the nation-state, residency, and national citizenship, and also to show that the process of hypersexualization works across a range of bodies and Black subject positions.

6. It is not clear that the desire for Black bodies and, in particular, the Black male body is attached to a particular class status. This desire has been part of popular culture, and its evolution coincides both with U.S. military occupation and the sexual revolution of the late 1960s and early 1970s. The sexual politics that emerged from the left (see Herzog 2005) coincided with an anti-racism that imagined it could achieve revolution

in part through sleeping with the Other (see Ege 2007). This fantasy persisted in the 1970s and 1980s as a group of German feminists began to see men from the Caribbean, West Africa, and other sites as alternatives to the White masculinity that was dominant even on the left (see Herzog 2005). As other authors have noted, "With new economic power, many Euro-American women are seeking an identity beyond the confines of the traditional gender scripts offered in their cultures" (Pruitt and LaFont 1995: 423).

7. Although the new *Zuwanderungsgesetz* (immigration law) that went into effect on January 1, 2005, formally acknowledges the possibility of immigration to Germany, particularly when tied to "highly qualified labor," the new law remains highly exclusionary (Die Bundesregierung 2004a, b).

8. I do not mean that Black men are literally dancing in exotic clubs as professional dancers, but I do want to highlight the relationship between the formal legal arena and the informal network of dance club encounters. Just as there is a space in the formal law for the exclusionary incorporation of foreign bodies, the same type of space exists in the broader social reality: "You can stay here, if (and only if) you dance." Of course, hardly anyone says this literally, but it is the effect of the social and legal conditions.

9. In this instance, one can see that formal policy is linked to an informal desire for Black men.

10. The term *economy of desire* alludes to the fact that there is more at work than innocent love in these relationships. There are social and state pressures; histories of desire; gender and racial investments, readings, and subjectivities; and social, juridical, and moral laws. This economy is based on the nexus between images and imaginations of Black bodies and the histories of German patriarchy, colonialism, and fascism. It is also intertwined with 1968 leftist and feminist resistances, Germany's 1990 unification, and possibilities to consume.

11. Even though Poland is now a member of the European Union, its entrance into the union did not immediately give its citizens the right to move through Germany without visas. Poland was not originally one of the Schengen states. Its borders with Germany were only opened (without restrictions to Polish visitors) in December 2007 (Ministry of Foreign Affairs of the Republic of Poland, n.d.).

12. Classically, the sovereign "decides on the state exception." See Agamben 1998, 2005; Schmitt 2006 [1922]. Following Walter Benjamin (1969 [1942]), Agamben (2005) links the state of exception to the state of emergency, which "has become the rule."

13. *Hypersexuality* refers to being extremely sexual.

14. For more on abjection in relation to Jewish and homosexual subjectivities in Austria, see Bunzl 2004. He argues that there has been a contemporary shift toward the recognition and incorporation of these subjects.

15. Even though many of the White German women who had been in relationships with Black men thought of themselves as resisting White male patriarchy and German racism, they were also involved, through these relationships and the difference implied in their descriptions of their Black partners, in producing new forms of Germanness. In a study of tourism, gender, and sex with "single" or "unaccompanied" women on Jamaican and Dominican beaches, which, in addition to ethnographic research, included a survey of 240 women, sociologist Jacqueline Sanchez Taylor reports:

White women, in particular, explained that they felt valued in the Caribbean in ways in which they are not back home. Their economic power and their whiteness means that they are not treated as local women but respected and protected. Their bodies are also valued over local women's bodies and they are offered a stage upon which they can simultaneously affirm their femininity through their ability to command local men and reject the white men. (2001: 760)

16. By referring to the "process of hypersexualization," I distinguish between the process in which normative sexuality and subjectivity are produced and the process in which Black subjects are made and incorporated into Germany. For another analysis of processes of differentiation at work in the German context, see Dominic Boyer's "On the Sedimentation and Accreditation of Social Knowledges of Difference: Mass Media, Journalism, and the Reproduction of East/West Alterities in Unified Germany" (2000).

17. The parade floats emphasize Black bodies as sites of desirable excess; they are not only not-German but also, in many ways, not modern, rational (boring) subjects. This was a point emphasized by an anonymous *Cultural Anthropology* reviewer. I saw more of these images when I visited women interlocutors at home.

18. I have reproduced the discussion here from my notes.

19. Once again, Blackness is understood as bodily movement as opposed to the cerebral distance of (boring) intellectual conversation (the way she describes her former White German boyfriend). In popular imagination and frequent performances in Berlin, Brazil, like Africa, represents good music and having a good time.

20. Fear versus contemporary interest points to earlier histories of the national reception of Black bodies.

21. She tells me that she doesn't know and doesn't want to know about his past. When it comes to the politics of asylum, in spite of her left-leaning politics in other areas, she takes up a normative story, assuming that his claim is false. The larger media and politically driven discourse understand Africans as economic and not "political" refugees.

22. Although I do not agree with their use of the term *fremdenfeindlich* (xenophobic), inasmuch as it naturalizes the opposition between "foreigner" and "native," Behrends and colleagues note (2003: 12), "Opfer einer fremdenfeindlich motiverten Straftat zu werden, ist im Osten der Republik ungefähr zwanzig Mal so groß wie im Westen" (The chance of becoming a victim of a xenophobic attack is twenty times greater in the East as opposed to the West of the Republic [Federal Republic of Germany]).

23. The letter was addressed to "The Chancellor of Germany, the President of Germany, the Parliament of Germany, the Supreme Court of Germany, the Media, the Human Rights Organizations, the United Nations High Commissioner for Refugees, the Churches"; 116 people signed the letter, which is dated April 26, 2000. See Rathenow Asylum Seekers 2000.

24. This emphasizes the stakes of recognition and the stakes of the performance. What types of bodies does a failed performance produce? How do failed performances emphasize discretionary power?

25. One should note here that the legal regime has psychological consequences.

26. It is interesting that she points out that he has a German passport as opposed to calling him a German citizen.

4. The Progeny of Guest Workers as Leftover Bodies

1. Rita Chin (2007) sees 1973, with the introduction of the *Anwerberstopp* (the ban on the recruitment of guest workers into Germany), as a major turning point.

2. In Germany, the liberal party (FDP) promotes policies to enhance free market possibilities.

5. Why Can't You Just Remove Your Headscarf So We Can See You?

1. The terms *Turkish* and *Muslim* are usually conflated in the German and broader European context. Writing about the French case, Joan Scott concludes:

> From the earliest days of conquest through decolonization and its aftermath, the veil has figured as a potent political emblem. It has conjured up fantasies of domination and submission as well as of seduction and terror; for some it is an expression of agency, for others a sign of victimization, and for many a practical instrument of warfare. . . . Drawing the line at wearing the veil is a way of drawing the line not only at Islam but at the differences Arab and Muslim populations represent, a way of insisting on the timeless superiority of French "civilization" in the face of a changing world. (2007: 89; see also Partridge 2003)

Esra Özyürek (2009) has pointed to the ways in which Islam has become a site of danger and desire via the "threat" of conversion from Christianity to Islam.

2. A political campaign in 2000 used the phrase "Kinder staat Inder" (Kids Instead of Indians) to challenge Chancellor Schröder's promotion of the German "green card."

3. In the 2005 federal campaign that eventually led to the election of Angela Merkel, the first female German chancellor, some campaign posters by Merkel's party, the Christian Democrats, simply showed the image of a blond, blue-eyed baby.

4. The official website's English summary explains the history of the carnival:

> After only six months of active preparation, the parade of the first Carnival of Cultures took place on May 16th, 1996. 50,000 visitors came to see the parade consisting of 2,200 performers accompanied by about 50 colourfully decorated floats. . . .
>
> In 1997—the second carnival year—a street festival was added to the programme. In the same year, the first Children's Carnival was celebrated. Since 1997 the Carnival of Cultures takes place over the Whitsun (Pentecost) weekend as a four-day celebration.
>
> Over the last nine years, the numbers of participants and visitors have risen continuously. In 2005, 1.5 million visitors celebrated at the street festival and the parade. . . .

> The Carnival of Cultures is open to everybody and all forms of cultural expression. It is regarded as a platform for a proud expression of hybrid cultural identities, containing traditional and contemporary elements. It includes and attracts all age groups, professional artists and amateurs, people from all walks of life. (Karneval der Kulturen 2006)

Readers of this text and the poster should note that the festival follows the Christian calendar and that using the image of a semi-nude Black female body ties this event to accessibility and sex (see Gilman 1985).

5. Turkey is a prime German tourist destination. In conversations with several White German acquaintances, many remarked that something was wrong with the Turks in Germany. In their estimation, the Turks in Turkey were fine.

6. Katherine Pratt Ewing (e.g., 2008) also writes extensively on this issue.

7. Care is the type of power Michel Foucault (1980) calls *pastoral*.

8. This sentiment is in line with the White German mother's sentiment during the first year of the TV show; she encourages her sixteen-year-old biological daughter to find a boyfriend and have sex.

9. The *Oxford English Dictionary* defines *pasha* as follows: "a Turkish officer of high rank, as a military commander or a provincial governor (now *hist.*)."

10. I borrow Michael Lipsky's (1980) term *street bureaucrats* to refer to those who manage and administer the welfare state on a day-to-day basis in direct relationships with state subjects.

11. I do not examine what Mahmood (2005) calls a "politics of piety" in any detail, but this is clearly another important dimension of this process.

12. The *Abitur* is the secondary school degree that allows its recipients to attend the university. Only one-third of secondary students in Germany receive this degree.

13. In a conversation with a White German schoolteacher, she says that in order to get a sense of the position of Turkish parents about the situation of German-language proficiency in the schools, "I asked the cleaning ladies." The naturalness of the link between Turkish heritage and working as a cleaning lady is consistent with Ludin's bitterness about her possibilities other than teaching, given her own bodily articulation as a formal German citizen who chooses to wear a headscarf.

14. For more on the "dangers" of conversion, see Özyürek (2009).

15. This interview took place before September 11, 2001, and the ensuing war.

16. I have edited the text here in order to make it more readable.

17. Referring to the expert testimony, which gave some evidence for why women in Germany wear headscarves, the court reveals:

> The expert witness Dr. Karakasoglu, who was heard in the oral hearing, carried out a survey of about twenty-five Muslim students at colleges of education, twelve of whom wore a headscarf, and on the basis of this survey she showed that the headscarf is also worn by young women in order to preserve their own identity and at the same time to show consideration for the traditions of their parents in a diaspora situation; in addition, another reason for wearing the headscarf . . . was the desire to obtain more independent protection by

signaling that they were not sexually available and integrating themselves into society in a self-determined way. . . . As understood by the women questioned, preserving their difference is a precondition for their integration. (51–52)

18. One should note, as I have been pointing out and as scholars such as Foucault (1990, 1991a) and Brown (1995) make clear, that rights, protection, and care themselves regulate the forms and possibilities of living. However, it should also be clear that non-citizens (or those perceived as such) are regulated differently from the "normal" citizen. To be regulated without the expectations of care, protection, and rights (even while being incorporated) has particular disabling effects.

Conclusion

1. One should note that the sovereign decision in contemporary life is constrained by international regimes such as the UN, national parliaments, congresses, and one's access to forceful implementation. Foucault's (1991a) triangle of governance, discipline, and sovereignty is probably a more accurate reflection of the calculations, rationalizations, and care reflected in contemporary forms of what he calls "governmentality," but again, this has to be considered in relation to "states of exception" (Agamben 2005).

2. By putting *sovereign* in the plural, I want to point to the ways in which the democratization of sovereignty has left subjects who are legally recognized as belonging to the nation-state with a degree of possibility to regularly make decisions about others beyond their family members or direct descendants (even without having to use force or threaten violence).

3. The *Oxford English Dictionary* defines *integration* as follows: "1.a. the making up or composition of a whole by adding together or combining the separate parts or elements; combination into an integral whole: a making whole or entire."

4. Taking from Agamben (1998, 2005): the *state of exception* refers to the situation in which killing (either directly or indirectly) does not count as a sacrifice. It refers to subjects who can be killed without mourning.

5. Here, *political life* is the life that when sacrificed can be mourned. *Bare life* is the opposite.

6. Similarly, as war broke out in Libya after the "Arab spring" in 2011, as African migrants began moving in large numbers from northern Africa through Italy to the rest of Europe, one began to see tensions and contradictions about the openness of European borders. The tensions were centered around the presence and mobility of African (both northern and sub-Saharan) subjects in Europe.

7. Rabinow (1996) argues that in the future, people will begin to identify in terms of their specific genetic makeup. This identification will be made possible by the increasing medical knowledge associated with gene mapping.

Epilogue

1. The full name of the foundation is Amadeu Antonio Stiftung: Initiativen für Zivilgesellschaft und Demokratische Kultur (Amadeu Antonio Foundation: Initiatives for Civil Society and Democratic Culture).

2. This position is supported by a press release from the organization Africavenir, one of the sponsors that worked with Rössel, announcing a forthcoming event on May 25, 2009 (around the same time that Ebéné says that she met with Africavenir to discuss the forthcoming exhibit). The press release makes no mention of the collaborator component, even when mentioning those nations from which the later exhibit suggests collaborators came: "India alone contributed 2.5 million colonial soldiers and China mourned more losses than Germany, Italy, and Japan combined" (Africavenir 2009). At the end of the release, Africavenir emphasizes: "It is important to us to make progress against the centrality of white expertise" (ibid.).

3. The director of the Ballhaus Naunynstrasse theater in Berlin, Langhoff explained her view of the term *post-migrant* as follows:

> Sie hat den Begriff der Postmigration zwar nicht erfunden aber mit den Stücken, die am Ballhaus inszeniert werden, erhält er eine neue Anschaulichkeit. "Der postmigrantische Raum ist der eigentlich neue deutsche Raum, das ist der Raum, in dem wir alle leben," sagt sie. Und in diesem Raum geht es um möglichst vielfältige Strategien der Partizipation. ("Preis für berliner Postmigrantisches Theater" 2011)

> She did not invent the term *post-migration*, but with the pieces that are being staged at the Ballhaus, the term takes on a distinctive meaning. "The post-migrant space is the new German space; it is the space in which we all live," she says. And as much as possible, this space advances diverse strategies of participation.

Elsewhere, she has noted:

> Den Begriff "postmigrantisch" hab ich über die angloamerikanischen Literaturwissenschaft vor etwa zehn Jahren kennen gelernt. Es scheint mir einleuchtend, dass wir die Geschichten der zweiten und dritten Generation anders bezeichnen. Die stehen im Kontext der Migration, werden aber von denen erzählt, die selber gar nicht mehr gewandert sind. Eben postmigrantisch. ("Wir inszenieren kein Getto-Theater" 2009)

> I learned about the term *post-migrant* from Anglo-American literary theory about ten years ago. It makes sense to me that we tell the stories of the third and fourth generation differently. These stories are placed in the context of migration, but are told by those who haven't personally experienced migration. So we use the term *post-migrant*.

4. In a compelling book about competing memory cultures and the possibilities for simultaneous memory under the rubric of "multidirectional memory," Michael Rothberg (2009) argues that social memory is not a zero-sum game. One memory, he notes, does not need to come at the expense of another. Viola Georgi has taken on this issue in *Entliehene Erinnerung* (Borrowed Memories, 2003) and in her work with Rainer Ohlinger, *Crossover Geschichte* (Crossover History, 2009). Elke Gryglewski (2009) has written about successfully working with Palestinian German youth to simultaneously attend to Holocaust memory and Palestinian histories.

References

Abu-Lughod, Lila. 2002. "Do Muslim Women Really Need Saving? Anthropological Reflections on Cultural Relativism and Its Others." *American Anthropologist* 104(3) (September): 783.

Adelson, Leslie. 2005. *The Turkish Turn in Contemporary German Literature: Towards a New Critical Grammar of Migration*. New York: Palgrave Macmillan.

Africavenir. 2009. "Informationsabend mit dem Journalisten Karl Rössel zum Thema 'Die Dritte Welt im Zweiten Weltkrieg.'" *openPR*. http://www.openpr.de /news/305442/Informationsabend-mit-dem-Journalisten-Karl-Roessel-zum-Thema -Die-Dritte-Welt-im-Zweiten-Weltkrieg.html, accessed March 27, 2010.

Agamben, Giorgio. 1998. *Homo Sacer: Sovereign Power and Bare Life*. Stanford, Calif.: Stanford University Press.

———. 2005. *State of Exception*. Chicago: University of Chicago Press.

Ahmed, Leila. 1992. *Women and Gender in Islam: Historical Roots of a Modern Debate*. New Haven, Conn.: Yale University Press.

Amadeu Antonio Foundation. 2010. "Who Was Amadeu Antonio?" http://www.amadeu -antonio-stiftung.de/eng/about-us/who-was-amadeu-antonio, accessed March 8, 2010.

Anderson, Benedict. 1991. *Imagined Communities: Reflections on the Origin and Spread of Nationalism*. London: Verso.

Appadurai, Arjun. 1991. "Global Ethnoscapes: Notes and Queries for a Transnational Anthropology." In *Recapturing Anthropology: Working in the Present*, ed. Richard G. Fox. Santa Fe, N.M.: School of American Research Press.

———. 1996. *Modernity at Large*. Minneapolis: University of Minnesota Press.

Asad, Talal. 1993. *Genealogies of Religion: Discipline and Reasons of Power in Christianity and Islam*. Baltimore, Md.: Johns Hopkins University Press.

———. 2002. "Muslims and European Identity: Can Europe Represent Islam?" In *The Idea of Europe*, ed. Anthony Pagden. New York: Cambridge University Press.

Asher, Andrew D. 2005. "A Paradise on the Oder? Ethnicity, Europeanization, and the EU Referendum in a Polish-German Border City." *City and Society* 17(1): 127–152.

Associated Press Worldstream: German. 1996. "Verleger haben es auf die Frauen abgesehen—Zeitschriftenmarkt ist hart umkaempft; Jede fuenfte Werbemark fliesst in Frauenmagazine." *Associated Press Worldstream: German* (March 10).

Attia, Iman. 2009. *Die "westliche Kultur" und ihr Anderes: Zur Dekonstruktion von Orientalismus und antmuslimischen Rassismus.* Berlin: Transcript.

Azevedo, Licinio, dir. 1991. *Farewell GDR.* New York: First Run Icarus Films.

Balibar, Etienne, and Immanuel Wallerstein. 1991 [1988]. *Race, Nation, Class.* London: Verso.

Beck, Ulrich. 2000. "The Cosmopolitan Perspective: Sociology of the Second Age of Modernity." *British Journal of Sociology* 51(1): 79–105.

Behrends, Jan, Thomas Lindenberger, and Patrice G. Poutrus. 2003. *Fremde und Fremd-Sein in der DDR: Zu historischen Ursachen der Fremdenfeindlichkeit in Ostdeutschland.* Berlin: Metropol.

Benjamin,Walter. 1969 [1942]. "Über den Begriff der Geschichte." In *Gesammelte Schriften,* vol. 2, pt. 2, ed. Rolf Tiedemann and Hermann Schweppenhäuser, trans. Harry Zohn, 253–264. New York: Schocken.

Berdahl, D. 1999. *Where the World Ended: Re-Unification and Identity in the German Borderland.* Berkeley: University of California Press.

———. 2001. "Go, Trabi, Go!": Reflections on a Car and Its Symbolization over Time. *Anthropology and Humanism* 25(2): 131–141.

———. 2005. "The Spirit of Capitalism and the Boundaries of Citizenship in Post-Wall Germany." *Comparative Studies in Society and History* 47(2) (April): 235.

Berger, John. 1975. *A Seventh Man.* Baltimore, Md.: Penguin.

Borneman, John. 1991. *After the Wall: East Meets West in the New Berlin.* New York: Basic.

———. 1992. "State, Territory, and Identity Formation in the Postwar Berlins, 1945–1989." *Cultural Anthropology* 7(1) (February): 45–62.

———. 1998. *Subversions of International Order: Studies in the Political Anthropology of Culture.* Albany: State University of New York Press.

Borneman, John, and Nick Fowler. 1997. "Europeanization." *Annual Review of Anthropology* 26 (October): 487–514.

Borneman, John, and Stefan Senders. 2000. "Politics without a Head: Is the 'Love Parade' a New Form of Political Identification?" *Cultural Anthropology* 15(2) (May): 294.

Bourdieu, Pierre, and Jean-Claude Passeron. 1977. *Reproduction in Education, Society and Culture.* London: Sage.

Bowen, John. 2008. *Why the French Don't Like Headscarves: Islam, the State, and Public Space.* Princeton, N.J.: Princeton University Press.

Boyer, Dominic. 2000. "On the Sedimentation and Accreditation of Social Knowledges of Difference: Mass Media, Journalism, and the Reproduction of East/West Alterities in Unified Germany." *Cultural Anthropology* 15(4) (November): 459.

———. 2005. "Welcome to the New Europe." *American Ethnologist* 32(4) (November): 521–523.

Brakalic, Slavenka. 1990. "In Their Own Words: Women of Eastern Europe." *Ms.* (July–August): 40, col. 1.

Bringa, Tone. 1995. *Being Muslim the Bosnian Way: Identity and Community in a Central Bosnian Village*. Princeton, N.J.: Princeton University Press.

Brown, Jacqueline Nassy. 1998. "Black Liverpool, Black America, and the Gendering of Diasporic Space." *Cultural Anthropology* 13(3): 291–325.

Brown, Wendy. 1995. *States of Injury*. Princeton, N.J.: Princeton University Press.

———. 2006. *Regulating Aversion: Tolerance in the Age of Identity and Empire*. Princeton, N.J.: Princeton University Press.

Brubaker, Rogers. 1992. *Citizenship and Nationhood in France and Germany*. Cambridge, Mass.: Harvard University Press.

Buck-Morss, Susan. 2000. "Hegel and Haiti." *Critical Inquiry* 26(4) (Summer): 821–865.

Bui, Pipo. 2004. *Envisioning Vietnamese Migrants in Germany: Ethnic Stigma, Immigrant Origin Narratives and Partial Masking*. Münster: Lit.

Bundesverfassungsgericht. 2003. BVerfG, 2 BvR 1436/02, September 24, pars. 1–138. http://www.bverfg.de/entscheidungen/rs20030924_2bvr143602en.html, accessed June 2, 2011.

Bunzl, Matti. 2004. *Symptoms of Modernity: Jews and Queers in Late Twentieth-Century Vienna*. Berkeley: University of California Press.

———. 2005. "Between Anti-Semitism and Islamophobia: Some Thoughts on the New Europe." *American Ethnologist* 32(4) (November): 499–508.

———. 2007. *Anti-Semitism and Islamophobia: Hatreds Old and New in Europe*. Chicago: Prickly Paradigm Press.

Butler, J. 1990. *Gender Trouble*. New York: Routledge.

———. 1993. *Bodies That Matter: On the Discursive Limits of "Sex."* New York: Routledge.

BZ. 2009. "Der Kniefall von Neukölln beunruhigt." *BZ* (August 27). http://www.bz-berlin.de/aktuell/berlin/der-kniefall-von-neukoelln-beunruhigt-article564377.html, accessed March 30, 2010.

Calhoun, Craig, ed. 1992. *Habermas and the Public Sphere*. Cambridge, Mass.: MIT Press.

Campt, Tina. 2004a. "Schwarze deutsche Gegenerinnerung: *Der Black Atlantic* als gegenhistoriografische Praxis." In *Der Black Atlantic*, ed. Tina Campt and Paul Gilroy. Berlin: Haus der Kulturen der Welt.

———. 2004b. *Other Germans: Black Germans and the Politics of Race, Gender, and Memory in the Third Reich*. Ann Arbor: University of Michigan Press.

Candan, Can, dir. 2000. *Walls, Mauern, Duvarlar*. United States and Turkey.

Çelebi-Gottschlich, Sevim. 1987. "Wahlrecht für Alle." 58. Sitzung, Abgeordnetenhaus von Berlin, 10 Wahlperiode, Drucksache 10 (August 4): 1667.

Çelick, Neco, dir. 2004. *Urban Guerrillas*. Berlin, Germany: 36 Pictures.

Chase, Cheryl. 1998. "Hermaphrodites with Attitude: Mapping the Emergence of Intersex Political Activism." *GLQ: A Journal of Gay and Lesbian Studies* 4(2): 189–211.

Chin, Rita. 2007. *The Guest Worker Question in Postwar Germany*. Cambridge: Cambridge University Press.

Christian Science Monitor. 2006. "Europe: Quizzes Probe Values of Potential Citizens." *Christian Science Monitor* (April 10). http://www.csmonitor.com/2006/0410/p01s04-woeu.html?s=widep, accessed July 7.

Çinar, Alev. 2005. *Moderninty, Islam, and Secularism in Turkey*. Minneapolis: University of Minnesota Press.

Cixous, H. 1988. "Sortie." In *Modern Criticism and Theory*, ed. David Lodge. London: Longman.

Clarke, Kamari Maxine. 2006. *Globalization and Race: Transformations in the Cultural Production of Blackness*. Durham, N.C.: Duke University Press.

Clifford, James. 1997. *Routes: Travel and Translation in the Late Twentieth Century*. Cambridge, Mass.: Harvard University Press.

Crenshaw, Kimberly. 1996. *Critical Race Theory*. New York: New Press.

Darnton, Robert. 1991. *Berlin Journal: 1989–1990*. New York: Norton.

de Lauretis, Teresa. 1987. *Technologies of Gender*. Bloomington: Indiana University Press.

Der Spiegel. 2001. "Der neue Mutterstolz: Kinder staat Karriere." *Der Spiegel* (July 16).

Die Bundesregierung. 2004a. "Zuwanderungsgesetz kann in Kraft treten." http://www. bundesregierung.de/Themen-A-Z/Innenpolitik-,6812/Zuwanderung.htm, accessed October 4, 2004.

———. 2004b. "Einzelheiten des Zuwanderungsgesetzes." http://www.bundesregierung.de/ artikel-,413.671622/Einzelheiten-des-Zuwanderungsg.htm, accessed October 4, 2004.

"Die Kopftuchlüge." 1999. *Emma* (January–February): 62–67.

Donle, Christian, and Peter Kather. 1993. "Germany." In *International Immigration and Nationality Law*, vol. 2, ed. Dennis Campbell. The Hague: Kluwer Law International.

Durkheim, Emile. 1938. *The Rules of Sociological Method*. Chicago: University of Chicago Press.

Ege, Moritz. 2007. *Schwarz werden: "Afroamerikanophilie" in den 1960er und 1970er Jahren*. Bielefed, Germany: Transcript.

Eggers, Maureen Maisha, et al., eds. 2005. *Mythen, Masken und Subjekte: Kritische weiszseinsforschung in Deutschland*. Münster: Unrast.

Eley, Geoff. 1990. "Foreword." In *A History of Foreign Labor in Germany, 1880–1980*, ed. Ulrich Herbert. Ann Arbor: University of Michigan Press.

El-Tayeb, Fatima. 2001. *Schwarze Deutsche: Der Diskurs um "Rasse" und nationale Identitat*. Frankfurt: Campus.

———. 2004. "Black Atlantic in Berlin? Queering Popular Culture, Afrikanische Diaspora und das Schwarze Europa." In *Der Black Atlantic*, ed. Tina Campt and Paul Gilroy. Berlin: Haus der Kulturen der Welt.

———. 2005. "Beyond the National? Interdisciplinary German Studies and the Global." Guest presentation to the German Academic Exchange Service Faculty Seminar, dir. Leslie Adelson, Cornell University, Ithaca, N.Y., July 22.

———. 2006. "Queering Ethnicity? Beyond the Black Paradigm." Paper presented at the conference "Remapping 'Black Germany': New Perspectives on Afro-German History, Politics, Culture," University of Massachusetts, Amherst, April 23.

Evans, J., and S. Hall, eds. 1991. *Visual Culture: The Reader*. London: Sage.

Ewald, F. 1990. "Norms, Discipline, and the Law." *Representations* 30 (Spring): 138–161.

Ewing, Katherine Pratt. 2000. "Legislating Religious Freedom: Muslim Challenges to the Relationship between 'Church' and 'State' in Germany and France." *Daedalus* 129(4) (Fall): 31–54.

———. 2003. "Living Islam in the Diaspora: Between Turkey and Germany." *South Atlantic Quarterly* 102(2–3) (Spring–Summer): 405–431.

———. 2008. *Stolen Honor: Stigmatizing Muslim Men in Berlin.* Stanford, Calif.: Stanford University Press.

Fanon, Frantz. 1965. *Studies in a Dying Colonialism.* New York: Monthly Review Press.

———. 1967. *Black Skin, White Masks.* New York: Grove.

Farocki, Harun, and Andrei Ujica, dirs. 1992. *Videograms einer Revolution.* Berlin: Harun Farocki Filmproduktion.

Fassbinder, Rainer Werner, dir. 1986 [1979]. *The Marriage of Maria Braun.* Burbank, Calif.: RCA/Columbia Pictures Home Video.

———. 1989 [1974]. *Ali, Fear Eats the Soul.* New York: New Yorker Video.

Fassin, Diddier. 2004. "Compassion and Repression: The Moral Economy of Immigration Policies in France." *Cultural Anthropology* 20(3): 362–387.

Fehrenbach, Heide. 1998. "Rehabilitating Fatherland: Race and German Remasculinization." *Signs* 24(1) (Autumn): 107–127.

———. 2005. *Race after Hitler: Black Occupation Children in Postwar Germany and America.* Princeton, N.J.: Princeton University Press.

Fikes, Kesha. 2009. *Managing African Portugal: The Citizen-Migrant Distinction.* Durham, N.C.: Duke University Press.

Focus. 1995. "Vietnamesen: Rueckkehr ohne 'Kopfgeld.'" *Focus* 3 (January 16): 26–27.

Foucault, Michel. 1975 [1973]. *The Birth of the Clinic: An Archaeology of Medical Perception.* New York: Vintage.

———. 1981. "Omnes et Singulatim." In *The Tanner Lectures on Human Values,* vol. 2, ed. Sterling M. McMurrin. Cambridge: Cambridge University Press.

———. 1990. *History of Sexuality,* vol. 1. New York: Vintage.

———. 1991a. "Governmentality." In *The Foucault Effect: Studies in Governmentality,* ed. G. Burchell, C. Gordon, and P. Miller. London: Harvester Wheatsheaf.

———. 1991b. *Remarks on Marx.* New York: Semiotext(e).

———. 1995 [1977]. *Discipline and Punish: The Birth of the Prison.* New York: Vintage.

———. 1997. *Ethics: Subjectivity and Truth.* New York: New Press.

———. 2003. *Society Must Be Defended.* New York: Picador.

———. 2007 [1997]. *The Politics of Truth.* New York: Semiotext(e).

Frankenberg, Ruth. 1993. *White Women, Race Matters.* Minneapolis: University of Minnesota Press.

Frankfurter Allgemeine Zeitung. 1993. "Vertragsarbeiter der DDR duerfen bleiben." *Frankfurter Allgemeine Zeitung* (May 17): 6.

———. 2007. "Sextourismus Schwarzer Mann, weiße Frau." *Frankfurter Allgemeine Zeitung* (June 18). http://www.faz.net/s/RubB4457BA9094E4B44BD26DF6DC-F5A5F00/Doc<E6948B4277C824428A7724F60C08ADD8E<ATpl<Ecommon<Scontent.html, accessed August 16, 2007.

Franks, Myfanwy. 2000. "Crossing the Borders of Whiteness? White Muslim Women Who Wear the *Hijab* in Britain Today." *Ethnic and Racial Studies* 23(5) (September): 917–929.

Friedrichsmeyer, Sara, Sara Lennox, and Susanne Zantop, eds. 1998. *The Imperialist Imagination: German Colonialism and Its Legacy.* Ann Arbor: University of Michigan Press.

Gal, Susan. 1991. "Bartok's Funeral: Representations of Europe in Hungarian Political Rhetoric." *American Ethnologist* 18(3) (August): 440.

Garton Ash, Timothy. 2009. "Ein neues Modell der Revolution." In *1989/Globale Geschichten,* ed. Susanne Stemmler, Valerie Smith, and Bernd M. Scherer. Göttingen: Wallstein.

Gates, Lisa. 1998. "Of Seeing and Otherness: Leni Riefenstahl's African Photographs." In *The Imperialist Imagination,* ed. Sara Friedrichsmeyer, Sara Lennox, and Susanne Zantop. Ann Arbor: University of Michigan Press.

Geddes, Andrew. 2000. *Immigration and European Integration: Towards Fortress Europe?* Manchester, England: Manchester University Press.

Georgi, Viola. 2003. *Entliehene Erinnerung: Geschictsbilder junger Migranten in Deutschland.* Hamburg: Hamburger Edition.

Georgi, Viola B., and Rainer Ohlinger. 2009. "Geschichte und Diversität: Crossover statt nationaler Narrative?" In *Crossover Geschichte: Historisches Bewusstsein Jugendlicher in der Einwanderungsgesellschaft,* ed. Viola B. Georgi and Rainer Ohlinger. Hamburg: Körberg-Stiftung.

Gilman, Sander L. 1985. *Difference and Pathology: Stereotypes of Sexuality, Race, and Madness.* Ithaca, N.Y.: Cornell University Press.

———. 1990. "The Jewish Body: A Foot-Note." *Bulletin of the History of Medicine* 64(4): 588–602.

———. 2000. "Are Jews White?" In *Theories of Race and Racism,* ed. Les Brack and Jon Solomos. London: Routledge.

Gilmore, Ruth Wilson. 2002. "Fatal Couplings of Power and Difference: Notes on Racism and Geography." *Professional Geographer* 54(1): 15–24.

Gilroy, Paul. 1993. *The Black Atlantic: Modernity and Double Consciousness.* Cambridge, Mass.: Harvard University Press.

———. 1997. *There Ain't No Black in the Union Jack: The Cultural Politics of Race and Nation.* London: Hutchinson.

———. 2000. *Against Race: Imagining Politics beyond the Color Line.* Cambridge, Mass.: Belknap.

Göktürk, Deniz, et al. 2007. "Introduction." In *Germany in Transit: Nation and Migration,* ed. Deniz Göktürk et al. Berkeley: University of California Press.

Goldberg, David T., ed. 1990. *Anatomy of Racism.* Minneapolis: University of Minnesota Press.

Gould, Stephen J. 1996. *The Mismeasure of Man.* New York: Norton.

Gryglewski, Elke. 2009. "Diesseits und jenseits gefühlter Geschichte: Zugänge von Jugendlichen mit Migrationshitergrund zu Schoa und Nahostkonflikt." In *Crossover Geschichte: Historisches Bewusstsein Jugendlicher in der Einwanderungsgesellschaft,* ed. Viola B. Georgi and Rainer Ohlinger. Hamburg: Körberg-Stiftung.

Habermas, Jürgen. 1997. *A Berlin Republic: Writings on Germany,* trans. Steven Rendall. Lincoln: University of Nebraska Press.

Hall, Stuart. 1990. "Cultural Identity and Diaspora." In *Identity: Community, Culture, Difference,* ed. Jonathan Rutherford. New York: New York University Press.

———. 1996. "The After-Life of Frantz Fanon: Why Fanon? Why Now? Why *Black Skin, White Masks?*" In *The Fact of Blackness: Frantz Fanon and Visual Representation*, ed. Alan Read, 12–37. London: Institute of Contemporary Arts.

Hall, Stuart, et al., eds. 1996. *Modernity: An Introduction to Modern Societies*. Cambridge: Blackwell.

Hall, S., D. Held, and T. McGrew, eds. 1992. *Modernity and Its Futures*. Cambridge: Polity.

Harvey, David. 1990. *The Condition of Postmodernity: An Enquiry into the Origins of Cultural Change*. Cambridge: Blackwell.

Hasselbach, Ingo. 1996. "How Nazis Are Made." *New Yorker* (January 8): 35–56.

Heldmann, Eva, dir. 1999. *Fremd Gehen: Gespräche mit meiner Freundin*. Germany: Eva Heldmann Film Produktion.

Hentschel, Tamara, ed. 1997. *Zweimal angekommen und doch nicht zu Hause: Vietnamesische Vertragsarbeiter in den neuen Bundesländern*. Berlin: Reistrommel.

Herbert, Ulrich. 1990. *A History of Foreign Labor in Germany, 1880–1980*. Ann Arbor: University of Michigan Press.

Herzog, Dagmar. 2005. *Sex after Fascism: Memory and Morality in Twentieth-Century Germany*. Princeton, N.J.: Princeton University Press.

Hirsi Ali, Ayaan. 2008. *Infidel*. London: Pocket.

Hockenos, Paul. 1993. *Free to Hate: The Rise of the Right in Post-Communist Eastern Europe*. New York: Routledge.

Höhn, Maria. 2002. *GIs and Fräuleins: The German-American Encounter in 1950s West Germany*. Chapel Hill: University of North Carolina Press.

Hovy, Bela. 2001. "Statistically Correct Asylum Data: Prospects and Limitations." http://www.unhcr.ch/cgi-bin/texis/vtx/home?page=search, accessed January 9, 2003.

Huntington, Samuel. 1993. "The Clash of Civilizations?" *Foreign Affairs* 72(3) (Summer): 22.

Ignatieff, Michael. 2001. *Human Rights*. Princeton, N.J.: Princeton University Press.

Ignatiev, Noel. 1995. *How the Irish Became White*. New York: Routledge.

Jürgensen, Havva. 2010. "Ich wünsche mir einmal eine Bundeskanzlerin mit türkischen oder arabischen Wurzeln." In *Unsere Geschicten—eure Geschichte? Neuköllner Sadtteilmütter und ihre Auseinadersetzung mit der Geschite des Nationalsozialismus*. Berlin: Aktion Sühnezeichen Friedensdienste.

Kaes, Anton. 1989. *From Hitler to Heimat: The Return of History as Film*. Cambridge, Mass.: Harvard University Press.

Kahane, Anetta. 2004. *Ich Sehe was, was du nicht siehst*. Berlin: Rowohlt.

Kaplan, Caren. 1996. *Questions of Travel: Postmodern Discourses of Displacement*. Durham, N.C.: Duke University Press.

Karneval der Kulturen. 2006. "English Summary." http://www1.spiegel.de/active/citizenship/fcgi/citizenship.fcgi, accessed August 18, 2006.

Kaschuba, Wolfgang, ed. 1995. *Kulturen, Identitäten, Diskurse: Perspektiven europäischer Ethnologie*. Berlin: Akademie.

Keaton, Trica Danielle. 2006. *Muslim Girls and the Other France: Race, Identity Politics and Social Exclusion*. Bloomington: Indiana University Press.

Kofman, Eleonore, Annie Phizacklea, Parvati Raghuram, and Rosemary Sales. 2000. *Gender and International Migration in Europe.* London: Routledge.

Krajewski, Markus, and Helmut Rittstieg. 1996. "German Nationality Law." In *Nationality Laws in the European Union,* ed. Bruno Nascimbene. Milan, Italy: Butterworths.

Krakauer, Sigfried. 1974 [1947]. *From Caligari to Hitler: A Psychological History of the German Film.* Princeton, N.J.: Princeton University Press.

Kühnel, Wolfgang. 1998. "Hitler's Grandchildren? The Reemergence of a Right-Wing Social Movement in Germany." In *Nation and Race: The Developing Euro-American Racist Subculture,* ed. Jeffrey Kaplan and Tore Bjorgo. Boston: Northeastern University Press.

Kürti, László. 1998. "The Emergence of Postcommunist Youth Identities in Eastern Europe: From Communist Youth, to Skinheads, to National Socialists and Beyond." In *Nation and Race,* ed. Jeffrey Kaplan and Tore Bjørgo. Boston: Northeastern University Press.

Lemon, Alaina. 2000. *Between Two Fires: Gypsy Performance and Romani Memory from Pushkin to Postsocialism.* Durham, N.C.: Duke University Press.

Lennox, Sara. 1998. "White Ladies and Dark Continents in Ingeborg Bachmann's *Todesarten.*" In *The Imperialist Imagination,* ed. Sara Friedrichsmeyer, Sara Lennox, and Susanne Zantop. Ann Arbor: University of Michigan Press.

Linke, Uli. 1999. "Formations of White Public Space: Racial Aesthetics, Body Politics, and the Nation." *Transforming Anthropology* 8(1–2): 129–161.

Lipsky, Michael. 1980. *Street-Level Bureaucracy: Dilemmas of the Individual in Public Services.* New York: Russell Sage Foundation.

Locke, Alaine, ed. 1992 [1925]. *The New Negro.* New York: Atheneum.

Locke, John. 1988 [1690]. *Two Treatises of Government.* Cambridge: Cambridge University Press.

Mahmood, Saba. 2005. *Politics of Piety: The Islamic Revival and the Feminist Subject.* Princeton, N.J.: Princeton University Press.

Maier, Charles. 1997. *Dissolution: The Crisis of Communism and the End of East Germany.* Princeton, N.J.: Princeton University Press.

Mandel, Ruth Ellen. 2008. *Cosmopolitan Anxieties: Turkish Challenges to Citizenship and Belonging in Germany.* Durham, N.C.: Duke University Press.

Mani, B. Venkat. 2007. *Cosmopolitical Claims: Turkish-German Literatures from Nadolny to Pamuk.* Iowa City: University of Iowa Press.

Marshall, T. H. 1992 [1950]. *Citizenship and Social Class.* London: Pluto Press.

Marx, Karl. 1978. *The Marx-Engels Reader,* ed. Robert C. Tucker. New York: Norton.

Massaquoi, Hans Jürgen. 1998. *Destined to Witness: Growing Up Black in Nazi Germany.* New York: Morrow.

Matyania, E. 1994. "Women after Communism: A Bitter Freedom." *Social Research* 61(2): 351–377.

McClintock, Anne. 1995. *Imperial Leather: Race, Gender and Sexuality in the Colonial Conquest.* New York: Routledge.

Merry, Sally Engle. 2006. *Human Rights and Gender Violence: Translating International Law into Local Justice.* Chicago: University of Chicago Press.

Miles, Robert. 1989. *Racism.* London: Routledge.

Ministry of Foreign Affairs of the Republic of Poland. n.d. "Schengen Zone: Poland Joins the Schengen Area." http://www.poland.gov.pl/Poland,in,Schengen,zone,1620 .html, accessed August 20, 2008.

Mitchell, Timothy. 1998. *Colonising Egypt.* Berkeley: University of California Press.

Moore, Henrietta L. 1999. "Anthropological Theory in the Turn of the Century." In *Anthropological Theory Today,* ed. Henrietta L. Moore. Cambridge: Polity.

Mosse, George L. 1985. *Nationalism and Sexuality.* New York: Fertig.

Müller, Ray, dir. 1995. *The Wonderful Horrible Life of Leni Riefenstahl.* New York: Kino International.

National Public Radio. 2005. "Photo Collection Tells Stories of Parsis in India." http://www.npr.org/templates/story/story.php?storyId=4223182, accessed January 20, 2005.

New York Times. 2002a. "Mocked in Europe of Old, African Is Embraced at Home at Last." May 4.

———. 2002b. "Finally Buried with Honor in Her Native Land." August 10.

———. 2004. "European Public Uneasy over Turkey's Bid to Join Union." October 2.

Ommer, Uwe. 1994. *Black Ladies.* Cologne: Taschen.

Ong, Aihwa. 1996. "Cultural Citizenship as Subject-Making: Immigrants Negotiate Racial and Cultural Boundaries in the United States." *Current Anthropology* 37(5): 737–762.

———. 1999. *Flexible Citizenship: The Cultural Logics of Transnationality.* Durham, N.C.: Duke University Press.

———. 2000. "Graduated Sovereignty in Southeast Asia." *Theory, Culture and Society* 17(4): 55–75.

———. 2003. *Buddha Is Hiding: Refugees, Citizenship, the New America.* Berkeley: University of California Press.

Opitz, May, Katharina Oguntoye, and Dagmar Schultz, eds. 1992. *Farbe bekennen: Afro-deutsche Frauen auf den Spuren ihrer Geschichte.* Frankfurt am Main: Fischer.

———. 1992. *Showing Our Colors: Afro-German Women Speak Out.* Amherst, Mass.: University of Massachusetts Press.

Özyürek, Esra. 2009. "Convert Alert: German Muslims and Turkish Christians as Threats to Security in the New Europe." *Comparative Studies in Society and History* 51(1) (January): 91–116.

Pagden, Anthony, ed. 2002. *The Idea of Europe: From Antiquity to the European Union.* New York: Cambridge University Press.

Partridge, Damani. 1996. "A 'Black' Coming Out: The Daily Life and Politicization of 'Afro-Germans.'" Paper presented at the American Anthropological Association meeting, San Francisco, Calif., November.

———. 2000. "Reflections on Citizenship and Exclusion: Ten Years after German Unification." *Reflections.* www.avh.de/de/programme/stip_aus/doc/buka/Berichte_99/ Partridge.doc, accessed April 30, 2003.

———. 2003. "Becoming Non-Citizens: Technologies of Exclusion and Exclusionary Incorporation after the Berlin Wall." Ph.D. diss., University of California, Berkeley, Department of Anthropology.

———. 2008a. "Citizenship and the Obama Moment in Berlin." *The Journal of the International Institute* (The University of Michigan, Ann Arbor), Fall 2008: 4–5.

———. 2008b. "We Were Dancing in the Club, Not on the Berlin Wall: Black Bodies, Street Bureaucrats, and Exclusionary Incorporation into the New Europe." *Cultural Anthropology* 23(4): 660–687.

———. 2010. "Holocaust *Mahnmal* (Memorial): Monumental Memory amidst Contemporary Race." *Comparative Studies in Society and History* 52(4): 820–850.

Partridge, Damani, dir. 2001. *Neo-Nazi Zone.* Berlin, Germany.

Pfeiffer, Christian. 1998. Talk delivered at "The Era of the New Tolerance" conference, Berlin, Germany, November 18–19.

Piesche, Peggy. 2003. "Black and German? East German Adolescents before 1989: A Retrospective View of a 'Non-Existent Issue' in the GDR." In *The Cultural After-Life of East Germany: New Transnational Perspectives,* ed. Leslie A. Adelson. Washington, D.C.: American Institute for Contemporary German Studies.

Poiger, Ute. 1998. *Jazz, Rock, and Rebels: Cold War Politics and American Culture in a Divided Germany.* Berkeley: University of California Press.

Povinelli, Elizabeth A. 2002. *The Cunning of Recognition: Indigenous Alterities and the Making of Australian Multiculturalism.* Durham, N.C.: Duke University Press.

Pred, Allan. 2000. *Even in Sweden: Racisms, Racialized Spaces, and the Popular Geographical Imagination.* Berkeley: University of California Press.

"Preis für berliner Postmigrantisches Theater: Formel 1 im Trabi." 2011. *Taz.de* (February 24). http://www.taz.de/1/leben/alltag/artikel/1/formel-1-im-trabi, accessed June 2, 2011.

Pruitt, Deborah, and Suzanne LaFont. 1995. "For Love and Money: Romance Tourism in Jamaica." *Annals of Tourism Research* 22(2): 422–440.

Rabinow, Paul. 1996. *Essays on the Anthropology of Reason.* Princeton, N.J.: Princeton University Press.

Rasmussen, Birgit Brander, et al., eds. 2001. *The Making and Unmaking of Whiteness.* Durham, N.C.: Duke University Press.

Rathenow Asylum Seekers. 2000. "An Appeal from the Asylum Seekers in Rathenow." http://www.nadir.org/nadir/aktuell/2000/05/11/742.html, accessed September 26, 2007.

Rau, Johannes. 2000. "Ohne Angst und ohne Träumereien: Gemeinsam in Deutschland leben." *Berliner Rede im Haus der Kulturen der Welt* (December 5). http://www.bundespraesident.de/frameset/index.jsp, accessed May 14, 2003.

Regis, Helen A. 1999. "Second Lines, Minstrelsy, and the Contested Landscapes of New Orleans Afro-Creole Festivals." *Cultural Anthropology* 14(4): 472–504.

Riefenstahl, Leni. 1982. *Leni Riefenstahl's Africa.* London: William Collins Sons.

———. 1992 [1987]. *Leni Riefenstahl: A Memoir.* New York: St. Martin's.

———. 1997 [1976]. *People of Kau.* New York: St. Martin's.

———. 1999. *Die Nuba.* Frechen: Komet.

Riefenstahl, Leni, dir. 2000 [1938]. *Olympia II: Festival of Beauty.* Chicago: Home Vision Cinema.

———. 2002 [1935]. *Triumph des Willens: Das Dokument vom Reichsparteitag 1934.* Bloomington, Ill.: Synapse Films.

Roedigger, D. 1991. *The Wages of Whiteness: Race and the Making of the American Working Class.* New York: Verso.

Rose, Nikolas. 2001. "The Politics of Life Itself." *Theory, Culture and Society* 18(6): 1–30.

———. 2003. "Governing Life: Biopolitics, Biocitizenship and Bioeconomics in a Global Age." Talk given in the Department of Anthropology, University of California, Berkeley, April 7.

Rose, Nikolas, and Paul Miller. 1992. "Political Power beyond the State: Problematics of Government." *British Journal of Sociology* 1(2) (June): 173–205.

Rössel, Karl. 2009. "Eröffnungsrede der Ausstellung 'Die Dritte Welt im Zweiten Weltkrieg.'" *Africavenir International.* http://www.africavenir.org/news-archive/newsdetails/datum/2009/09/12/karl-roessel-eroeffnungsrede-der-ausstellung-die-dritte-welt-im-zweiten-weltkrieg-am-1-september-2.html?tx_ttnews%5BbackPid%5D=34&cHash=5eab91b84d, accessed March 27, 2010.

Rothberg, Michael. 2009. *Multidirectional Memory: Remembering the Holocaust in the Age of Decolonization.* Stanford, Calif.: Stanford University Press.

Sanchez Taylor, Jacqueline. 2001. "Dollars Are a Girl's Best Friend: Female Tourists' Sexual Behaviour in the Caribbean." *Sociology* 35(3): 749–764.

Sawyer, Lena. 2006. "Racialization, Gender, and Consumption among West Indian Girls in Brooklyn." In *Globalization and Race: Transformations in the Cultural Production of Blackness,* ed. Kamari Maxine Clarke and Deborah A. Thomas. Durham, N.C.: Duke University Press.

Scheper-Hughes, Nancy. 2002. *Ethnografeast.* Berkeley: University of California Press.

Scheper-Hughes, Nancy, and M. Locke. 1987. "The Mindful Body: A Prolegomena to Future Work in Medical Anthropology." *Medical Anthropology Quarterly* 1(1): 1–39.

Schiffauer, Werner. 1997. "Islam as a Civil Religion: Political Culture and the Organisation of Diversity in Germany." In *Politics of Multiculturalism in the New Europe: Racism, Identity and Community,* ed. Tariq Modood and Prina Jane Werbner. New York: Zed.

Schmitt, Carl. 1996 [1932]. *The Concept of the Political.* Chicago: University of Chicago Press.

———. 2006 [1922]. *Political Theology: Four Chapters on the Concept of Sovereignty.* Chicago: University of Chicago Press.

Schoelzel, Andreas. 2009. "Demonstration in Berlin gegen das Ausländergesetz, April 1990." In *1989/Globale Geschichten,* ed. Susanne Stemmler, Valerie Smith, and Bernd M. Scherer. Göttingen: Wallstein.

Scott, J. 1985. *Weapons of the Weak.* New Haven, Conn.: Yale University Press.

———. 1990. *Domination and the Arts of Resistance.* New Haven, Conn.: Yale University Press.

Scott, Joan Wallach. 2007. *The Politics of the Veil.* Princeton, N.J.: Princeton University Press.

Senders, S. 1996. "Laws of Belonging: Legal Dimensions of National Inclusion in Germany." *New German Critique* 67 (Winter): 147–176.

Shively, Kim. 2005. "Religious Bodies in Secular States: The Veil in Turkey and France." Paper presented at "Summer Institute of Teaching and Research on Women: Turkey at the Crossroads: Women, Women's Studies and State." http://pages.towson.edu/ncctrw/summer%20institutes/Papers-Website/Shively%2005.pdf, accessed August 25, 2006.

Sieg, Katrin. 2002. *Ethnic Drag: Performing Race, Nation, Sexuality in West Germany.* Ann Arbor: University of Michigan Press.

Silverstein, Paul. 2004. *Algeria in France: Transpolitics, Race, and Nation.* Bloomington: Indiana University Press.

———. 2005. "Immigrant Racialization and the New Savage Slot: Race, Migration, and Immigration in the New Europe." *Annual Review of Anthropology* 34: 363–384.

Soysal, Yasemin. 1994. *Limits of Citizenship: Migrants and Postnational Membership in Europe.* Chicago: University of Chicago Press.

Spennemann, Nozomi. 1997. "Aufbauhelfer für eine bessere Zukunft: Die vietnamessischen Vertragsarbeiter in der ehemaligen DDR." In *Zweimal Angekommen und doch nicht zu Hause,* ed. Tamara Hentschel, Magnar Hirschberger, Lars Liepe, and Nozomi Spennemann. Berlin: Reistrommel.

Spiegel Online. 2006. "Take Baden-Württemberg's New Citizenship Test." *Spiegel Online.* http://www1.spiegel.de/active/citizenship/fcgi/citizenship.fcgi?a=1212, accessed July 7, 2006.

Spivak, Gayatri Chakravorty. 1988. "Can the Subaltern Speak?" In *Marxism and the Interpretation of Culture,* ed. Cary Nelson and Lawrence Grossberg. Champaign: University of Illinois Press.

Stoler, A. 1995. *Race and the Education of Desire: Foucault's History of Sexuality and the Colonial Order of Things.* Durham, N.C.: Duke University Press.

Süddeutsche Zeitung. 1996. "Amica, das neue Frauenmagazin mit dem EQ." *Süddeutsche Zeitung* (January 13).

Tagesspiegel. 2009a. "Mörder äußerte vor Attacke Sympathie für NPD." *Tagesspiegel* (July 8). http://www.tagesspiegel.de/politik/Aegypterin-Gerichtssaal-Mord;art771 ,2842897, accessed March 29, 2010.

———. 2009b. "Werkstatt der Erinnerungskulturen." *Tagesspiegel* (October 2). http://www.tagesspiegel.de/kultur/ausstellungen/Ausstellung-DritteWelt;art2652,2913879, accessed March 26, 2010.

Tageszeitung. 2002. "Zur Sache, Schätzchen! Der Erfolg der Reiseindustrie verdankt sich nicht zuletz ihrer unterschwellingen erotischen Botschaft. Eine Spurensuche der Erotik beim Reisen. Ist der Sextourismus ein Schmuddelthema?" *Tageszeitung* (June 15). http://www.taz.de/index.php?id=archivseite&dig=2002/06/15/a0222, accessed August 12, 2007.

Tawada, Yoko. 1996. *Talisman.* Tübingen, Germany: Konkursbuchverlag.

Taylor, Charles. 1994. "Multiculturalism." In *Multiculturalism,* ed. Amy Gutman. Princeton, N.J.: Princeton University Press.

Thomas, Deborah A. 2002. "Democratizing Dance: Institutional Transformation and Hegemonic Re-Ordering in Postcolonial Jamaica." *Cultural Anthropology* 17(4): 512–550.

Tibi, Bassam. 1998. *Europa ohne Identitat? Die Krise der multikulturellen Gesellschaft.* Munchen: Bertelsmann.

Ticktin, Miriam. 2006. "Where Ethics and Politics Meet: The Violence of Humanitarianism in France." *American Ethnologist* 33(1): 33–49.

Tißberger, Martina, et al. 2006. *Weiß—Weißsein: Whiteness Kritische Studien zu Gender und Rassismus.* Frankfurt am Main: Peter Lang.

Till, Karen E. 2005. *The New Berlin: Memory, Politics, Place.* Minneapolis: University of Minnesota Press.

Turner, B. 1993. "Contemporary Problems in the Theory of Citizenship." In *Citizenship and Social Theory,* ed. Bryan S. Turner. London: Sage.

Verdery, Katherine. 1994. "From Parent-State to Family Patriarchs: Gender and Nation in Contemporary Eastern Europe." *East European Politics and Societies* 8(2) (Spring): 231.

———. 1996. *What Was Socialism? What Comes Next?* Princeton, N.J.: Princeton University Press.

Verwaltungsgerichtshof Baden-Württemberg. 2001. "Religiös motiviertes Kopftuch im öffentlichen Schuldienst." *DVBL: Deutsches Verwaltungsblatt* 19: 1534.

Walther, Joseph Daniel. 2003. *Creating Germans Abroad: Cultural Policies and National Identity in Namibia.* Athens: Ohio University Press.

Willis, D., and C. Williams. 2002. *The Black Female Body.* Philadelphia: Temple University Press.

"Wir inszenieren kein Getto-Theater." 2009. *Taz.de* (April 18). http://www.taz.de/1/archiv/print-archiv/printressorts/digi-artikel/?ressort=ku&dig=2009%2F04%2F18%2Fa0036&cHash=e75e8d7fc2, accessed June 2, 2011.

Wright, Michelle M. 2004. *Becoming Black: Creating Identity in the African Diaspora.* Durham, N.C.: Duke University Press.

Zhang, Li. 2001. *Strangers in the City: Reconfigurations of Space, Power, and Social Networks within China's Floating Population.* Stanford, Calif.: Stanford University Press.

Zizek, Slavoj. 1993. *Tarrying with the Negative: Kant, Hegel, and the Critique of Ideology.* Durham, N.C.: Duke University Press.

Index

New Anthropologies of Europe

Damani J. Partridge is Associate Professor in the Department of Anthropology and in the Department of Afroamerican and African Studies at the University of Michigan.

Lightning Source UK Ltd.
Milton Keynes UK
UKHW020646250421
382482UK00023B/576